Contemporary Issues
in Leadership

About the Book

Leadership is an elusive attribute: hard to define, difficult to practice and to teach, and endlessly fascinating to observe and study.

In this new and extensively revised second edition of *Contemporary Issues in Leadership*, Professors Rosenbach and Taylor describe the phenomenon of leadership and identify what makes an individual a strong leader. They examine the complexity of various leadership tasks and look at how performance is influenced by such factors as personality, gender, and aspirations of both leaders and followers.

For this lively anthology, Rosenbach and Taylor have gathered articles containing the best examples of effective leadership. Over half of the selections are new to this second edition; many are original contributions, written specifically for this collection. Recommendations from the many readers of the first edition have helped shape the updating of the rest of the articles, making an excellent book even better. Altogether the essays are a blend of classic and contemporary literature, and of scholarly and journalistic writing.

Trenchant and provocative, *Contemporary Issues in Leadership* illustrates the importance of a leader's vision and how it can empower followers with meaning, commitment, and confidence. The authors clearly portray the challenges that present and future leaders must face as they respond to increasingly complex issues and more demanding constituencies. The approach of the book remains firmly interdisciplinary, appealing to a broad range of students and scholars.

Contemporary Issues in Leadership

SECOND EDITION

——— □ ———

edited by William E. Rosenbach and Robert L. Taylor

Foreword by Thomas E. Cronin

Westview Press
BOULDER □ SAN FRANCISCO □ LONDON

HM
141
·C69
1989

Copyright © 1989 by Westview Press, Inc.

Published in 1989 in the United States of America by Westview Press, Inc., 5500 Central Avenue, Boulder, Colorado 80301, and in the United Kingdom by Westview Press, Inc., 13 Brunswick Centre, London WC1N 1AF, England

Library of Congress Cataloging-in-Publication Data
Contemporary issues in leadership / edited by William E. Rosenbach and
   Robert L. Taylor; foreword by Thomas E. Cronin.—2nd ed.
      p. cm.
   Includes bibliographies.
   ISBN 0-8133-0829-1—ISBN 0-8133-0830-5 (pbk.)
   1. Leadership. I. Rosenbach, William E. II. Taylor, Robert L.
(Robert Lewis), 1939–   .
HM141.C69 1989
303.3′4—dc20   89-5718
                                                                              CIP

Printed and bound in the United States of America

The paper used in this publication meets the requirements of the American National
Standard for Permanence of Paper for Printed Library Materials Z39.48-1984.

10   9   8   7   6   5   4   3   2   1

To my parents and Denise O'Brien
—W.E.R.

To Linda and Kara
—R.L.T.

Contents

Preface

In the first edition of this work, we presented a collection of readings from a variety of disciplines to help provide a broad and integrated understanding of that elusive and mysterious concept—leadership. Our purpose for the second edition remains the same. We continue to acknowledge that there are many legitimate ways to approach the study of leadership, and, to that end, we review here the literature of business, education, psychology, history, sociology, philosophy, politics, religion, and the military. If, in this multidisciplinary overview, we have presented viewpoints that both support and contradict your particular perception of leadership, we have accomplished at least one of our goals.

Based on response from readers, we have included in the present version five chapters from the first edition. Another five readings that appear in this edition are original pieces that have not been previously published. Some of the articles are old—classic, if you will; others are quite current. There is an interesting blend of scholarly and nonacademic presentations, all well written and thought provoking. The new contributions should significantly add to the usefulness of the book.

There are four parts to the book. Part 1 explores the nature of the leadership paradox: Why is it that we cannot easily define leadership even though we recognize, appreciate, and expect it? The personal qualities of leadership are the focus of Part 2, in which we look at individual differences as they relate to leadership. The concept of followership is also examined, including its implications for leader development. In Part 3 we recognize the importance not only of what leaders do, but of how they do it. Substance relates to goals and objectives; style reflects the process by which the leader interacts with others to get the job done under various circumstances. Part 4 concludes the discussion by examining the importance of the leader's role in defining the future by creating and articulating a vision that empowers the followers to transform the vision into action.

We hope that you share the feeling of excitement and growth that we experienced as a result of studying leadership from perspectives unfamiliar to us. We have found that leadership is hard work and sometimes disappointing. But most often it is challenging, exciting, and fun.

We are indebted to the authors and publishers of the readings included here as well as to our students, who, over the years, have asked questions about leadership that we could not adequately answer. We wish to thank our colleagues and friends David Campbell, Earl Potter, Larry Cummings, Kerry Walters, Leah Cox Hoopfer, Virginia Schein, and Marshall Sashkin for their advice and assistance. This book would never have been completed without Judy Hepler's patience and expertise at transforming illegible scribbling and fragmented thoughts into a complete manuscript despite unreasonable deadlines. Finally, as two individuals who recognize good leadership when we see it, we gratefully acknowledge Miriam Gilbert's superb leadership of a very professional staff at Westview Press.

William E. Rosenbach
Robert L. Taylor

Foreword

Leadership is all about making things happen that otherwise might not happen and preventing things from happening that ordinarily would happen. It is the process of getting people to work together to achieve common goals and aspirations. It involves the infusion of vision and purpose into an enterprise and entails mobilizing both people and resources to undertake and achieve desired ends.

Leadership defies easy analysis, for it is ultimately a relationship or a chemistry between leaders and their associates. We understand much of what is involved in leadership—vision, strategy, trust, cooperation, high motivation, productivity, and renewal—but paradoxically, however much we admire and study it, precise definitions and measurements remain elusive. Individuals with ample leadership qualities do not necessarily become effective leaders. The genius of leadership sometimes comes too early or too late, and an effective person in one setting can be a failure in another.

A second paradox of leadership is that strong leaders can lead us astray as well as aright. Arthur M. Schlesinger has observed that while leaders have been responsible for moving humanity toward individual freedom, social justice, and religious and racial tolerance, they have also been responsible for the most horrible crimes and extravagant follies that have disgraced the human race. For better, or for worse, leaders and leadership make a difference. Without leadership, there would be little movement or progress in human affairs.

As most of the chapters in this valuable book emphasize, the effective modern leader is also an effective learner, an effective teacher, and an effective mentor or coach. Increasingly, leadership needs in contemporary organizations—public and private—are being reconceptualized as an *engagement* between partners and collaborators. To study leaders separate from the loyalties and complex interactions they have with followers, constituents, and team members is to miss the most important aspects of leadership. Scholars and students of leadership agree that it is the two-way loyalty, the two-way communication, and the mutual engagement of leaders and "led" that are crucial for leadership effectiveness. Thus leadership is essentially a collective enterprise: the ongoing, if subtle, interplay between common needs and wants and a leader's capacity to understand and respond to those collective aspirations.

Effective leadership remains in many ways the most baffling of the performing arts. There is an element of mystery about it. Intuition, flare, and sometimes even theatrical ability come into play. Can leadership be taught? It is said some things can be better learned than taught, and I believe that this is the case with leadership. There is no easy way. Learning to be a leader, like learning an art or becoming a gifted performer, requires concentration, internal self-discipline, practice, patience, and the experience of trying and testing in the crucible of real organizations faced with real problems.

Students of leadership must develop their capacities for observation, reflection, imagination, invention, and judgment. They must also learn to think, write, communicate, and listen effectively and hone their abilities to gather and interpret evidence, marshal facts, and employ the most rigorous methods in the pursuit of knowledge. They need to develop an unyielding commitment to the truth, balanced with a full appreciation of what remains to be learned. Students of leadership learn from mentors who lead by example, who succeed in solving problems, and who make desirable things happen.

Would-be leaders will find in this volume some of the best examinations of effective leadership available. Professors Rosenbach and Taylor are two of the country's best informed students of leadership, and they have gathered diverse essays and research reports that point to both what we know and what remains puzzling about effective leadership. For students of leadership, this book is an excellent place to start.

Thomas E. Cronin
McHugh Professor of American Institutions and Leadership
The Colorado College

PART ONE

UNDERSTANDING LEADERSHIP

There are almost as many definitions of leadership as there are people who have attempted to describe the concept. We have great difficulty defining the term, and we are frustrated at attempts to measure leadership effectiveness. Yet, we all seem to know good leadership when we see it. Leadership, one of the most observed and studied concepts in the modern world, is also one of the least understood of all social processes.

An emerging consensus describes leadership as a process of social influence. However, profiles of leader behaviors do not yield any common threads. Institutional settings are so dissimilar that we are unable to formulate a set of common assumptions that apply to every situation. The result is that many scholars question whether the study of leadership is productive or worthwhile.

Yet, in an increasingly complex world we find a greater need to understand the process of leadership. Groups and organizations are attempting to cope with rapidly changing environments. Limited resources and the need to link diverse cultures throughout the world have placed great pressures on individuals to assume leadership responsibilities. The problems, uncertainties, and opportunities in today's world cause us to search for people who have the vision and energy to take us from where we are to where we want to be.

We long for leaders who are capable of addressing economic and social crises. At the same time, we often reject political candidates because they cannot build a consensus among those who want to be led. Contemporary leaders in business and politics often find themselves impotent; their sphere of influence is so severely constrained and the expectations of their followers so unrealistic that they are rendered ineffective. The question becomes, Can *anyone* lead?

A number of seminars and programs have been developed to educate and train people to be leaders. None have proven successful in taking ordinary people and transforming them into leaders. There are no precise solutions to a process that seems to be based upon the personality of

1

the individual, the collective culture of a group, and the situation at hand. All three of these elements are found in every leadership situation, but there is no prescription that guarantees success in producing leaders.

A great deal of energy has been focused on separating leadership from management. We are not convinced that this is a worthwhile endeavor. Management functions such as planning, organizing, and controlling cannot be separated from the influence process necessary in leadership. Whether a leader must be a good manager or vice versa is a moot question. The real issue is whether a group of people can achieve a common goal with the advice, assistance, and direction of an individual (or group). It means little whether they followed an established procedure or arrived at their destination without design. What makes the difference is that someone helped them create a vision, energized the group to use the available resources for action, and kept the vision alive so that progress was made toward achieving the desired goal.

Thus, our first objective is to provide a scenario for understanding leadership and developing a basis for understanding the phenomenon as it affects today's world. We suggest that self-knowledge, combined with an awareness of the world, will provide the necessary insights to help you appreciate successful leadership. Armed with this knowledge, you can then assess historical and current situations in such a way that the ingredients can be analyzed and understood.

Leadership Perspectives

In "Where Have All the Leaders Gone?" (Chapter 1), Warren Bennis states that our disenchantment with many of today's leaders is partly the result of unfulfilled expectations for both leaders and those being led. He also feels many people confuse administration, management, and leadership. Finally, he suggests that some members of organizations really do not want leadership. Our challenge is to reinstitute leadership in ways that we have tended to ignore but desperately need.

John W. Gardner theorizes in Chapter 2, "The Tasks of Leadership," that we can differentiate between those who are leaders and those who are not by their actions. Using examples of successful male and female leaders, he relates their actions to our lives. Gardner suggests that the significant functions of leadership are envisioning goals, affirming values, motivating, managing, achieving a workable level of unity, explaining, serving as a symbol, representing the group externally, and renewing (leaders, followers, and organizations). He points out that leadership is a social process and that defining its tasks may make it appear more orderly than it actually is.

In "The Leadership Gap," Abraham Zaleznik (Chapter 3) suggests that during periods of uncertainty and change society experiences an inherent tension between the need for leaders and the need for managers. Zaleznik argues that managerial goals are based in the structure of the organization, whereas leadership goals focus on the people. Leaders work to bring about change, are willing to take risks, and have great self-confidence. Managers are perhaps less willing to take risks; they tend toward careerism, and emphasize management skills at the expense of good leadership. Both leaders and managers are needed, says Zaleznik, but we need to merge personal and organizational values in order to develop a stronger sense of true leadership.

In Chapter 4, "Thinking and Learning About Leadership," Tom Cronin provides an adept analysis of the issues associated with trying to define leadership. He questions whether we can teach leadership and, by doing so, raises several important issues for discussion. First, Cronin suggests that we cannot understand leadership without understanding followership. Second, he challenges us to recognize that leaders may be dispersed throughout society, that we may not be able to find leaders by looking in a logical, practical way. He concludes his essay with a set of leadership qualities, bringing into perspective the questions raised in earlier articles.

In Chapter 5, David Van Fleet and Gary Yukl present a comprehensive summary of the significant leadership research over the past one hundred years. In "A Century of Leadership Research," they have taken all of the classic articles and books and distilled them into a concise summary that portrays the evolution of theoretical research in leadership. Their major theme is that although leadership appears to be a relatively simple topic, it is really a complex social phenomenon. This piece weaves together the assumptions and understandings of today's leadership research.

The Issues

The frustration of this initial inquiry is that we come to no clear conclusions. We chose these different perspectives to highlight the fact that our understanding of leadership is characterized by ambiguity, inconsistency, and paradox. Leadership is an elusive concept, and the uncertainties associated with it are constantly challenged and enlivened by the realities of a leader's achievements. It is important at this point not to attempt a definition. Rather, we must think about a conceptual framework within which we can address the issues raised in the remainder of the book.

Several common themes will emerge. The leader has a vision—he or she sees something that others cannot: a future state of affairs for the group or organization. The first task of the leader is to communicate this vision and "co-create" an organizational vision with group members. The vision then becomes independent of the leader and becomes something that everyone shares. The leader emerges as the "vision keeper" and is constantly challenged to energize everyone toward achievement of the desired result.

Developing alternatives of action to turn the vision into reality is the leader's second major challenge. Creativity and innovation are the keys. Once again, everyone in the group or organization must get involved and participate. The leader becomes "producer-director," and everyone works on achieving the goal.

The third challenge is to sustain the activity; during this phase, the leader must be in constant touch with the environment so that necessary changes can be made. Thus, a leader must be flexible or adaptable. The leader pursues not a plan, but, rather, a constant understanding because, as the environment changes, so does the vision. There are no tried and true techniques; intuition, feelings, and belief in the vision guide the leader in the right direction.

Address each of the articles in this book with an open mind, and you will find that the construct of leadership will fall into place. Although you will see dichotomies and contradictions, we are confident that from all of these you will get a clear definition of what *you* believe leadership to be. It is, after all, your definition of leadership in the context of what you understand about yourself, the areas in which you operate, and the aspirations that you hold, that is important in understanding this complex topic.

1

Where Have All
the Leaders Gone?

WARREN G. BENNIS

Where have all the leaders gone? They are, as a paraphrase of that haunting song reminds us, "long time passing."

All the leaders whom the young respect are dead. F.D.R., who could challenge a nation to rise above fear, is gone. Churchill, who could demand and get blood, sweat, and tears, is gone. Eisenhower, the most beloved leader since Washington, is gone. Schweitzer, who from the jungles of Lambarene could inspire mankind with a reverence for life, is gone. Einstein, who could give us that sense of unity in infinity, is gone. Gandhi, the Kennedys, Martin Luther King, all lie slain, as if to prove the mortal risk in telling us that we can be greater, better than we are.

The landscape is littered with fallen leaders. A President re-elected with the greatest plurality in history resigns in disgrace. The Vice President he twice chose as qualified to succeed him is driven from office as a common crook. Since 1973 the governments of all nine Common Market countries have changed hands—at least once. In the last year over a dozen major governments have fallen. Shaky coalitions exist in Finland, Portugal, Argentina, Belgium, Holland, and Israel. Minority governments rule precariously in Britain, Denmark, and Sweden. In Ethiopia, the King of Kings died captive in his palace.

The leaders who remain, the successors and the survivors—the struggling corporate chieftains, the university presidents, the city managers and mayors, the state governors—all are now seen as an "endangered species" because of the whirl of events and circumstances beyond rational control.

Reprinted with permission from *Technology Review*, 75:9 (March-April 1977), pp. 3–12. Copyright © 1977.

There is a high turnover, an appalling mortality—whether occupational or actuarial—among leaders. In recent years the typical college president has lasted about four years; in the decade of the 1950s, the average tenure was over eleven years. Men capable of leading institutions often refuse to accept such pressures, such risks. We see what James Reston of the *New York Times* calls "burnt out cases," the debris of leaders. We see Peter Principle leaders rising to their final levels of incompetence. It has been said that if a Martian were to demand, "Take me to your leader," Earthlings would not know where to take him. Administrative sclerosis around the world, in political office, in all administrative offices, breeds suspicion and distrust. A bumper sticker in Massachusetts summed it up: "Impeach Someone!"

In business the landscape is equally flat. The great leaders that come to mind—Ford, Edison, Rockefeller, Morgan, Schwab, Sloan, Kettering—are long gone. Nixon's business chums were either entrepreneurs "outside" the business Establishment, like Aplanalp the Aerosol King, or they had no widespread acceptance as business leaders or spokesmen. President Ford seemed to get on best with the Washington vice presidents of major corporations (a vice president syndrome as it were). *Fortune* magazine reveals the absence of business leaders in New York University's Hall of Fame. Of the ninety-nine individuals selected, only ten are business leaders.

The peril of the present situation is not exaggerated. Dr. John Platt, a scientist at the University of Michigan, recently stated what he considers to be the ten basic dangers to world survival. Of greatest significance was the possibility of some kind of nuclear war or accident which would destroy the entire human race. The second greatest danger is the possibility of a worldwide epidemic, famine or depression. He sees as the world's third greatest danger a general failure in *the quality of the management and leadership of our institutions.*

Where have all the leaders gone? Why have they become "endangered species"?

Falling Out of Control

Something's happened, that's clear; something that bewilders. As I write this, for example, it can be noted that our technology brings together, at 600 m.p.h. speeds, people who left Los Angeles, San Francisco, Denver, Chicago, Atlanta, at lunch, only to have them all blown to smithereens by a bomb left in a baggage locker at an airport.

It's as if mankind, to paraphrase Teilhard de Chardin, is *falling suddenly out of control of its own destiny.* Perhaps only a new Homer or Herodotus would be able, later on, to show us its patterns and designs, its coherences and contours. We still lack that historical view. What we hear and discern now is not one voice or signal but a confusing jim-jangle of chords. All we know for sure is that we cannot wait a generation for the historian to tell us what happened; we must try to make sense out of the jumble of voices now. Indeed, the first test for any leader today is to discover just *what* he or she does confront; only then will it be possible to devise the best ways of making that reality—the multiple realities—potentially manageable.

The most serious threat to our institutions and the cause of our diminishing sense of able leadership is the steady erosion of institutional autonomy. Time was when the leader could decide—period. A Henry Ford, an Andrew Carnegie, a Nicholas Murray Butler, could issue a ukase—and all would automatically obey. Their successors' hands are now tied in innumerable ways—by governmental requirements, by various agencies, by union rules, by the moral and sometimes legal pressures of organized consumers and environmentalists. For example, before David Mathews became Secretary of Health, Education, and Welfare, and speaking as President of the University of Alabama, he characterized federal regulations as threatening to

> . . . bind the body of higher education in a Lilliputian nightmare of forms and formulas. The constraints emanate from various accrediting agencies, Federal bureaucracies, and state boards, but their effects are the same . . . a loss of institutional autonomy, and a serious threat to diversity, creativity, and reform. Most seriously, that injection of more regulations may even work against the accountability it seeks to foster, because it so dangerously diffuses responsibility.

The external forces that impinge and impose upon the perimeter of our institutions—the incessant concatenation of often contrary requirements—are the basic reasons for the loss of their self-determination. Fifty years ago this external environment was fairly placid, like an ocean on a calm day, forecastable, predictable, regular, not terribly eventful. Now that ocean is turbulent and highly inter-dependent—and makes tidal waves. In my own institution right now the key people for me to reckon with are not only the students, the faculty, and my own management group, but people external to the university—the city manager, city council members, the state legislature, accrediting and professional associations, the federal government, alumni, and parents. There is an incessant, dissonant clamor out there. And because the university is a brilliant example of an institution that has blunted and diffused its main purposes through a proliferation of dependence on "external patronage structures," its autonomy has declined to the point where our boundary system is like Swiss cheese. Because of these pressures, every leader must create a department of "external affairs," a secretary of state, as it were, to deal with external constituencies.

Accompanying all this is a new kind of populism, not the barn burners of the Grange days, not the "free silver" of Bryanism ("The crown of thorns"), but the fragmentation, the caucusization of constituencies. My own campus is typical; we have over 500 organized governance and pressure groups. We have a coalition of women's groups, a gay society, black organizations for both students and faculty, a veterans' group, a continuing education group for women, a handicapped group, a faculty council on Jewish affairs, a faculty union organized by the American Association of University Professors, an organization for those staff members who are neither faculty nor administrators, an organization of middle-management staff members, an association of women administrators, a small, elite group of graduate fellows.

This fragmentation, which exists more or less in all organizations, marks the end not only of community, a sense of shared values and symbols, but of consensus, an agreement reached despite differences. It was Lyndon Johnson's tragedy to plead, "Come let us reason together," at a time when all these groups scarcely wanted to *be* together, much less reason together.

These pressure groups are fragmented. They go their separate and often conflicting ways. They say: "No, we don't want to be part of the mainstream of America—we just want to be us," whether they're blacks, Chicanos, women, the third sex, or Menominee Indians seizing an empty Catholic monastery. They tell us that the old dream of "the melting pot," of assimilation, does not work—or never was. They have never been *"beyond* the melting pot" (as Glazer and Moynihan wrote about it); they have been *behind* it.

So what we have now is a new form of politics—King Caucus, who has more heads than Cerberus, and contending Queens who cry, "Off with their heads!" as they play croquet with flamingos. It is *the politics of multiple advocacies*—vocal, demanding, often "out of sync" with each other. They represent people who are fed up with being ignored, neglected, excluded, denied, subordinated. No longer do they march on cities, on bureaus, or on organizations they view as sexist, racist, anti-Semitic, or whatever. Now, they file suit. The law has suddenly emerged as the court of first resort.

A Litigious Society: "Is the Wool Worth the Cry?"

And so, we have become a litigious society where individuals and groups—in spectacularly increasing numbers—bring suits to resolve issues which previously might have been settled privately. A hockey player, injured in his sport, bypasses the institutional procedures to bring formal suit. The club owners are outraged that one of "its own" would take the case "outside." College students, unhappy with what they are learning on campus, are turning to the courts as well. A lawsuit against the University of Bridgeport may produce the first clear legal precedent. It was filed last spring by a woman seeking $150 in tuition, the cost of her books, and legal fees because a course required of secondary education majors was "worthless" and she "didn't learn anything." A law review has been sued for rejecting an article. In New Jersey, a federal judge has ordered twenty-eight state Senators to stand trial for violating the constitutional rights of the twenty-ninth member, a woman, by excluding her from their party caucus. They did so because, they claimed, she was "leaking" their deliberations to the press. In a Columbus, Ohio, test case, the U.S. Supreme Court recently ruled that secondary-school students may not be suspended, disciplinarily, without formal charges and a hearing, that the loss of a single day's education is a deprivation of property. A federal court in Washington has just awarded $10,000 to each of the thousands of May, 1970, anti-war demonstrators whom it found had been illegally arrested and confined at the behest of Attorney General Mitchell.

Aside from the merits of any particular case, the overriding fact is clear that the hands of all administrators are increasingly tied by real or potential legal issues. I find I must consult our lawyers over even small, trivial decisions. The university has so many suits against it (40 at last count) that my mother calls me "my son, the defendant."

The courts and the law are, of course, necessary to protect individual rights and to provide recourse for negligence, breach of contract, and fraud. But a "litigious society" presents consequences that nobody bargained for, not the least the rising, visible expense of legal preparation plus the invisible costs of wasted time.

Far more serious than expense, however, is the confusion, ambiguity, and lack of subtlety of the law and what that does to institutional autonomy and leadership. To take the example of consumer protection, we see that lawsuits are forcing universities to insert a railroad-timetable disclaimer in their catalogues—e.g., "Courses in this catalogue are subject to change without notice"—in order to head off possible lawsuits. At the same time, the Federal Trade Commission is putting pressure on doctors, architects, lawyers, and other professionals to revise their codes of ethics forbidding advertising. The Buckley amendment, which permits any student to examine his own file, tends to exclude from the file any qualitative judgments which would provide even the flimsiest basis for a suit.

The confusion, ambiguity, and complexity of the law—augmented by conflicting court interpretations—tend toward institutional paralysis. Equally forbidding is the fact that the courts are substituting their judgments for the expertise of the institution. Justice may prevail but at a price to institutional leadership so expensive, as we shall see, that one has to ask if the "wool is worth the cry."

One for the Seesaw

The incessant external forces and the teeming internal constituencies, each with their own diverse and often contrary expectations, demands, and pressures, are difficult enough for any leader to understand, let alone control: at their best, leaders serve as quiet and efficient custodians.

The problem is made infinitely more complex when the goals and values of the internal and external forces seem not merely divergent, but irreconcilable. Their collision, or "boundary clash," tends to isolate or crush the "man at the top."

The College of Medicine of a large urban, but state affiliated, university accepts 187 applicants out of 8,000. Immediately some 23,000 people are angered, the rejected applicants and their parents. Although admissions decisions are the prerogative of the faculty, the president of the university finds himself deluged by phone calls and letters from parents, alumni, friends of the regents, and legislators. He feels, however, that "the president shouldn't butt in. . . ." Meanwhile, the issue grows more political. Disgruntled persons write their legislators. The legislators demand an informal commitment that the College of Medicine accept only state residents. Next they propose a bill that only state residents receive support. The president is forced to become involved. He talks to the governor, the legislators, and the media, and he amasses political support to oppose the state-only bill. Eventually, the bill is dropped.

The legislators provide a large share of the revenues of the university (which happens to be the University of Cincinnati—but it could be legion), and their support has a direct relation to how their constituents react to our internal decisions. Patronage structures blanket the social geography of our environment, as they do that of other institutions. Whether these structures consist of taxpayers or consumers, they are demanding, often fickle, and always want their way. In any case, their generosity or miserliness reflects the degree of respect which they feel for the institution, and whether they like what we're doing for them or their relatives. It's as simple as that.

Let me cite a classic confrontation between these internal and external constituencies, mirroring a divergence in their goals and values. It concerns the policy of "open admission" which has created bewilderment and confusion on many campuses. Open admission makes it difficult to understand what we're about, what our "basic" mission is. It makes it almost impossible to define with any precision the educational stands that we must take from time to time. It's hard to determine just what students need or want and what our responsibility to them should be. As one Appalachian student told his humanities professor: "Sure, I'll be glad to read Dante with you, as soon as everybody in my family has a pair of shoes."

The public's uneasiness is often verbalized through code words or phrases (at least according to my mail and the letters-to-the-editor columns) like "lowering of academic standards" or "cheapening the degree." These concerns often (but not always) reflect the public's foreboding about mass education and its concomitant "equal opportunity" for minorities and women in higher education. While "Affirmative Action" is the mandated vehicle for implementing equal education and work opportunities, in practice it has proved to be more a case study of how difficult it is to force profound changes in an institution as complex, prestigious, slow-moving—and sensitive to economic forces—as a university.

Whatever the reality of Affirmative Action, some citizens are uneasy about this development and use the rhetoric of "lowering standards" or "quotas" to question sharply its validity. And to make matters more complicated, another, increasingly vocal, group feels dissatisfied at the seeming lack of progress. Each of these viewpoints is held by our various publics, and this in turn leads to a situation where "both sides" are dissatisfied with our progress—some because we are doing too little, others because we are trying too much. In either case, we are in the middle and neither side is happy with the university. Or its president.

The university is, in a sense, an anvil on which a fragmented society hammers.

Yes, provide a broad, liberal arts, humanistic education.

No, teach people practical things, so as to guarantee them jobs.

Yes, focus on research and education for the elite.

No, train dental technicians, hotel managers, accountants, but also provide professional education for lawyers, doctors, and engineers.

Yes, stop lowering academic standards, but be sure and enroll more minorities and the poor as a way of creating a more egalitarian society.

And also, while you're at it, provide compensatory education for those victimized by inadequate public schooling, provide opportunities for part-time students, especially for women caught in the homemaker's trap, provide continuing education as job enrichment for workers and executives, and, by the way, become the vehicle through which income redistribution can be achieved.

Obviously, we do not possess the resources to achieve all of these aims. We couldn't, even if we wanted to. By providing a complete menu for every taste we would inevitably and quickly alienate one or another public who would feel disaffected or threatened by one or another of our academic programs and would, actively or passively, turn off its support.

All of our institutions, both public *and* private, confront similar conflict between internal and external environments. In Cincinnati, Procter and Gamble and Federated Department Stores, two of our nation's most successful and well-managed enterprises, must now consider (indeed, are on occasion forced by law to consider) *both* external and internal conflicts, whether nitrates or price-labeling.

The root problem contains profound and grave consequences. It isn't only a matter of a loss of *consensus* over basic values; it is a *polarization* of these values. The university problem is basically a reflection of society's problems, a fact so obvious that we tend to forget it. Education and society are indivisible and cannot be detached from each other. Similarly, Business, with a large "B," is the concentrated epitome of our culture— and is inseparable from it. Coolidge was right that America's business *is* business, and Engine Charlie Wilson was not far wrong with his memorable "what's good for General Motors" remark: business thrives or sickens along with our nation's destiny. All of our institutional fates are correlated with our nation's.

What seems to have happened is this: the environmental encroachments and turbulence, the steady beat of litigation, the fragmentation of constituencies along with their new found eloquence and power, multiple advocacy, win-lose adversarial conflicts between internal and external forces—all of this—has led to a situation where our leaders are "keeping their heads below the grass," as L.B.J. once put it, or paralyzed, or resembling nothing so much as acrobatic clowns. Whatever metaphor one prefers, to grow and stay healthy an institution must strike a proper balance between openness to the environment and protection from too much permeability. Achieving the proper trading relationship without being colonialized is the delicate balance leaders must achieve.

Having to look both ways—in and out, back and forth—was the special gift of Janus, and is required for all leaders today. The "Janus Phenomenon" is a relatively new example of organizational turbulence and leadership optics. Today's leader is surrounded by constituent groups, from inside and outside, as well as by numerous individuals who at any moment, discovering some supposed mutual interest, may suddenly coalesce into some new constituency. In either case, people need slight stimulus to become vocal, organized advocates and activists.

The Cat's Cradle

We know what overstimulation by external forces does to an individual; a total reliance on external cues, stimuli, rewards, and punishments leads to an inability to control one's own destiny. People in this state tend to avoid any behavior for which there is no external cue. Without signals, they vegetate. With contrary signals, they either become catatonic—literally too paralyzed to choose, let alone *act* on a choice, for fear of risk—or, conversely, they lunge at anything and everything, finally contorting themselves into enervated pretzels.

When we apply this analysis to organizations and their leadership, we can observe the same effects. While these coercive political and legal regulations are more pronounced in the public sector than in the private sector, in the latter area the market mechanism has heretofore been the linking pin between the firm and environment, the source of feedback regarding rewards and punishments, and the reflection of the success or failure of decisions. Whether the organization is private or public, whether the controls are legitimate or not, there is only one natural conclusion: an excess of (even well-intended) controls will lead inexorably to lobotomized institutions.

What neither lawmakers nor politicians seem to realize is that law and regulation deal primarily with sins of commission. Sins of omission are more difficult to deal with, partly, as Kenneth Boulding points out, because it is just damned hard in practice to distinguish between honest mistakes and deliberate evil. Which is another way of saying that legitimate risk-taking can land you in jail. On the other hand, by "playing it safe," by living up to the inverted proverb, "Don't just do something, sit there," an institution, a leader, a person, can avoid error, and if continued long enough, they can *almost* avoid living.

As the legal and political systems become increasingly concerned with sins of commission—a fact exemplified in the dramatic switch from *caveat emptor* to *caveat vendor*, in the deluge of consumer protection legislation, in malpractice suits, in the environmental protection movement, in the court decisions awarding damages to purchasers of faulty products—we can get to a point where no producer, no organization, will do anything at all, like the California surgeons who quit operating on any but emergency patients. Why should they? The costs of uncertainty and honest mistakes are now unbearable and far too costly.

At my own and many other universities, for example, we are now in the process of rewriting our catalogues so carefully that it will be virtually impossible for any student (read: consumer) to claim that we haven't fulfilled our end of the bargain. At the same time, because we have to be so careful, we can never express our hopes, our dreams, and our bold ideas of what a university experience could provide for the prospective student. I suspect that in ten years or so, college catalogues, rarely a publication which faculty, students, or administrators are wild about in any case, will devolve into statements that resemble nothing more than the finely printed cautions and disclaimers on the back of airline tickets—just the opposite of what education is all about: an adventurous and exciting odyssey of the mind.

All this—all of the litigation, legislation, and *caveat vendor*—not only diminishes the potency of our institutions, but leads to something more pernicious and possibly irrecoverable. We seek comfort in the delusion that all of our troubles, our failures, our losses, our insecurities, our "hangups," our missed opportunities, our incompetence, can be located "somewhere else," can be blamed on "someone else," can be settled in the seamless, suffocating, and invisible "system." How convenient, dear Brutus.

Just think: at a certain point, following our current practices and national mood, any sense of individual responsibility will rapidly erode. And along with that, the volume of low-level "belly-aching" and vacuous preaching about "the system" will grow more strident. The result: those leaders who are around either will be too weak or will shy away from the inevitable risks involved in doing anything good, bad, or indifferent.

I am *not* arguing the case against regulations and controls. I am painfully conscious that some of them are necessary if we are to realize our nation's values (e.g., equality of opportunity for all); without them, I fear, our basic heritage would have long ago been indelibly corrupted. (And it is not hard to understand why campaign finances have come under control recently. How do we deal with Gulf's $12 million bribes, including one to L.B.J. in 1962 when he was Vice President?) I am also aware that many of our institutions have, through inactive, corrupt, and inhumane actions, brought on themselves regulations which today they claim are unnecessary.

All the same, when it comes to protecting people from their exploiters we have an extra responsibility to be so vigilant, so careful that we don't end up in a situation where *everyone* is enmeshed by a cat's cradle of regulations erratically tangled together with the filaments of "good intentions."

As Justice Brandeis put it many years ago:

> Experience should teach us to be most on guard to protect liberty when the governments' purposes are beneficent. Men born to freedom are naturally alert to repel invasion of their liberty by evil-minded rulers. The greatest dangers to liberty lurk in insidious encroachments by men of zeal, well-meaning, but without understanding.

Variations on a Theme

Memorandum to the People of Ohio's 13th Congressional District:

Summary: Being the Congressman is rigorous servitude, ceaseless enslavement to a peculiar mix of everyone else's needs, demands and whims, plus one's own sense of duty, ambition or vanity. It is that from which Mrs. Mosher and I now declare our personal independence, to seek our freedom, as of January 3, 1977.

It is a Congressman's inescapable lot, his or her enslavement, to be never alone, never free from incessant buffeting by people, events, problems, decisions. . . . It is a grueling experience, often frustrating, discouraging, sometimes very disillusioning. . . . House debates, caucuses, briefings, working breakfasts, working lunches, receptions, dinners, homework study, and even midnight collect calls from drunks. . . . You name it!

I am for opting out. I shall not be a candidate for reelection in 1976.

Charles A. Mosher,
Representative
13th Congressional District
State of Ohio
December 19, 1975

The basic problem is that leaders are facing a set of conditions that seemed to take shape suddenly, like an unscheduled express train looming out of the night. Whoever would have forecast the post-Depression development in the public sector of those areas of welfare, social service, health, and education? Who, save for a Lord Keynes, could have predicted the scale and range of the multinational corporations? Prophetically he wrote: "Progress lies in the growth and the recognition of semi-autonomous bodies within the states. Large business corporations, when they have reached a certain age and size, approximate the status of public corporations rather than that of the individualistic private enterprise."

The Keynesian prophecy is upon us. When David Rockefeller goes to London, he is greeted as if he were a chief of state (and some of his empires *are* bigger than many states). But in addition to the growth of semi-autonomous, often global, corporations which rival governments, we also have public-sector institutions which Keynes could scarcely have imagined. The largest employment sector of our society, and the one growing at the fastest rate, is local and state government. Higher education, which less than twenty years ago was 50 percent private–50 percent public, is now about 85 percent public and is expected to be 90 percent public by 1980. And, where a century ago 90 percent of all Americans were self-employed, today 90 percent work in what can be called bureaucracies, members of some kind of corporate family. They might be called "juristic" persons who work within the sovereignty of a legal entity called a corporation or agency. Juristic persons, not masters of their own actions, cannot place the same faith in themselves that self-employed persons did.

These are the problems of leadership today. We have the important emergence of a Roosevelt-Keynes revolution, the new politics of multiple advocacy, new dependencies, new constituencies, new regulatory controls, new values. And how do our endangered species, the leaders, cope with these new complications and entanglements? For the most part, they do not; that is, they are neither coping nor leading. One reason, I fear, is that many of us misconceive what leadership is about. Leading does not mean managing; the difference between the two is crucial. I know many institutions that are very well *managed* and very poorly *led*. They may excel in the ability to handle the daily routine, and yet they may never ask whether the routine should be done at all. To lead, the dictionary informs us, is to go in advance of, to show the way, to influence or induce, to guide in direction, course, action, opinion. To manage means to bring about, to accomplish, to have charge of or responsibility for, to conduct. The difference may be summarized as activities of vision and judgment versus activities of efficiency.

In his decisionmaking, the leader today is a multidirectional broker who must deal with four estates—his own management team, constituencies within his organization, forces outside his organization, and the media. While his decisions and actions affect the people of these four estates, their decisions and actions, too, affect him. The fact is that the concept of "movers and shakers"—a leadership elite that determines the major decisions—is an outdated notion. Leaders are as much the "shook" as the shakers. Whether the four estates force too great a quantity of problems on the leader or whether the leader takes on too much in an attempt to prove himself, the result is what I call "Bennis' First Law of Pseudodynamics," which is that routine work will always drive out the innovational.

When the well-known author John Hersey was permitted to sit for a week in the Oval Office and its antechambers, recording all he saw and heard, he counted (in five working days) more than 4,000 visitors—Indian tribal chiefs, bishops and rabbis, woolgrowers and cattlemen, labor leaders and businessmen, students, blacks—flowing through the President's office in an unending stream. Just to handle the millions of pieces of mail pouring in and out of the White House took some 250 employees. The daily "news summary" occupied six full-time staffers. To collect and screen the names of possible candidates for the 4,000 positions the President controls, there was a staff of 30. The speech-writing team, which turned out 746,000 words during Ford's first 10 months in office, numbered 13, and Ron Nessen's news staff included eight deputies plus 38 other assistants apparently needed to handle the 1,500 news correspondents covering the White House.

During Lincoln's presidency there was a total of 50 on the White House staff—and that included telegraph operators and secretaries. Roosevelt inherited three secretaries from Hoover; now there are over 3,000. During the Eisenhower and Kennedy years, the staff of the Office of the President increased 13 percent under each. L.B.J. increased his another 13 percent, and Nixon increased his by 25 percent in his first term. Unhappily, the White House overload can be duplicated over the entire corporate and public bureaucratic landscapes. Little wonder there are burnt-out cases or that Congressman Mosher should declare his independence from "rigorous servitude, ceaseless enslavement."

Leading Through Limits

We are now experiencing a transition period that may aptly be called an "era of limits." After the Club of Rome warned us of *The Limits of Growth*, the Arab petroleum boycott, soaring fuel costs, and the continuing energy crisis have confirmed the brutal fact that our national goals have outrun our present means. Some political and institutional leaders exploit this mood by turning the public's disenchantment with growth into a political asset. They want to follow the popular mood, rather than lead it.

The National Observer calls California's young Governor Edmund G. Brown "the hottest politician in America," and quotes him thus: "Growth in California has slowed down . . . the feeling is strongly antigrowth. Once people seemed to think there were no limits to the growth of California. Now Californians are moving to Oregon and Colorado. . . . There are limits to everything—limits to this planet, limits to government mechanisms, limits to any philosophy or idea. And that's a concept we have to get used to. Someone called it the Europeanization of America. That's part right. You take an empty piece of land and you fill it up with houses and soon the land is more scarce and the air is more polluted and things are more complicated. That's where we are today. . . ." *The National Observer* says his rhetoric works: "Over 90 percent of the people in California applaud his performance" (November 29, 1975, pp. 1, 16).

Compared with the grandiose rhetoric of a quarter-century about the apostolic conviction that size and scale plus technological "know-how" could solve all of society's basic problems, the management of decline, as presented by Governor Brown, sounds at least respectably sane, and especially so when compared with a pronunciamento by one of the leaders of the European Economic Community, Dr. Sicco Mansholt: "More, further, quicker, richer are the watchwords of present day society. We must adapt to this for there is no alternative." *That* kind of rhetoric, especially when at brutal odds with present reality, denies the very nature of the human condition.

Thus, growing in popularity, and becoming more sophisticated in its approach, is a new movement. I call it "cameo leadership," which aspires to carve things well, but smaller. It preaches a "homecoming," a less complicated time, a communal life, a radical decentralization of organizational life, a return to Walden before the Pond was polluted, before the Coke stand made its appearance, before *Walden* itself was required reading . . . when things were compassable.

A chief spokesman for this counter-technology movement is E. F. Schumacher, a former top economist and planner for England's National Coal Board. In his book, *Small Is Beautiful*, he writes: "We are poor, not demi-gods. . . . We have plenty to be sorrowful about, and are not emerging into a golden age. . . . We need a gentle approach, a nonviolent spirit, and small is beautiful. . . ."

Governor Brown of California is an avid disciple of Dr. Schumacher's "Buddhist economics." Small *is* beautiful. Sometimes. Perhaps it is beautiful more often than big is beautiful. When big gets ugly, we see human waste, depersonalization, alienation, possibly disruption. When small gets ugly, which never crosses Schumacher's mind, it leads to a decentralization bordering on anarchy; also to poverty, famine, and disease.

Small is beautiful. The era of limits is upon us. Who can argue? Nevertheless, these are slogans as empty as they are both appealing and timely. Because they are appealing we fail to see that they represent no specific programs for change. In fact, rather than opening up the possibilities for solutions, they close them with brevity and an exclamation mark. Basically, they reflect the symptoms now afflicting us by setting rhetorical opposites against each other. Small is beautiful, so big must be ugly. A grain of sand may be more beautiful than a pane of glass. But must we trade the glass for sand (as well as the life expectancy of those protected by glass for that of a Bedouin out admiring that ultimate decentralization, the desert)?

The real point is not one of beauty. The real point is whether leaders can face up to and cope with our present crises, worries, and imperatives. The real problem is how we can lead institutions in a world of over three billion people, millions of whom will starve while other millions can't find work; and for many who do find work it's either boring or underpaid. Many whose work is exciting and provides meaning live with quiet desperation in armed fortresses in fear of "the others." The real question is: How do we provide the needed jobs, and, after that, how do we learn to lead so that people can work more cooperatively, more sensibly, more humanely with one another? How can we lead in such a way that the requisite interdependence—so crucial for human survival and economic resilience—can be realized in a humane and gentle spirit?

Coda

Where have all the leaders gone? They're consulting, pleading, trotting, temporizing, putting out fires, either avoiding or—more often—taking too much heat, and spending too much energy in doing both. They are peering at a landscape of "bottom lines," ostentatiously taking the bus to work (with four bodyguards, rather than the one chauffeur they might need if they drove) to demonstrate their commitment to energy conservation. They are money changers lost in a narrow orbit. They resign. They burn out. They decide not to run or serve. They read Buddhist economics, listen to prophets of decentralization and then proceed to create new bureaucracies to stamp out old ones. (Nixon's "Anti-Big Government" one was bigger than Johnson's.) They are organizational Houdinis, surrounded by sharks or shackled in a water cage, and manage to escape, miraculously, while the public marvels at the feat and then longs for something more than "disappearing acts." They are motivating people through fear, or by cautiously following the "trends," or by posing as Reality through adopting a "Let's Face It" cynicism. They are all characters in a dreamless society. Groping in the darkness, learning how to "retrench," as if that were an art like playing the violin. And they are all scared.

And who can blame them? Sweaty palms are understandable, even natural. That is the final irony. Precisely at the time when the trust and credibility of our leaders is at an all-time low and when survivors in leadership feel most inhibited in exercising the potentiality of power, we most need individuals who can lead. We need people who can shape the future, not just barely manage to get through the day.

There is no simple solution. But there are some things we must recognize:

• Leaders must develop the vision and strength to call the shots. There are risks in taking the initiative. The greater risk is to wait for orders. We need leaders at every level who can lead, not just manage.

• This means that institutions (and followers) have to recognize that they *need* leadership, that their need is for vision, energy, and drive, rather than for blandness and safety.

• This means that the leader must be a "conceptualist" (not just someone to tinker with the "nuts and bolts"). A conceptualist is more than an "idea man." He must have an entrepreneurial vision, a sense of perspective, the time and the inclination to think about the forces and raise the fundamental questions that will affect the destiny of both the institution and the society within which it is embedded.

• This means that he must have a sense of continuity and significance in order, to paraphrase the words of Shelley, to see the present in the past and the future in the present. He must, in the compelling moments of the present, be able to clarify problems—elevate them into understandable choices for the constituents—rather than exploit them; to define issues, not aggravate them.

In this respect leaders are essentially educators. Our great political leaders, such as Jefferson, Lincoln, and Wilson, tried to educate the people about problems by studying the messy existential groaning of the people and transforming murky problems into understandable issues. A leader who responds to a drought by attacking the lack of rainfall is not likely to inspire a great deal of confidence. What we see today is sometimes worse: leaving the problem as a problem (e.g., "the economy" or "the energy crisis") or allowing the problem to get out of control until it sours and becomes a "crisis." What is essential, instead, are leaders who will get at the underlying issues and present a clear alternative. Dr. Martin Luther King, Jr., provided this perspective for black people. We sorely need the same leadership for the whole nation.

• A leader must get at the truth and learn how to filter the unwieldy flow of information into coherent patterns. He must prevent the distortion of that information by over-eager aides who will tailor it to what they consider to be his prejudices or vanities. The biggest problem of a leader—any leader—is getting the truth. Pierre du Pont said well in a long-ago note to his brother Irenée, "One cannot expect to know what will happen, one can only consider himself fortunate if he can know what *has* happened." The politics of bureaucracy tend to interfere with rather than facilitate truth gathering.

That's mainly true because the huge size of our organizations and the enormous overload burdening every leader make it impossible for [a leader] to verify all his own information, analyze all of his own problems, or always decide who should or should not have his ear or time. Since he must rely for much of this upon his key assistants and officers, he would not feel comfortable in so close and vital a relationship with men (women, unfortunately, would not even be considered!) who were not at least of kindred minds and of compatible personalities.

Of course, this is perfectly human, and up to a point understandable. But the consequences can be devastating for it means that the leader is likely to see only that highly selective information, or those carefully screened people that his key assistants decide he should see. And he may discover too late that he acted on information that was inadequate or inaccurate, or that he has been shielded from "troublesome" visitors who wanted to tell him what he should have known, or that he had been protected from some problem that should have been his primary concern.

Given the character of today's institutions with their multiple dependencies and advocacies, picking a team of congenial and compatible associates may be deadly, a replay of Watergate. The most striking thing and most obvious impression I remember from the early Watergate hearings is how much all the Nixon aides looked alike. I had trouble telling Dean from Magruder, Porter from Sloan, Strachan from Haldeman. In appearance, they are almost mirror images of the younger Nixon of the 1940s, as if they were that spiritual or ghostly double called doppelganger. It is easy enough to cry shame on Watergate without perceiving its interconnections with our own lives and organizations and, in lesser degree, our conduct.

For in too many institutions a very few people are filtering the facts, implicitly skewing reality, and selecting information that provides an inaccurate picture on which decisions may be based. Such skewing can affect history: Barbara Tuchman in her recent book on China tells how, in the 1940s, Mao Tse Tung wanted very much to visit Roosevelt, but Roosevelt cancelled the proposed meeting on the basis of incredibly biased information from Ambassador Pat Hurley. It was nearly thirty years later that another President sought out the meeting with Mao, which earlier conceivably could have averted many subsequent disasters.

So the leader cannot rely exclusively on his palace guards for information. Hard as it is to do, he must have multiple information sources and must remain accessible, despite the fact that accessibility in modern times seems one of the most underrated political virtues. The Romans, who were the greatest politicians of antiquity, and probably also the busiest men, valued that quality highly in their leaders. Cicero, in praising Pompey, commented on his ready availability, not only to his subordinates, but to the ordinary soldiers in his command.

A later Roman historian recounted this even more telling anecdote about the Emperor Hadrian. The emperor, who at that time ruled almost the entire civilized world, was riding into Rome in his chariot when an old woman blocked his path. The woman asked him to hear a grievance. Hadrian brushed her aside, saying that he was too busy. "Then you're too busy to be emperor," she called after him. Whereupon he halted his chariot and heard her out.

A pebble dropped in Watergate has its ripple throughout the complex organizational society, and by the same token it is the excesses, the concealments, the arrogance and half-truths of a thousand faceless doppelgangers, in innumerable large organizations, that make a Watergate, an Attica, a Selma possible.

• The leader must be a social architect who studies and shapes what is called the "culture of work"—those intangibles that are so hard to discern but are so terribly important in governing the way people act, the values and norms that are subtlely transmitted to individuals and groups and that tend to create binding and bonding. In whatever goals and values the leader pursues he must proceed toward their implementation by designing a social architecture which encourages understanding, participation, and ownership of the goals. He must, of course, learn about and be influenced by those who will be affected by the decisions which contain the day-to-day realization of the goals. At the very least, he must be forever conscious that the culture can facilitate or subvert "the best laid plans. . . ."

The culture of an organization dictates the mechanisms by which conflict can be resolved, and how costly, humane, fair, and reasonable the outcomes will be. It can influence whether or not there is a "zero-sum" mentality that insists upon an absolute winner or an absolute loser or whether there is a climate of hope. There can be no progress without hope, and there can be no hope if our organizations view conflict as a football game, a win-lose (or possibly tie) situation. While zero-sum situations are extremely rare, most leaders (and followers) tend to respond to most conflicts as if there has to be only one winner and only one loser. In reality, organizations and nations are involved in a much different kind of contest, resembling not so much football as it does the remarkable Swedish game, Vasa Run, in which many take part, some reach the finish line earlier than others and are rewarded for it, but all get there in the end.

Lots of things go into producing a culture: the particular technology of the institution, its peculiar history and geography, the characteristics of the people, and its social architecture. The leader must understand these things; he must have the capacities of an amateur social anthropologist so that he can understand the culture within which he works and which he himself can have some part in creating and maintaining.

• The task of the leader is to lead. And to lead others he must first of all know himself. His ultimate test is the wise use of power. As Sophocles says in *Antigone*: "It is hard to learn the mind of any mortal, or the heart, till he be tried in chief authority. Power shows the man."

So he must learn, most of all, to listen to himself. He must integrate his ideal with his actions and, even when a crackling discrepancy exists, learn how to tolerate this ambiguity between the desirable and the necessary, but [have] not so much tolerance that the margins between them become undiscernible. When that happens, the leader is unwittingly substituting an authentic ideal for an evasion of convenience. Soon he'll forget about the goal—and even feel "comfortable" with an illusion of progress. He must learn how to listen to understand, not to evaluate. He must learn to play, to live with ambiguity and inconsistency. And, most of all, the test of any leader is whether he can ride and direct the process of change and, by so doing, build new strengths in the process.

2

The Tasks of Leadership

JOHN W. GARDNER

Examination of the tasks performed by leaders takes us to the heart of some of the most interesting questions concerning leadership. It also helps to distinguish among the many kinds of leaders, who differ strikingly in how well they perform various functions.

I shall deal with nine tasks: envisioning goals, affirming values, motivating, managing, achieving a workable level of unity, explaining, serving as a symbol, representing the group externally, and renewing. These seem to me to be the most significant functions of leadership, but I encourage readers to add to the list or to describe the tasks in other ways.

It is convenient to use as examples men and women whose names are known to everyone; such people are generally leaders at a fairly lofty level. But the leadership tasks in question are performed at many levels. Every thoughtful parent, teacher, foreman, and county supervisor understands that.

Envisioning Goals

If one asks people what leaders do, the answers tend to focus on two functions: goal-setting and motivating. As a high school senior put it, "Leaders point us in the right direction and tell us to get moving." We shall have to take a more complicated view of the tasks of leadership, but it is appropriate that we begin with envisioning goals.

Leaders perform the function of goal-setting in diverse ways. Some assert a vision of what the group (organization, community, nation) can be at its best. For Americans, one of the earliest such assertions was John Winthrop's "We shall be as a city on a hill, the eyes of all people

Reprinted with permission from *New Management*, 4:4 (Spring 1987), pp. 9–14.

upon us." Other leaders point us toward solutions to our problems. Still others, presiding over internally divided groups, are able to define overarching goals that unify constituencies and focus energies.

Obviously, a constituency is not a blank slate on which a leader may write. Any collection of people sufficiently related to be called a community has many shared goals—some explicit, some unexpressed (perhaps even unconscious)—that are as basic as better prices for their crops and as intangible as a better future for their children. In defining objectives the leader must take such shared goals into account.

The relative roles of leader and followers in determining goals vary from group to group. The teacher of first-grade children and the sergeant training recruits do not do extensive consulting as to goals; congressional candidates do a great deal. In the case of many leaders, goals are handed to them by higher authority. The factory manager and the combat commander may be superb leaders, but many of their goals will have been set at higher levels.

Finally, there is inevitable tension between long- and short-term goals. Constituents are not comfortable with the jerkiness of short-term goal-seeking, and they value the stability that comes with a vision of far horizons. But leaders who hold to long-term goals must ask constituents to defer immediate gratification on at least some fronts, and that does not build popularity. When citizens enter the voting booth, they are apt to remember the deferral of gratification more vividly than they remember the reason for it.

Affirming Values

A great civilization is a drama lived in the minds of a people. It is a shared vision, shared norms, expectations, and purposes. When one thinks of the world's great civilizations, the most vivid images are of the monuments left behind: the Pyramids, the Parthenon, the Mayan temples. But in truth all the physical splendor was the merest by-product. The civilizations themselves, from beginning to end, existed in the minds of men and women.

If we look at ordinary human communities, we see the same reality. A community lives in the minds of its members: in shared assumptions, beliefs, customs, and ideas that give meaning and motivate. And among those ideas are norms or values. In any healthy and reasonably coherent community, people decide what things they will define as legal or illegal, virtuous or vicious, in good taste or in bad.

These values are embodied in the society's religious beliefs and its secular philosophy. Over the past century, many intellectuals have looked down on the celebration of society's values as an unsophisticated and often hypocritical activity. But every healthy social celebrates its values. They are expressed in art, song, and ritual. They are stated explicitly in historic documents, ceremonial speeches, and textbooks.

However expressed, values carry the message of shared purposes, standards, and conceptions of what is worth living and striving for; and they have immense motivating power. People will accept pain and frustration and will strive mightily to meet required standards, all on the condition that the denials and exertions exist within a framework of shared meaning.

There will be vigorous conflicts over specific values in a pluralistic community. At best that is a sign of vitality; at worst it is the price of pluralism. But conflict is one thing, disintegration is something else. When the community's broad consensus disintegrates or loses its force, the society sickens. Nothing holds together.

The leaders whom we admire the most help to revitalize our shared beliefs and values. They have always spent a portion of their time teaching the value framework. It didn't stop with Moses. Jefferson was at it constantly, so were Lincoln, Gandhi, and Martin Luther King.

Sometimes the leader's affirmation of values challenges entrenched hypocrisy or conflicts with the values held by a segment of the constituency. Elizabeth Cady Stanton, nineteenth-century women's rights leader, speaking for now-accepted values, was regarded as a thoroughgoing radical in her day. Jesus not only comforted the afflicted but afflicted the comfortable. Values decay "out there"—in the marketplace, the law office, the press—and they must be regenerated out there. They must be reflected in actual behavior and embedded in our laws and institutions. People who remind us of that are rarely popular.

Motivating

Leaders do not normally create motivation out of thin air. They unlock or channel existing motives. To accomplish that they must understand the hopes and fears and bread-and-butter needs of their constituents.

Any group has a great tangle of motives. Effective leaders tap those motives that serve the purposes of collective action in pursuit of significant shared goals. They accomplish the alignment of individual and group goals. They deal with the circumstances that often lead group members to withhold their best efforts. They call for the kind of effort and restraint, drive and discipline that make for great performance. They create a climate in which there is pride in making significant contributions to shared goals.

Positive Attitudes

At the heart of sustained morale and motivation lie two ingredients that appear somewhat contradictory: on the one hand, positive attitudes toward the future and what one can accomplish through one's own intentional acts; and, on the other hand, recognition that life is not easy and that nothing is ever finally safe.

Students of the American westward movement are familiar with the powerful sense of the future that characterized so many of the pioneers, the belief that they were part of an immensely exciting drama just begun. The sense of having the *Zeitgeist* on one's side is an intoxicating thing.

Somewhat more complex than simple attitudes toward the future are the attitudes individuals have toward their own capacity to affect that future. Psychologists have ways of measuring the extent to which people believe they control (or can influence) the circumstances of their lives and the world around them. Some feel utterly powerless, victims of fate. Others have varying degrees of conviction that they do indeed have some capacity to control their own lives and influence the world around them. This confidence greatly increases the likelihood of sustained, highly motivated effort.

Loss of Confidence

The opposite of positive attitudes is not adequately captured by the word pessimism. Loss of confidence brings images of defeat and failure, helplessness, even self-contempt. Among the direct consequences are an incapacity to summon energy on behalf of purposeful effort, an unwillingness to take risks, and a fatal timidity when the moment of opportunity breaks. The effect on an organization can be devastating. As negative attitudes rise, bureaucratic defensiveness rises along with them, and the whole system becomes rigid.

Creativity within an organization is to be found among men and women who are considerably removed from the fatalistic end of the scale. People have to believe in their capacity to act and bring about a good result. Leaders must help them keep that enlivening belief. Loss of it is one of the most poignant contemporary problems. There are innumerable factors in contemporary life that leave people with a sense of puzzlement and impotence about their relationship to the whole. Leaders must help us believe that we can be effective, that we can achieve a better future by our own efforts.

Managing

Most managers exhibit some leadership skills, and most leaders on occasion find themselves managing. Leadership and management are not the same thing, but they overlap. What follows is a list of those aspects of leadership that one might describe as managing.

1. *Planning and Priority-Setting.* Assuming that broad goals have been set, someone has to plan, fix priorities, choose means, and formulate policy. These are functions often performed by leaders. When Lyndon B. Johnson said, early in his presidency, that education was the nation's number one priority, he galvanized the nation's educational leaders and released constructive energies far beyond any governmental action that had yet been taken.

2. *Organizing and Institution-Building.* We have all seen leaders enjoy their brilliant moment and then disappear without a trace because they had no gift for building their purposes into institutions. Someone has to design the structures and processes through which substantial endeavors get accomplished over time. Many who have written on leadership have noted that, ideally, leaders should not regard themselves as indispensable but should enable the group to carry on. Institutions are a means to that end.

3. *Keeping the System Functioning.* Presiding over the arrangements through which individual energies are coordinated to achieve shared goals sounds like a quintessential management task. But it is clear that most leaders find themselves occasionally performing one or another of the essential chores: mobilizing and allocating resources, ensuring the continuing vitality of the team, creating and maintaining appropriate procedures, delegating and coordinating, providing a system of incentives, supervising, evaluating, and holding accountable.

4. *Agenda-Setting and Decision-Making.* The goals may be clear, the organization well set up and smoothly operating, but there remain agenda-setting and decision-making functions that must be dealt with. The announcement of goals without a proposed program for meeting them is a familiar enough political phenomenon, but not one that builds credibility.

5. *Exercising Political Judgment.* In our pluralistic society, persons directing substantial enterprises find that they are presiding over many constituencies within their organization and contending with many outside. Each has its needs and claims. One of the tasks of the leader/manager is to make the political judgments necessary to prevent secondary conflicts of purpose from blocking progress toward primary goals.

Achieving Workable Unity

A pluralistic society is, by definition, one in which there are many different groups, each with its own purposes. Collisions are inevitable and often healthy, as in commercial competition, the settlement of civil suits, and efforts to redress grievances through the political process. Conflict is necessary in the case of oppressed groups that must fight for the justice that is due them. Indeed, one could argue that willingness to engage in battle when necessary is a *sine qua non* of leadership.

But most leaders most of the time are striving to diminish conflict rather than increase it. Some measure of cohesion and mutual tolerance is an absolute requirement of social functioning.

Leaders must deal with both external and internal conflict. The time is past—if it ever existed—when leaders could confine their attention to the system over which they have jurisdiction. Today they live in a world of interacting, colliding systems. Leaders of any particular system have no choice but to take into account the need for mutually workable arrangements with systems external to their own. Leaders unwilling to do so are not serving the long-term interests of their own constituents.

Leaders in this country today must cope with the fragmentation of the society into groups that have great difficulty in understanding one another or agreeing on common goals. It is a fragmentation rooted in the pluralism of our society, in the obsessive specialization of modern life, in the multiple, interlocking systems through which we conduct our affairs, and in the skill with which groups in the society organize to advance their concerns.

Under the circumstances, all our leaders must spend part of their time building community, dealing with polarization, and creating loyalty to the larger venture. There is a false notion that this is a more bland, less rigorous task than leadership of one of the combative segments. In fact, the leader willing to tackle polarization is the braver person and is generally under fire from both sides.

Explaining

"Explaining" sounds too pedestrian to belong on a list of the tasks of leadership, but every leader will recognize it. People want to know what the problem is, why they are being asked to do certain things, how they relate to the larger picture. Thurman Arnold said, "Unhappy is a people that has run out of words to describe what is happening to them." Leaders find the words.

To be heard above the hubbub in the public forum today, explaining generally requires more than clarity and eloquence. It requires effective access to the media of communication or broad alliances among those segments of the population that keep ideas in circulation: editors, writers, intellectuals, association leaders, advocacy groups, chief executive officers, and the like.

The task of explaining is so important that some who do it exceptionally well play a leadership role even though they are not leaders in the conventional sense. When the American colonies were struggling for independence, Thomas Paine was a memorable explainer. In the powerful environmentalist surge of the 1960s and 1970s, no activist leader had as pervasive an influence on the movement as did Rachel Carson, whose book *Silent Spring* burst on the scene in 1963. Betty Friedan's *The Feminine Mystique* played a similar role for the women's movement.

Serving as a Symbol

The leader is inevitably a symbol. The worker singled out to be foreman discovers with some discomfort that he is set apart from his old comrades in subtle ways. He tries to keep the old camaraderie but things have changed. He is now a symbol of management.

In a group threatened with internal strife the leader may be a crucial symbol of unity. In a minority group's struggle to find its place, combative leaders—troublesome to others—may be to their own people the perfect symbol of their anger and their struggle.

The top leader of a community or nation symbolizes the group's collective identity and continuity. It is for this reason that the death of a president produces a special reaction of grief and loss. Americans who were beyond childhood when John F. Kennedy was assassinated remember, despite the passage of decades, precisely where they were and what they were doing when the news reached them. Even for many who did not admire him, the news had the impact of a blow to the solar plexus. And those old enough to remember Franklin D. Roosevelt's death recognize the reaction.

Most leaders become quite aware of the symbolic aspects of their role and make effective use of them. One of the twentieth-century leaders who did so most skillfully was Gandhi. In the issues he chose to do battle on, in the way he conducted his campaigns, in the jail terms and the fasting, and in his manner of dress he symbolized his people, their desperate need, and their struggle against oppression.

Representing the Group

In quieter times (we love to imagine that there were quieter times) leaders could perhaps concentrate on their own followers. Today, representing the group in its dealings with others is a substantial leadership task.

It is a truism that all of the human systems that make up the society (and the world) are increasingly interdependent. The corporate CEO is constantly coping with external groups: all levels of government, competitors, the investment community, the media, consumers' advocacy groups, environmental groups, and foreign governments.

People who have spent their careers in the world of the specialist or within the boundaries of a narrow community (their firm, their profession) are ill-equipped for such leadership tasks. The young potential leader must learn early to cross boundaries and to know many worlds.

Given those realities, it is not easy to hold fast to the traditional idea of a leader with a clearly defined constituency. Those who exercise leadership in dealing with systems external to their own are doing so without a grant of authority over those external groups. The attributes that enable them to reach and lead their own constituencies may be wholly ineffective in external dealings.

A distinctive characteristic of the ablest leaders is that they do not shrink from external representation. They see the long-term needs and goals of their constituency in the broadest context, and they act accordingly. The most capable mayors think not just of the city but of the metropolitan area and the region. Able business leaders are alert to the political climate and to world economic trends.

The most remarkable modern example of a leader carrying out the representative function is Charles de Gaulle. De Gaulle has his detractors, but none can fail to marvel at his performance in successfully representing the once and future France-as-a-great-power at a time when the nation itself was a defeated, demoralized, enemy-occupied land.

Renewing

Leaders need not be renewers. They can lead people down old paths, using old slogans, toward old objectives. Sometimes that is appropriate. But the world changes with disconcerting swiftness. Too often paths are blocked, and the old solutions no longer solve anything.

Change is not to be sought for its own sake. The consequences of change may be very good, very bad, or something in-between. All renewal is a blend of continuity and change. Our problem is that to forgo change is not an option today. We are buffeted by events over which we have no control, and change will occur. The question is: Will it be the kind of change that will preserve our deepest values, enhance the vitality of the system, and ensure its future? All intelligent efforts to accomplish renewal are attempts to bring about those consequences.

All effective performance depends on the refinement of methods for reaching whatever goals are sought. But when new realities call for new methods, it turns out that the old ways of doing things have hardened into inviolable routines. Innovation is blocked by a thicket of fixed attitudes, habits, perceptions, assumptions, and unwritten rules. The consequence is that although renewal seems like a motherhood issue—who could oppose it in principle?—it is rarely popular in practice.

The Trance of Nonrenewal

The problem is systemic. It is not a question of healthy systems whose leaders happen to lack creativity. If we could pump creativity into the leaders, they would still be faced with the reality of systemic stagnation. Organizational arrangements and strategies designed to deal with old realities must be redesigned to cope with new challenges. Individuals who are functioning far below their potential must be awakened.

In some systems that have gone too long without renewal, people understand that change is needed and are restless. This was spectacularly true of Turkey when Kemal Ataturk, one of the great leader/renewers of modern times, was a young officer. Long before World War I he had joined the Young Turks who sought a constitutional government for the decaying 600-year-old Ottoman Empire. After the war he drove out the various foreign powers threatening Turkey's autonomy, created the Turkish Republic, and then, as president, launched an extraordinary series of reforms. He disestablished Islam as the state religion; abolished old codes subordinating women; instituted a new civil and penal code; abolished the traditional—mainly religious—educational system; and established secular schools.

Such far-reaching changes would have been quite impossible had there not been an influential body of Turks who were ready for change. Humiliated by defeat in the war, alienated by the decay of the sultanate, and acutely conscious of their country's backwardness, they were eager to put the past behind them.

But such readiness for change is not a common circumstance. In most systems needing renewal, people are satisfied with things as they are, and the leaders are satisfied too. It is as though the system were asleep under a magic spell.

But the spell can be broken. Disaster is a spell-breaker. (Of course, the disaster is often brought on by the nonadaptive ways of the system.) Competition from rival systems may break the spell. Cold reality can be a spell-breaker, and leaders can help by cutting through all the organizational filters and getting back in touch with what actually goes on. That is why generals should visit the front lines and business executives should mingle with customers.

A strategy for avoiding the trance of nonrenewal is to keep a measure of diversity and dissent in the system. Dissent isn't comfortable, but generally it is simply the proposing of alternatives: a system that isn't continuously examining alternatives is not likely to evolve creatively.

A feature of the trance of nonrenewal is that individuals can look straight at a flaw in the system and not see it as a flaw. The organization that is gravely in need of renewal shows plenty of signs of its threatened condition, but the signs can't be seen by those who are "under the spell." The future generally announces itself from afar. But most people are not listening. Others are listening but cannot bestir themselves to act. Leaders who can listen and bestir themselves will be credited with an uncanny gift for prophecy.

So much for the tasks of leadership. Any attempt to describe a social process as complex as leadership inevitably makes it seem more orderly than it is. Leadership is not tidy. Decisions are made and then revised or reversed. Misunderstandings are frequent; inconsistency is inevitable. Achieving a goal may simply make the next goal more urgent: inside every solution are the seeds of new problems. And as Donald Michael has pointed out, most of the time most things are out of hand. No leader enjoys that reality, but every leader knows it.

3

The Leadership Gap

ABRAHAM ZALEZNIK

Five years ago in the *Harvard Business Review (HBR)*,[1] I raised the question of whether managers and leaders have distinctly different types of personality. I said that American business had created a new breed called the manager, whose function is to ensure the "competence, control, and the balance-of-power relations among groups with the potential for rivalry." The managerial ethic has fostered a bureaucratic culture that minimizes imaginative capacity and the ability to visualize purposes and to generate values at work, all important attributes of leaders who interact with followers.

The manager was seen as a person with practical responsibilities, who sees that problems are resolved in such a way that people at different levels of responsibility will continue to contribute effectively to the organization. Managerial practice focuses on the decisionmaking process rather than ultimate events, and managers themselves are typically hard working, intelligent, analytical, and tolerant of others. Individuals who are usually thought of as leaders, on the other hand—more dramatic in style and unpredictable in behavior—seem to dominate the swirl of power and politics with an authority that stems from personal magnetism and commitment to their own undertakings and destinies.

During periods of stress and change, society feels an inherent tension between its need for both managers and leaders, for both stability and innovation, and shows symptoms of the deficiency it may have created by stimulating an adequate supply of one type at the expense of the other.

Managerial goals are deeply embedded in the structure of the organization, in contrast to entrepreneurial or individual leadership goals, which actively attempt to shape public ideas and tastes. Instead of boldly

Reprinted from *The Washington Quarterly, A Review of Strategic and International Issues,* 6:1 (Winter 1983), by permission of the MIT Press, Cambridge, Massachusetts.

adopting technical innovation or taking risks with untested ideas, managers tend to survey constituents' needs and build their goals on a rational anticipation of the response. They tend to avoid direct confrontation or solutions that could stir up strong feelings of support or opposition. To reconcile differences among people they often seek ways to convert win-lose situations into win-win situations. They focus subordinates' attention on procedures rather than on the substance of decisions, communicate in signals rather than in clearly stated messages, and play for time to take the sting out of win-lose. These tactics frequently create a climate of bureaucratic intrigue and control, which may account for subordinates often viewing managers as inscrutable, detached, and manipulative.

A leader is more interested in what events and decisions mean to people than in his own role in getting things accomplished. The atmosphere leaders create is often one of ferment, which intensifies individual motivation and often results in unanticipated outcomes. Risk is involved in the uncertainty of whether this intensity produces innovation and high performance, or is just wasted energy.

A sense of belonging, of being part of a group or organization, is important to a manager. Perpetuating and strengthening existing institutions enhances his sense of self-worth: he is performing in a role that harmonizes with the ideals of duty and responsibility. Leaders tend to feel somewhat apart from their environment and other people; their relationship toward individuals in a group and their own approach to work are more important to them than group membership and work roles. It is this separate sense of self that makes leaders agents of change, whether technological, political, or ideological.

Even great talent will not guarantee that a potential leader can achieve his ambitions, or that what he achieves will benefit the world. Leaders, like artists, are inconsistent in their ability to function well, and some may give up the struggle.

Is the Distinction Valid?

Our recent concern over declining U.S. productivity, declining standards of quality, and the low state of our work ethos testifies to some missing element in the way we organize economic activity in our society. I think this is directly related to the failure of modern bureaucracies to make use of one kind of leadership talent. If managers and leaders are both needed—one to maintain order by controlling the processes of strategy and operations, the other to effect necessary change by raising standards and defining future goals—we now face the serious challenge of how to build alliances or coalitions not merely between people who work at different jobs but between different kinds of personality types. Leadership involves the personal effect of the leader as an instrument of change on the thinking and behavior of other people.

In my *HBR* article, I used the example of Alfred P. Sloan, whose genius for management was responsible for introducing such new concepts as marketing programs related to product line segmentation, a new kind of distribution organization, and a balanced program of centralization and decentralization that is still a classic model of formal organizational structure. I showed how he handled a conflict between the heads of the manufacturing companies in General Motors, who wanted to go ahead with production of a water-cooled engine that they could make easily and take to market, and Charles Kettering, who was the head of research and development (R&D) and wanted more time and resources to develop an air-cooled engine. Sloan needed a solution that would not alienate Kettering or his ally, Pierre S. du Pont. Instead of exercising his authority to make the practical decision in favor of the manufacturing heads, he threaded his way through the problem by creating a new structure, a mythical organization called the air-cooled engine company, with Kettering in charge. Sloan knew that Kettering was an inventor and not a manager and that the air-cooled engine would probably not materialize, but his maneuver was brilliant because it solved the problem so everyone concerned accepted the process rather than saw it as a win-lose situation.

Such manipulations are useful to managers when the only apparent alternative solutions would hurt the organization or interfere with its output. A leader might have plunged headlong into the conflict, relying on his own powers to steer things through to what he saw as a sound long-range solution, but he might only have aggravated the problem by holding the manufacturers at bay and blocking production in the waiting factories.

Most American managers would probably take umbrage at the notion their profession overlooks any important element. To understand why effective management is not enough, I would like to point out four management assumptions that seem to me mistaken.

One assumption is that the goals of the organization are inherently sound. Managers do not think of themselves as having responsibility for rapid changes in orientation and attitudes, but instead they perpetuate existing goals. One of the elements missing in management, as well as in our economic institutions, is a willingness to question the goals inherent in organizations.

A second assumption is that setting up structures and forms to solve problems involves no cost to the organization. There is in fact a cost that should be calculated for every structural innovation, and if we were able to calculate these, managers would less frequently manipulate structures and think more directly about the nature of the problem they are trying to solve.

A third assumption that may be wrong is that the motivations, beliefs, needs, and desires of human beings are constants and will automatically support the structures that managers try to implement. I think this assumption should be questioned very seriously. There is ample evidence that human motivations vary not only according to incentives and rewards, but also with the social setting and culture of the organization.

The fourth and weakest link in the whole foundation of ideas that supports the management ethos is the assumption that behavior is predictable. We do not yet know enough about behavior, and I do not think we ever will. If behavior could be predicted, organizations could be run with a great deal more assurance than is actually possible simply by calculating the likely effects of doing certain things.

Leadership involves more of the personal effect of the leader as an instrument of change in raising the aspirations and values of other people. Leaders center their assumptions on people—why they act as they do, what they think, what is important to them—rather than on structures.

Leaders assume they can and will be responsible for directing and bringing about any appropriate change. Their primary job is to work persuasively on the values, beliefs, and ideas of people who are going to be part of this change. James MacGregor Burns, in his impressive synthesis drawn from a broad range of disciplines that have tackled the subject of leadership, shows how this "transforming" process worked in the lives of dominant world figures who changed the course of events.[2] During periods of upheaval the leaders tapped the immediate needs and desires of constituencies and transformed them into a higher stage of aspiration and expectation that led to effective action. Burns distinguished this transforming from a transactional kind of leadership, which is kept within contractual boundaries and is based on exchange of one thing for another, such as services rendered in return for money or responsibility accepted in exchange for tenured rank. This corresponds more to the work of managers and their concern with the orderly processes and getting things done through contractual relationships in a structure with a minimum of emotional engagement.

In his book *Leadership*, Professor Burns points out that in the past there have been two approaches to the subject: leaders are viewed either as heroic and famous figures, which is essentially an elitist and exclusive point of view, or as agents from the perspective of followers. He proposes a more realistic concept for the twentieth century, uniting these two views, in which the processes and interplay of leadership are seen as part of the dynamics of conflict and power, with leadership as something more than power holding. In the more complex and potent form of transformational leadership, a leader's power is based on an inherent sensitivity to followers' latent ideas, and his ability to raise them toward higher goals. Interaction between leader and followers is mutually stimulating and elevating, and the change in motives and goals of both has a direct effect on social relations—and morale—ranging from the small and hardly noticed to the creative and historic.

Leadership also involves risk. In contrast to the manager's reliance on structure, the leader risks losing his authority or an erosion of his power base by putting his personal desires on the line. Nothing is as perishable as power if it is used unwisely, or held without being used. The conservatism of managers may well be based on the necessity of guarding the extent to which they risk erosion of their power base. But leaders assume, more often than not, that the impetus for action comes from within themselves rather than from an imposed structure, and accept this inner challenge.

Probably the most important characteristic of leaders is that they must understand themselves before they can work on others. Because they view themselves as instruments of action, Socrates' maxim "Know thyself" is fundamental to leadership. Whereas the burden of responsibility for managers is basically on the structural network of people contributing to output, the essential responsibility of a leader is to himself and to effective interaction with his constituents. Leadership is meaningless without values. An organization or hierarchy can set its values and hope to develop leaders who will articulate them, but values cannot be imposed. They must correspond to the values latent in leaders and followers that can mesh with those of the organization.

The only values that can be relied on are those that are deeply felt and have been absorbed from experience. The styles and standards that evolve from the experience of a functioning relationship between leader and followers will survive even though they may be diverse and occasionally conflicting. The healthy expression of a loyal opposition strengthens the development of durable policies in well-run governments and institutions. There is no reason why democratic institutions, including corporations, cannot thrive by accepting the positive value of different attitudes, expressions, styles, opinions, and personalities.

Is There a Leadership Gap?

The increasing imbalance in our society weighted toward management has created a shortage of leaders in American institutions. One prevalent symptom of this gap is the loss of confidence in authority. Without the bond of confidence between those in authority and those responsive to it, achieving unity of purpose or any common understanding of what a business enterprise, university, or government is trying to accomplish becomes difficult.

Simultaneous with a decline in confidence, a dangerous trend toward careerism has developed. More often than not, people think of their own advancement or personal goals in terms of salary and status rather than the long-range effects of their work on others or on larger organizational objectives. Nothing destroys mutual confidence between a person in authority and the subordinates more than an awareness that the supervisor, executive, or officer is fundamentally looking out for his own self-interest. We must find ways to counteract careerism. I think it is a dangerous symptom—at least as destructive at middle and lower levels as at the top—reflecting deterioration in a culture that does not adequately recognize the importance of personal or human values. If we respect power and money above personality, intelligence, and ideas, we establish careerist incentives and rewards that blur the significance of personal accomplishment or of higher social goals.

Executives often reject my view that managers and leaders are different. Because complexity makes their jobs so extremely demanding, they feel that being a top manager takes more talent and ability than I appreciate. Others contend that real managers have to *be* leaders to cope with elaborate, accumulated layers of hierarchies, especially in the defense area where the structure has been described as "just there." Layers of management and review and the anonymity of upper echelon staffs make it difficult to run a sprawling enterprise encompassing a tremendous range of personnel, operations, equipment, and supplies and seem to require leadership in managers as well as managerial expertise in leaders. I certainly would not minimize the burdens of responsibility at these levels, or the need for talent. The anonymity so keenly felt even by top officials in the defense organization is, however, the product of a managerial culture that has restricted the development of networks of individual leaders as an integral force in the organization.

Does not the mobility of people in responsible positions—the general lack of anchors—again indicate that our institutions have encouraged management at the expense of leadership? We find an illustration of this in the army's attempt to encourage unit cohesion by introducing a cohort system to keep enlisted men committed to their units and to the goals of the military organization. A military sociologist's observation that the . . . system has promoted positive mentor relationships between unit leaders and soldiers demonstrates again that a leadership gap has had its demoralizing causal effects.

The application of systems analysis and econometric models to the All-Volunteer force is, of course, another structural attempt at solving the problems of efficiency in a large multiunit organization. That it is a civilian-imposed change, a deviation from the long-time military tradition, makes it no less a characteristically managerial structural solution, stressing skills over rank but neglecting to incorporate subjective, qualitative factors like cohesion and commitment on the very mechanistic ground that such factors don't lend themselves to the quantitative analysis.

Looking closely at the issues of leadership in organizations, I come back to the concept that it is essential and possible to underline the necessity for a coherent structure of authority in which individuals view themselves as major agents of action without readily shifting responsibility on to structures over which they have no feeling of control or personal investment. We could enhance our work ethos and our quality of production if organizations emphatically adopted the point of view that to direct people and communicate policy you must believe what you say and say only what you believe. Production indicators might rise dramatically when supervisors are encouraged to probe problems, propose improvements, and stimulate those working under them to adopt new attitudes and practices. It could reasonably be expected that through more widespread use of individual example and engagement the transformational process would prove far more efficient than consultants' surveys or organizational directives.

We all know by now that the American automobile industry, for instance, cannot be turned around by cautious piecemeal solutions or structural adjustments. Not only will bold decisions have to be made, but many risks will have to be taken in adopting technical innovations. The kind of initiative needed may be outside the experience of U.S. managers, but it can be found in the personality pattern of leaders whose self-reliance and ties with their followers give them the power to steer through problems toward the decisions that must be made for long-range solutions.

The complaint is made that Americans will not become followers because they have lost a sense of values. It has even been proposed that we should organize followers first around a set of goals or programs before leaders step forward to attach themselves to the appropriate cause. But as I have said, these proposals fail to consider the overriding aspect of leadership: the leader's intuitive abilities and personal qualities are essential in eliciting a response from followers in order to extend their energies and attitudes toward larger goals and values. Organizational attempts to prefabricate scenarios or instill prescribed values are futile, because they dodge the issue of personal influence and engagement by leaders and draw one more veil of anonymity between people and programs.

Can We Educate for Leadership?

Historians note that leaders emerge in times of crisis, as if the crisis itself had brought them forth to satisfy a public yearning for one individual to symbolize people's hopes, desires, ambitions, and determination. Apart from the disadvantages of waiting for crises to produce leaders, we can in our own time wonder whether the apparent phenomenon of crisis leadership is as dependable as it seems to have been in the past. The opposing influence of man-made bureaucratic structures may have been too effective. Our institutions will have to reassess their needs and determine not only how they can encourage and develop leaders at many different levels, but where the particular gaps are that leaders could most effectively fill.

"How do we recognize leadership? And do we understand it?" managers ask. It is true that we cannot pinpoint potential leaders in advance, but we can give them opportunities. Mentors can test the willingness of younger people to shape and mediate conflict and to step forward with their own criticisms and proposals for work problems— especially where structural solutions have not worked.

In the early days of the American republic an astonishing number of great men were prominently active in public life. Before schools of law, medicine, science, and technology had been established, the political arena was virtually the only field open to men of talent, so they concentrated there and shone brilliantly. The talent they represented is widely diffused today through many specialties in the arts, sciences, and professions, but it is far less conspicuous in the bureaucracies of those institutions that shape our social standards: business, education, government.

It is a mistake to assume that people have changed from one generation to another and can no longer respond to initiative. Our system of training and educating people has denied [those with] a certain kind of leadership talent enough significant participation in the life of the organization. Managers, teachers, and people in responsible positions in the society can recognize potential leaders more easily when they understand that freely developed personal relationships between supervisors and subordinates can benefit the culture of the group, that questions and challenges can yield results, and that encouraging experimentation can produce a more dynamic environment where talent can grow.

Is it an elitist concept to train selected individuals to become leaders because of talent, personality, and potential influence over followers? Americans have always felt a tension between the polarized ideals of looking up to a select group of leaders and participation in a democracy.

The fundamental tension in our society between elitist and populist viewpoints tends to focus on a version of leadership representing either extreme. As a result we do not think much about the many effective leaders who have not captured headlines or appeared in history books. I think it is time to separate the term "charisma" from the concept of leadership. Charisma leads but can also mislead followers. It is not a necessary ingredient of leadership and certainly inclines toward elitist and mystical conceptions, as well as singles out certain leaders and diminishes others whose influence on followers may have been as enduring and significant.

Above all, charismatic leadership as a concept diverts attention from the important educational function of leadership. The energy and time expended in trying to bring out a talent for management in leaders, or leadership traits in good managers, could be allocated more realistically to teaching managers and leaders to understand their different approaches to work relationships without becoming destructively competitive, and for each to see the need for the other. This would also focus more attention on how to overcome the many obstacles to early identification of leaders.

Manager and Leader Orientations— Both Have Value

Our management culture is based on the rational principle of contract, which binds individuals to terms covering an exchange of something for something else without further infringements on their freedom. Contractual relationships are the key to a democratic economy and the free enterprise system, although extending the principle of contract into all family or community relationships tends to leave people deprived of the benefits of important human relationships.

The leader-manager distinction has been viewed by the sociologist Charles Moskos as a contrast between commitment to the institution, whose purpose and values transcend self-interest, and to occupational categories, where responsibilities are purely contractual, exchanging work for cash. I think this may miss the important potential synergistic effects of leadership and management in improving the ways in which people approach work and the solution of problems. Although executives' personal goals, according to this proposed theory, are more explicitly linked to institutional goals, the relationship with followers that leaders can develop in the professional and occupational categories could be at least as significant to the character and quality of the organization.

A more useful analogy might compare the effects of leaders and managers to those of strategy and operations, with strategists staking out the direction, relative position, and objectives of the organization in its competitive setting, and operations managers dealing with current applications and implementation of specifications and programs. Strategy is the job of projecting into the future: surveying a company's situation and deciding between alternative courses of action with many possible consequences. Operations coordinates the work of implementing decisions that have been made and getting the job done. Strategy corresponds to leadership in making decisions and taking actions that affect others, while operations corresponds to the many interrelating responsibilities of management.

This analogy suggests how the synergistic relationship between strategy and operations would apply also in a fully functioning relationship of mutual respect between leaders and managers in large organizations. To view the distinction as one between ideals and commitment, on one hand, and occupations and material self-interest, on the other, seems to oversimplify and even distort the real difference.

The notion that managers deal with things and leaders deal with people is another oversimplification. Managers deal with a great many people and have to be aware of their needs. The difference I would stress is that managers deal with people in interacting groups, aiming at consensus agreement and on the whole minimizing the one-to-one relationship that is essential to a leader's makeup and development. Both managers and leaders can contribute to a society and its institutions. The art of business management has obscured the importance of personal initiative and leadership by its emphasis on structural arrangements, processes, and order, to the point where personal leadership needs to be retrieved and drawn out in individuals whose talents predispose them in that direction.

Experimenting with one-to-one relationships, such as apprenticing junior executives to senior mentors, could inject a healthy elixir into the managerial culture. Peer alliances, through which corporations attempt to differentiate responsibilities equally among persons of equal status, theoretically promote learning uninhibited by the restraints of authority or criticisms of superiors, but I believe such alliances consistently develop team players rather than the kind of individual who might become a leader. In a one-to-one relationship with a superior, a junior executive can learn first hand about power, performance, and integrity. These relationships could teach senior executives that a direct exchange of ideas, open challenges, and the competitive impulses of subordinates can be creative and stimulating without shattering their own authority. Furthermore, apprenticeships prepare individuals to move more rapidly into strategy-related positions where they can put their ideas to work.

To undergo the necessary transformation in this decade, management will have to accept the feasibility of working alliances with leaders who question old practices and propose new solutions, and to think of the link between them as essential as the link between strategy and operations. While guarding against the cult of elitism, managers must nevertheless lean toward a culture of individualism. Only when the values of an organization also can be expressed as the personal values of those within the organization can they have any real meaning.

Notes

1. Abraham Zaleznik,"Managers and Leaders: Are They Different?" *Harvard Business Review*, May-June 1977, pp. 67–68.

2. James MacGregor Burns, *Leadership* (New York: Harper & Row, 1978), chapters 1, 3, 6, 7, 9, 11.

4

Thinking and Learning About Leadership

THOMAS E. CRONIN

Introduction

Leadership is one of the most widely talked about subjects and at the same time one of the most elusive and puzzling. Americans often yearn for great, transcending leadership for their communities, companies, the military, unions, universities, sports teams, and for the nation. However, we have an almost love-hate ambivalence about power wielders. And we especially dislike anyone who tries to boss us around. Yes, we admire the Washingtons and Churchills, but Hitler and Al Capone were leaders too—and that points up a fundamental problem. Leadership can be exercised in the service of noble, liberating, enriching ends, but it can also serve to manipulate, mislead and repress.

"One of the most universal cravings of our time," writes James MacGregor Burns, "is a hunger for compelling and creative leadership." But exactly what is creative leadership? A *Wall Street Journal* cartoon had two men talking about leadership. Finally, one turned to the other in exasperation and said: "Yes, we need leadership, but we also need someone to tell us what to do." That is to say, leadership for most people most of the time is a rather hazy, distant and even confusing abstraction. Hence, thinking about or defining leadership is a kind of intellectual leadership challenge in itself.

What follows are some thoughts about leadership and education for leadership. These thoughts and ideas are highly personal and hardly scientific. As I shall suggest below, almost anything that can be said about leadership can be contradicted with counter examples. Moreover, the whole subject is riddled with paradoxes. My ideas here are the

Reprinted from *Presidential Studies Quarterly*, 14:1 (Winter 1984), pp. 22–34, by permission of the Center for the Study of the Presidency.

product of my studies of political leadership and my own participation in politics from the town meeting level to the White House staff. Some of my ideas come from helping to advise universities and foundations and the Houston-based American Leadership Forum on how best to go about encouraging leadership development. Finally, my thoughts have also been influenced in a variety of ways by numerous conversations with five especially insightful writers on leadership—Warren Bennis, James MacGregor Burns, David Campbell, Harlan Cleveland and John W. Gardner.

Teaching Leadership

Can we teach people to become leaders? Can we teach leadership? People are divided on these questions. It was once widely held that "leaders are born and not made," but that view is less widely held today. We also used to hear about "natural leaders" but nowadays most leaders have learned their leadership ability rather than inherited it. Still there is much mystery to the whole matter. In any event, many people think colleges and universities should steer clear of the whole subject. What follows is a set of reasons why our institutions of higher learning generally are "bashful about teaching leadership." These reasons may overstate the case, but they are the objections that serious people often raise.

First, many people still believe that leaders are born and not made. Or that leadership is somehow almost accidental or at least that most leaders emerge from circumstances and normally do not create them. In any event, it is usually added, most people, most of the time, are not now and never will be leaders.

Second, American cultural values hold that leadership is an elitist and thus anti-American phenomenon. Plato and Machiavelli and other grand theorists might urge upon their contemporaries the need for selecting out and training a select few for top leadership roles. But this runs against the American grain. We like to think that anyone can become a top leader here. Hence, no special training should be given to some special select few.

Third is the complaint that leadership training would more than likely be preoccupied with skills, techniques, and the *means* of getting things done. But leadership for what? A focus on *means* divorced from *ends* makes people—especially intellectuals—ill at ease. They hardly want to be in the business of training future Joe McCarthys or Hitlers or Idi Amins.

Fourth, leadership study strikes many as an explicitly vocational topic. It's a practical and applied matter—better learned in summer jobs, in internships or on the playing fields. You learn it on the job. You learn it from gaining experience, from making mistakes and learning from these. And you should learn it from mentors.

Fifth, leadership often involves an element of manipulation or deviousness, if not outright ruthlessness. Some consider it as virtually the same as learning about jungle-fighting or acquiring "the killer instinct." It's just not "clean" enough a subject matter for many people to embrace. Plus, "leaders" like Stalin and Hitler gave "leadership" a bad name. If they were leaders, then spare us of their clones or imitators.

Sixth, leadership in the most robust sense of the term is such an ecumenical and intellectually all-encompassing subject that it frightens not only the timid but even the most well educated of persons. To teach leadership is an act of arrogance. That is, it is to suggest one understands far more than even a well educated person can understand—history, ethics, philosophy, classics, politics, biography, psychology, management, sociology, law, etc. . . . and [is] steeped deeply as well in the "real world."

Seventh, colleges and universities are increasingly organized in highly specialized divisions and departments all geared to train specialists. While the mission of the college may be to educate "the educated person" and society's future leaders, in fact the incentive system is geared to training specialists. Society today rewards the expert or the super specialist—the data processors, the pilots, the financial whiz, the heart surgeon, the special team punt returners, and so on. Leaders, however, have to learn to become generalists and usually have to do so well after they have left our colleges, graduate schools and professional schools.

Eighth, leadership strikes many people (and with some justification) as an elusive, hazy and almost mysterious commodity. Now you see it, now you don't. So much of leadership is intangible, you can't possibly define all the parts. A person may be an outstanding leader here, but fail there. Trait theory has been thoroughly debunked. In fact, leadership is highly situational and contextual. A special chemistry develops between leaders and followers and it is usually context specific. Followers often do more to determine the leadership they will get than can any teacher. Hence, why not teach people to be substantively bright and well-read and let things just take their natural course.

Ninth, virtually anything that can be said about leadership can be denied or disproven. Leadership studies, to the extent they exist, are unscientific. Countless paradoxes and contradictions litter every manuscript on leadership. Thus, we yearn for leadership, but yearn equally to be free and left alone. We admire risk-taking, entrepreneurial leadership, but we roundly criticize excessive risk-taking as bullheadedness or plain stupid. We want leaders who are highly self-confident and who are perhaps incurably optimistic—yet we also dislike hubris and often yearn for at least a little self-doubt (e.g., Creon in *Antigone*). Leaders have to be almost singleminded in their drive and commitment but too much of that makes a person rigid, driven and unacceptable. We want leaders to be good listeners and represent their constituents, yet in the words of Walter Lippmann, effective leadership often consists of giving the people not what they want but what they will learn to want. How in the world, then, can you be rigorous and precise in teaching leadership?

Tenth, leadership at its best comes close to creativity. And how do you teach creativity? We are increasingly made aware of the fact that much of creative thinking calls upon unconscious thinking, dreaming and even fantasy. Some fascinating work is being done on intuition and the nonrational—but it is hardly a topic with which traditional disciplines in traditional colleges are comfortable.

Leaders themselves often complain that the incentives for leadership are not as great as the disincentives. Many people shy away from leadership responsibilities saying it "just isn't worth it." A survey of some 1700 business, government and professional leaders revealed a number of striking reasons. . . . See Table 1.

Relationships

A few other initial observations need to be made about leadership. Chief among these is that the study of leadership needs inevitably to be linked or merged with the study of followership. We cannot really study leaders in isolation from followers, constituents or group members. The leader is very much a product of the group, and very much shaped by its aspirations, values and human resources. The more we learn about leadership, the more the leader-follower linkage is understood and reaffirmed. A leader has to resonate with followers. Part of being an effective leader is having excellent ideas, or a clear sense of direction, a sense of mission. But such ideas or vision are useless unless the would-be leader can communicate them and get them accepted by followers. A two-way engagement or two-way interaction is constantly going on. When it ceases, leaders become lost, out of touch, imperial or worse.

The question of leaders linked with followers raises the question of the transferability of leadership. Can an effective leader in one situation transfer this capacity, this skill, this style—to another setting? The record is mixed indeed. Certain persons have been effective in diverse settings. George Washington and Dwight Eisenhower come to mind. Jack Kemp and Bill Bradley, two well-known and respected members of Congress, were previously successful professional athletes. Scores of business leaders

TABLE 1
What Leaders Say Are the Obstacles to Leadership in America

	Very Important	Somewhat Important	Not Important
The system does not favor the most capable individuals	54%	35%	11%
Our educational system does not provide people with leadership skills	48	37	15
American voters look for the wrong qualities in leaders	46	44	10
Leaders are not fully appreciated	23	49	28
Leaders are not given enough financial compensation	21	48	31
The pressures of leadership positions are too great	18	51	31
Leadership roles demand too much time	17	45	38
Potential leaders are deterred by fears of lack of privacy	16	43	41
The responsibilities of leadership roles appear too great	14	44	42
The times make effective leadership impossible	10	39	51

Source: The Connecticut Mutual Life Report on American Values in the '80s (Hartford, Conn. 1981), p. 188.

have been effective in the public sector and vice versa. Scores of military leaders have become effective in business or politics. Some in both. However, there are countless examples of those who have not met with success when they have tried to transfer their leadership abilities from one setting to a distinctively different setting. Sometimes this failure arises because the new group's goals or needs are so different from the previous organization. Sometimes it is because the leadership needs are different. Thus, the leadership needs of a military officer leading a platoon up a hill in battle may well be very different from the leadership requirements of someone asked to change sexist attitudes and practices in a large corporation or racist and ethnic hatred in an inner city. The leadership required of a candidate for office is often markedly different from that required of a campaign manager. Leadership required in founding a company may be exceedingly different from that required in the company's second generation.

Another confusing aspect about leadership is that leadership and management are often talked about as if they were the same. While it is true that an effective manager is often an effective leader and leadership requires, among other things, many of the skills of an effective manager, there are differences. Leaders are the people who infuse vision into an organization or a society. At their best, they are preoccupied with values and the longer range needs and aspirations of their followers. Managers are concerned with doing things *the right way*. Leaders are more concerned with identifying and then getting themselves and their organizations focused on *doing the right thing*. John Quincy Adams, Herbert Hoover and Jimmy Carter were often good, sometimes excellent, managers. Before coming to the White House, they were all recognized for being effective achievers. As businessmen, diplomats, governors or cabinet members, they excelled. As presidential leaders, they were found wanting. None was invited back for a second term. While none was considered an outright failure, each seemed to fail in providing the vision needed for the times. They were unable to lift the public's spirit and get the nation moving in new, more desirable directions.

As this brief digression suggests, being a leader is not the same thing as being holder of a high office. An effective leader is someone concerned with far more than the mechanics of office. While a good manager is concerned, and justifiably so, with efficiency, with keeping things going, with the routines and standard operating procedures, and with reaffirming ongoing systems, the creative leader acts as an inventor, risk taker and generalist entrepreneur—ever asking or searching for what is right, where are we headed, and keenly sensing new directions, new possibilities and welcoming change. We need all the talented managers we can get, but we also need creative leaders. Ironically, too, an effective leader is not very effective for long unless he or she can recruit managers to help make things work over the long run.

Characteristics

One of the most important things to be said about leadership is that it is commonly very dispersed throughout a society. Our leadership needs vary enormously. Many of the great breakthroughs occur because of people well in advance of their time who are willing to agitate for change and suggest fresh new approaches that are, as yet, unacceptable to majority opinion. Many of the leadership needs of a nation are met by persons who do not hold high office and who often don't look or even act as leaders. Which brings us to the question of defining leadership. Agreement on a definition is difficult to achieve. But for the purposes at hand, leaders are people who perceive what is needed and what is right and know how to mobilize people and resources to accomplish mutual goals.

Leaders are individuals who can help create options and opportunities—who can help clarify problems and choices, who can build morale and coalitions, who can inspire others and provide a vision of the possibilities and promise of a better organization, or a better community. Leaders have those indispensable qualities of contagious self-confidence, unwarranted optimism and incurable idealism that allow them to attract and mobilize others to undertake demanding tasks these people never dreamed they could undertake. In short, leaders empower and help liberate others. They enhance the possibilities for freedom—both for people and organizations. They engage with followers in such a way so that many of the followers become leaders in their own right.

As implied above, many of the significant breakthroughs in both the public and private sectors of this nation have been made by people who saw all the complexities ahead of them, but so believed in themselves and their purposes that they refused to be overwhelmed and paralyzed by doubts. They were willing to invent new rules and gamble on the future.

Good leaders, almost always, have been get-it-all-together, broken-field runners. They have been generalists. Tomorrow's leaders will very likely have begun life as trained specialists. Our society particularly rewards the specialist. John W. Gardner puts it well:

> All too often, on the long road up, young leaders become "servants of what is rather than shapers of what might be." In the long process of learning how the system works, they are rewarded for playing within the intricate structure of existing rules. By the time they reach the top, they are very likely to be trained prisoners of the structure. This is not all bad; every vital system re-affirms itself. But no system can stay vital for long unless some of its leaders remain sufficiently independent to help it to change and grow.

Only as creative generalists can these would-be leaders cope with the multiple highly organized groups—each fighting for special treatment, each armed with its own narrow definition of the public interest, often to the point of paralyzing *any* significant action.

Overcoming fears, especially fears of stepping beyond the boundaries of one's tribe, is a special need for the leader. A leader's task, as a renewer of organizational goals and aspirations, is to illuminate goals, to help reperceive one's own and one's organization's resources and strengths, to speak to people on what's only dimly in their minds. The effective creative leader is one who can give voice and form so that people say, "Ah, yes—that's what I too have been feeling."

Note too, however, that leaders are always aware of and at least partly shaped by the higher wants and aspirations and common purposes of their followers and constituents. Leaders consult and listen just as they educate and attempt to renew the goals of an organization. They know how "to squint with their ears." Civic leaders often emerge as we are able to agree upon goals. One analyst has suggested that it is no good for us to just go looking for leaders. We must first rediscover our own goals and values. If we are to have the leaders we need, we will first have to agree upon priorities. In one sense, if we wish to have leaders to follow, we will often have to show them the way.

In looking for leadership and in organizational affiliations—people are looking for *significance, competence, affirmation, and fairness.* To join an organization, an individual has to give up some aspect of his or her uniqueness, some part of his or her soul. Thus, there is a price in affiliating and in following. The leader serves as a strength and an attraction in the organization—but psychologically there is also a *repulsion* to the leader—in part because of the dependence on the leader. John Steinbeck said of American presidents that the people believe that "they were ours and we exercise the right to destroy them." Effective leaders must know how to absorb these hostilities, however latent they may be.

The leader also must be ever sensitive to the distinction between *power* and *authority.* Power is the strength or raw force to exercise control or coerce someone to do something, while authority is power that is *accepted* as legitimate by subordinates. The whole question of leadership raises countless issues about participation and the acceptance of power in superior-subordinate relationships. How much participation or involvement is needed, is desirable? What is the impact of participation on effectiveness? How best for the leader to earn moral and social acceptance for his or her authority? America generally prizes participation in all kinds of organizations, especially civic and political life. Yet, we must realize too that a part of us yearns for charismatic leadership. Ironically, savior figures and charismatic leaders often, indeed almost always, create distance and not participation.

One of the most difficult tasks for those who would measure and evaluate leadership is the task of trying to look at the elements that make up leadership. One way to look at these elements is to suggest that a leader has various *skills,* also has or exercises a distinctive *style* and, still more elusive, has various *qualities* that may be pronounced. By skill, I mean the capacity to do something well. Something that is learnable and can be improved, such as speaking or negotiating or planning. Most leaders need to have *technical skills* (such as writing well); *human relations skills,* the capacity to supervise, inspire, build coalitions and so on; and also what might be called *conceptual* skills—the capacity to play with ideas, shrewdly seek advice and forge grand strategy. Skills can be examined. Skills can be taught. And skills plainly make up an important part of leadership capability. Skills alone, however, cannot guarantee leadership success.

A person's leadership style may also be critical to effectiveness. Style refers to how a person relates to people, to tasks and to challenges. A person's style is usually a very personal and distinctive feature of his or her personality and character. A style may be democratic or autocratic, centralized or decentralized, empathetic or detached, extroverted or introverted, assertive or passive, engaged or remote. This hardly exhausts the diverse possibilities—but is meant to be suggestive. Different styles may work equally well in different situations. However, there is often a proper fit between the needs of an organization and the needed leadership style. A fair amount of research has been done in this area—but much more remains to be learned.

A person's *behavioral style* refers to one's way of relating to other people—to peers, subordinates, rivals, bosses, advisers, the press. A person's *psychological style* refers to one's way of handling stress, tensions, challenges to the ego, internal conflicts. Considerable work needs to be done in these areas—particularly if we are to learn how best to prepare people for shaping their leadership styles to diverse leadership situations and needs. But it is a challenge worth accepting.

James MacGregor Burns, in his book *Leadership*, offers us yet one additional distinction worth thinking about. Ultimately, Burns says, there are two overriding kinds of social and political leadership: *transactional* and *transformational leadership*. The transactional leader engages in an exchange, usually for self-interest and with short-term interests in mind. It is, in essence, a bargain situation: "I'll vote for your bill if you vote for mine." Or "You do me a favor and I will shortly return it." Most pragmatic officeholders practice transactional leadership most of the time. It is commonly a practical necessity. It is the general way people do business and get their jobs done—and stay in office. The transforming or transcending leader is the person who, as briefly noted earlier, so engages with followers as to bring them to a heightened political and social consciousness and activity, and in the process converts many of those followers into leaders in their own right. The transforming leader, with a focus on the higher aspirations and longer range, is also a teacher, mentor and educator—pointing out the possibilities and the hopes and the often only dimly understood dreams of a people—and getting them to undertake the preparation and the job needed to attain these goals.

Of course, not everyone can be a leader. And rarely can any one leader provide an organization's entire range of leadership needs. Upon closer inspection, most firms and most societies have all kinds of leaders and these diverse leaders, in turn, are usually highly dependent for their success on the leadership performed by other leaders. Some leaders are excellent at creating or inventing new structures. Others are great task leaders—helping to energize groups at problem solving. Others are excellent social (or affective) leaders, helping to build morale and renew the spirit of an organization or a people. These leaders are often indispensable in providing what might be called the human glue that holds groups together.

Further, the most lasting and pervasive leadership of all is often intangible and noninstitutional. It is the leadership fostered by ideas embodied in social, political or artistic movements, in books, in documents, in speeches, and in the memory of great lives greatly lived. Intellectual or idea leadership at its best is provided by those—often not in high political or corporate office—who can clarify values and the implications of such values for policy. The point here is that leadership is not only dispersed and diverse, but interdependent. Leaders need leaders as much as followers need leaders. This may sound confusing but it is part of the truth about the leadership puzzle.

Leadership Qualities

In the second half of this essay, I will raise, in a more general way, some of the qualities I believe are central to leadership. Everyone has his or her own list of leadership qualities. I will not be able to discuss all of mine, but permit me to offer my list and then describe a few of the more important ones in a bit more detail.

Leadership Qualities—A Tentative List
- Self-knowledge/self-confidence
- Vision, ability to infuse important, transcending values into an enterprise
- Intelligence, wisdom, judgment
- Learning/renewal
- Worldmindedness/a sense of history and breadth
- Coalition building/social architecture
- Morale-building/motivation
- Stamina, energy, tenacity, courage, enthusiasm
- Character, integrity/intellectual honesty
- Risk-taking/entrepreneurship
- An ability to communicate, persuade/listen
- Understanding the nature of power and authority

- An ability to concentrate on achieving goals and results
- A sense of humor, perspective, flexibility

Leadership consists of a spiral upwards, a spiral of self-improvement, self-knowledge and seizing and creating opportunities so that a person can make things happen that would not otherwise have occurred. Just as there can be a spiral upwards, there can be a spiral downwards— characterized by failure, depression, self-defeat, self-doubt, and paralyzing fatalism.

If asked to point to key qualities of successful leadership, I would suggest [the following].

Leaders Are People Who Know Who They Are and Know Where They Are Going

"What a man thinks about himself," Thoreau wrote, "that is what determines, or rather indicates, his fate." One of the most paralyzing of mental illnesses is wrong perception of self. This leads to poor choosing and poor choosing leads to a fouled-up life. In one sense, the trouble with many people is not what they don't know, it is what they do know, but it is misinformed or misinformation.

Leaders must be self-reliant individuals with great tenacity and stamina. The world is moved by people who are enthusiastic. Optimism and high motivations count for a lot. They can lift organizations. Most people are forever waiting around for somebody to light a fire under them. They are people who have not learned the valuable lesson that ultimately you are the one who is responsible for you. You don't blame others. You don't blame circumstances. You simply take charge and help move the enterprise forward.

I am sure many of you have been puzzled, as I have been, about why so many talented friends of ours have leveled off earlier than needs to be the case. What is it that prevents people from becoming the best they could be? Often it is a lack of education, a physical handicap or a disease such as alcoholism. Very often, however, it is because people have not been able to gain control over their lives. Various things nibble away at their capacity for self-realization or what Abraham Maslow called self-actualization. Family problems, inadequate financial planning, and poor health or mental health problems are key factors that damage self-esteem. Plainly, it is difficult to handle life, not to mention leadership responsibilities, if people feel they do not control their own lives. This emotional feeling of helplessness inevitably leads people to believe they aren't capable, they can't do the job. It also inhibits risk-taking and just about all the qualities associated with creativity and leadership.

Picture a scale from, at one end, an attitude of "I don't control anything and I feel like the bird in a badminton game"—to the other end of the scale where there is an attitude of "I'm in charge." Either extreme may be pathological, but plainly the higher up, relatively, toward the "I'm in charge" end of the scale, the more one is able to handle the challenges of transforming or creative leadership.

Thus, the single biggest factor is motivating or liberating would-be leaders in their attitude toward themselves and toward their responsibilities to others.

Leaders also have to understand the situations they find themselves in. As observed in *Alice in Wonderland*, before we decide where we are going, we first have to decide where we are right now. After this comes commitment to something larger and longer term than just our own egos. People can achieve meaning in their lives only when they can give as well as take from their society. Failure to set priorities and develop significant personal purposes undermines nearly any capacity for leadership. "When a man does not know what harbor he is making for, no wind is the right wind."

Leaders Set Priorities and Mobilize Energies

Too many people become overwhelmed with trivia, with constant close encounters of a third rate. Leaders have always to focus on the major problems of the day, and on the higher aspirations and needs of their followers. Leadership divorced from important transcending purpose becomes manipulation, deception and, in the extreme, is not leadership at all, but repression and tyranny.

The effective modern leader has to be able to live in an age of uncertainty. Priorities have to be set and decisions have to be made even though all the information is not in—this will surely be even more true in the future than it has been in the past. The information revolution has tremendously enlarged both the opportunities and the frustrations for leaders. Knowing what you don't know becomes as important as knowing what you do know. A willingness to experiment and explore possible strategies even in the face of uncertainty may become a more pronounced characteristic of the creative leader.

The creative priority setter learns both to encourage and to question his or her intuitive tendencies. Oliver Wendell Holmes, Jr., said that "to have doubted one's own first principles is the mark of a civilized man" and so it continues to be. The ability to look at things differently, and reach out for more and better advice, is crucial. The ability to admit error and learn from mistakes is also vitally important.

Leaders need to have considerable self-confidence, but they also must have a dose of self-doubt. Leaders must learn how to communicate the need for advice and help, how to become creative listeners, how to empathize, and understand. In Sophocles' compelling play, *Antigone*, the tragic hero, King Creon, hears his son's advice but imprudently rejects it or perhaps does not even hear it. But it, Haemon's, is advice any leader should take into account:

> Let not your first thought be your only thought. Think if there cannot be some other way. Surely, to think your own the only wisdom, and yours the only word, the only will, betrays a shallow spirit, an empty heart. It is no weakness for the wisest man to learn when he is wrong, know when to yield. . . .
> So, father, pause and put aside your anger. I think, for what my young opinion's worth, that good as it is to have infallible wisdom, since this is rarely found, the next best thing is to be willing to listen to wise advice.

Leaders need to be able to discover their own strengths and the strengths of those with whom they work. They have to learn how to share and to delegate. They have to be able to make people believe they are important, that they are or can be winners. People yearn to think that what they are doing is something useful, something important. The transforming or creative leader knows how to nourish conviction and morale within an organization.

Good leaders know how to serve as morale-builders and renewers of purpose, able to get people to rededicate themselves to long-cherished but sometimes dimly understood values. Motivation is sometimes as much as 40 to 50 percent of the leadership enterprise. You can do very little alone with just faith and determination, yet you can do next to nothing without them. Organizations of all kinds need constantly to rediscover or renew their faith, direction, and sense of purpose.

Leaders Have to Provide the Risk-Taking, Entrepreneurial Imagination for Their Organizations and Communities

Leaders are able to see things in a different and fresh context. Warren Bennis suggests that creative leadership requires the capacity to recontextualize a situation. Willis Harmon suggests a leader is one who reperceives situations and challenges and comes up with new approaches, insights and solutions.

A third-grade class begins and the teacher says: "Class, take out your pencils and paper and draw a picture of anything you can think of." Students begin to draw balls, trees, automobiles, and so forth. Teacher asks Sally, in the second row: "What are you drawing?" Sally says, "I'm drawing a picture of God." Teacher says: "But no one has ever seen

God; we don't know what he looks like." An undaunted Sally responds: "Well, they sure will when I get through!"

This little story illustrates the sometimes irrational self-confidence and "failure is impossible" factor that motivates the galvanizing leader. The founding revolutionaries in America, Susan Anthony, Martin Luther King, Jr., Saul Alinsky and countless others had the vision of a better and newer society and they, in effect, said, "They'll know a better or more just society when we get through."

Mark Twain once said, "a man is viewed as a crackpot until his idea succeeds." We need a hospitable environment for the dissenter and the creative individual. We need to avoid killing the spark of individuality that allows creativity to flourish. We kill it with rules, red tape, procedures, standard operating restrictions and countless admonitions "not to rock the boat."

Creativity is the ability to recombine things. To see a radio here and a clock there and put them together. Hence, the clockradio. Openmindedness is crucial. Too many organizations are organized with structures to solve problems that no longer exist. Vested interest grows up in every human institution. People all too often become prisoners of their procedures.

Psychologist David Campbell points out that history records a long list of innovations that come from outside the "expert" organization. (See also John Jewkes, *The Sources of Invention.*) The automobile was not invented by the transportation experts of that era, the railroaders. The airplane was not invented by automobile experts. Polaroid film was not invented by Kodak. Handheld pocket calculators were not invented by IBM, digital watches were not invented by watchmakers. Apple computers and herbal tea are yet two more examples. The list is endless and the moral is vivid.

Leaders get organizations interested in what they are going to become, not what they have been. Creative leadership requires also not being afraid to fail. An essential aspect of creative leadership is curiosity. The best way to have inventive ideas is to have lots of ideas, and to have an organization that welcomes fresh ideas—whatever their merit. As any scientist knows, the art of research requires countless experimentation and failure before you get the results you want, or sometimes the unexpected result that constitutes the true breakthrough.

Leaders recognize the utility of dreaming, fantasy and unconscious thinking. One advocate of creative thinking writes,

> Production of dramatically new ideas by a process of purely conscious calculation rarely seems to occur. Unconscious thinking, thinking which

you are unaware of, is a major contribution to the production of new ideas. . . .

Leaders Need to Have a Sense of Humor and a Sense of Proportion

Leaders take their work seriously, but do not take themselves too seriously. Humor relieves strain and enables people to relax and see things in a slightly different or fresh light. Effective leaders usually can tell a joke, take a joke, and tell a good story. They also usually know the art of telling parables. Lincoln, FDR and JFK come quickly to mind, while Hoover, Nixon and Carter were humorless men. Adlai Stevenson put it this way: "If I couldn't laugh, I couldn't live—especially in politics."

In this same light, leaders need to be able to share the credit. Leadership sometimes consists of emphasizing the dignity of others and of keeping one's own sense of importance from becoming inflated. Dwight Eisenhower had a slogan he tried to live by which went as follows: "There's no telling how much one can accomplish so long as one doesn't need to get all the credit for it."

Thus, leaders need to have a sense of proportion and a sense of detachment. They must avoid being workaholics and recognize that they will have to be followers in most of the enterprises of life and leaders only a small fraction of the time. Emerson put it well when he tried to answer the question, "What is Success?"

To laugh often and love much, to win the respect of intelligent persons and the affection of children; to appreciate beauty; to find the best in others; to give one's self; to leave the world a lot better whether by a healthy child, a garden patch, or a redeemed social condition; to have played and laughed with enthusiasm and sung with exaltation, to know even one life has breathed easier because you have lived—that is to have succeeded.

Humor, proportion and also *compassion*. A person able to understand emotions and passion and at least on occasion to express one's self with passion and conviction. Enthusiasm, hope, vitality and energy are crucial to radiating confidence.

Leaders Have to Be Skilled Mediators and Negotiators, But They Also Have to Be Able to Stir Things Up and Encourage Healthy and Desired Conflict

An old Peanut's cartoon has a dejected Charlie Brown coming off a softball field as the game concludes. In exasperation he whines, "How can we lose when we are so sincere?" Sincerity and purity of heart are not enough to succeed in challenging leadership jobs.

The strength of leaders often lies in their tenacity, in knowing how to deal with competing factions, knowing when to compromise, when to amplify conflict, and when to move an organization or a community away from paralyzing divisiveness and toward a vision of the common good.

Most citizens avoid conflict and find conflicts of any kind painful. The truly effective leader welcomes several kinds of conflict and views conflict as an opportunity for change or revitalization.

Stirring things up is often a prerequisite for social and economic breakthrough. Women's rights, black rights, consumer protection, tax reform movements and even our election campaigns are occasions for division and conflict. They are a reality the leader has to learn to accept, understand and turn to his advantage. Harry Truman said:

> A President who's any damn good at all makes enemies, makes a lot of enemies. I even made a few myself when I was in the White House, and I wouldn't be without them.

George Bernard Shaw and others have put it only slightly differently. Reasonable people, they observe, adjust themselves to reality and cope with what they find. Unreasonable people dream dreams of a different, a better, world and try to adapt the world to themselves. This discontent or unreasonableness is often the first step in the progress of a person as well as for a community or nation.

But be aware that "stirrer uppers" and conflict-amplifiers are often threatening in any organization or society. In the kingdom of the blind, the one-eyed man is king. This may well be, as the proverb has it. But in the kingdom of the one-eyed person, the two-eyed person is looked upon with considerable suspicion and may even be considered downright dangerous.

Thus, it takes courage and guts as well as imagination and stamina to be the two-eyed person in a one-eyed world. Harlan Cleveland points out that just about every leader has had the experience of being in an office surrounded by experts. The sum of the meeting will be, "Let's do nothing cautiously." The leader is the one who has to say, "Let's take the first step." He or she is the functional equivalent of the first bird off the telephone wire, or what Texans call the "bell cow." The experts always have an excuse. They are like the losing tennis player whose motto is: "It's not whether you win or lose, it's how you place the blame."

An Effective Leader Must Have Integrity

This has been suggested earlier in several implicit ways, but it is perhaps the most central of leadership qualities. A leader must be able to see people in all of their relationships, in the wholeness of their lives and not just as a means to getting a job done, as a means for enhanced productivity.

Some may call it character, others would call it authenticity, compassion or empathy. Whatever we call it, character and integrity are much easier kept than recovered. People can see through a phony. People can readily tell whether a person has respect for others. Respect and responsibility generally migrate to those who are fair, compassionate and care about values, beliefs and feelings of others. People who cannot rise above their prejudices usually fail. People who permit a shell to be built up around their heart will not long be able to exercise creative leadership. Michael Maccoby captures this concern.

> The exercise of the heart is that of experiencing, thinking critically, willing, and acting, so as to overcome egocentrism and to share passion with other people . . . and to respond to their needs with the help one can give. . . . It requires discipline, learning to concentrate, to think critically, and to communicate. The goal, a developed heart, implies integrity, a spiritual center, a sense of "I" not motivated by greed or fear, but by love of life, adventure and fellow feelings.

A leader's integrity requires also that he or she not be captured by peer pressures, protocol, mindless traditions or conventional rules. The truly effective leader is able to see above and beyond normal constraints and discern proper and desirable ends. The leader also possesses a sense of history and a concern for posterity. This ability, an exceptional capacity to disregard external pressures, is the ability that separates leaders from followers.

The Leader Has to Have Brains and Breadth

In the future, even more so than in the past, only the really bright individuals will be leaders.

Harlan Cleveland highlights this quality well when he writes:

> It used to be that a leader was a two-fisted businessman who chopped up the jobs that needed to be done, then left everyone alone and roared at them if they didn't work right. . . .

> Loud commands worked if one person knew all things, but because of
> the way we [now] make decisions, through committees, a person charging
> around with a loud voice is just in the way.

Today's leaders must widen their perspectives and lengthen the focal
point of their thinking. Leaders today have to learn how to thread or
weave together disparate parts and move beyond analytical to integrative
thinking. This will require well-read, well-traveled persons who can rise
above their specialities and their professions. It will require as well
persons who are not afraid of politics, but who rather view the art of
politics as the art of bringing about the difficult and the desirable.

American Leadership

The creative political leader must work in a tension-filled world
between unity and dissent, majority rule and minority rights and countless
other contradictions. Tocqueville said of us, "These Americans yearn for
leadership, but they also want to be left alone and free." The political
leader is always trying to reconcile this and other paradoxes—but the
important point is to be able to live with the paradoxes and dilemmas.
And beyond this, the political leader must also be able to create, and
preserve, a sense of community and shared heritage, the civic bond that
ties us—disparate and fiesty, rugged individualists—together.

Effective leaders of today and tomorrow also know how to vary their
styles of leadership depending on the maturity of their subordinates.
They involve their peers and their subordinates in their responsibility
networks. They must be good educators and good communicators. They
also have to have that spark of emotion or passion that can excite others
to join them in the enterprise.

Most effective leaders will also be effective communicators: good
writers, good speakers and good conversationalists. A few noted scientists
may get by with mumbling, but they are the exception. For so much
of leadership consists nowadays in persuading and informing that someone
who cannot communicate well, cannot succeed. To paraphrase George
Orwell, "If people cannot communicate well, they cannot think well,
and if they cannot think well, others will do their thinking for them."

America is especially good at training experts, specialists and managers.
We have plenty of these specialist leaders, but they are almost always
one-segment leaders. We are in special need of educating multi-segment
leaders. Persons who have a global perspective and understand that the
once tidy lines between domestic and international, and public and
private, are irretrievably blurred. Indispensible to a leader is a sense of
breadth, the intellectual capacity to handle complex mental tasks, to see

relationships between apparently unrelated objects, to see patterns in incomplete information, to draw accurate conclusions from inchoate data.

Vision is the ability to see all sides of an issue and to eliminate biases. Vision and breadth of knowledge put one in a strategic position— preventing the leader from falling into the traps that short-sightedness, mindless parochialism often set for people.

None of these qualities can guarantee creative leadership, but they can, when encouraged, provide a greater likelihood of it. We need all the leadership we can get—in and out of government. The vitality of nongovernmental America lies in our ability to educate and nourish more citizen-leaders. Those of us who expect to reap the blessings of freedom and liberty must undergo the fatigues of supporting them and provide the leadership to sustain them.

Learning About Leadership

Permit me to return again to the question of whether leadership can be learned, and possibly taught. My own belief is that students cannot usually be taught to be leaders. But students, and anyone else for that matter, can profitably be exposed to leadership, discussions of leadership skills and styles, and leadership strategies and theories. Individuals can learn in their own minds the strengths as well as limitations of leadership. People can learn about the paradoxes and contradictions and ironies of leadership, which, however puzzling, are central to appreciating the diversity and the dilemmas of problem-solving and getting organizations and nations to function.

Learning about leadership means recognizing bad leadership as well as good. Learning about leadership means understanding the critical linkage of ends and means. Learning about leadership also involves the study of the special chemistry that develops between leaders and followers, not only the chemistry that existed between Americans and Lincoln, but also between Mao and the Chinese peasants, Lenin and the Bolsheviks, between Martin Luther King, Jr., and civil rights activists, between Jean Monnet and those who dreamed of a European Economic Community.

Students can learn to discern and define situations and contexts within which leadership has flourished. Students can learn about the fallibility of the trait theory. Students can learn about the contextual problems of leadership, of why and when leadership is sometimes transferable, and sometimes not. Students can learn about the crucial role that advisors and supporters play in the leadership equation. Students can also learn about countless problem-solving strategies and theories, and participate in role playing exercises that sharpen their own skills in such undertakings.

Students of leadership can learn widely from reading biographies about both the best and the worst leaders. Plutarch's *Lives* would be a good place to start. Much can be learned from mentors and from intern-participant observing. Much can also be learned about leadership by getting away from one's own culture and examining how leaders in other circumstances go about the task of motivating and mobilizing others. Countless learning opportunities exist that can sharpen a student's skills as a speaker, debater, negotiator, problem clarifier and planner. Such skills should not be minimized. Nor should anyone underestimate the importance of history, economics, logic, and a series of related substantive fields that help provide the breadth and the perspective indispensible to societal leadership.

Above all, students of leadership can make an appointment with themselves and begin to appreciate their own strengths and deficiencies. Personal mastery is important. So too the ability to use one's intuition, and to enrich one's creative impulses. John Gardner suggests, "It's what you learn after you know it all that really counts." Would-be leaders learn to manage their time more wisely. Would-be leaders learn that self-pity and resentment are like toxic substances. Would-be leaders learn the old truth that most people are not for or against you but rather preoccupied with themselves. Would-be leaders learn to break out of their comfortable imprisonments; they learn to cast aside dull routines and habits that enslave most of us. Would-be leaders learn how to become truly sharing and caring people—in their families, their professions and in their communities. And would-be leaders constantly learn too that they have more to give than they have ever given, no matter how much they have given.

Let me conclude by paraphrasing from John Adams:

> We must study politics [and leadership] and war [and peace] that our sons [and daughters] have the liberty to study mathematics and philosophy, geography, natural history and naval architecture, navigation, commerce, and agriculture, in order to give their children a right to study painting, poetry, music, architecture, statuary, tapestry, and porcelain.

5

A Century of
Leadership Research

DAVID D. VAN FLEET
GARY A. YUKL

Leadership research seems to have many of the characteristics of research in nuclear physics. The atom was long thought to be the simplest, single indivisible particle of matter. Knowledge of the atom, it was believed, would enhance our mastery of nature. However, it was eventually demonstrated that there was not one or even just a few such particles; indeed, there were many. Subsequent research showed that atoms were not the primary building blocks of matter but were themselves composed of even smaller particles—protons, neutrons, and electrons. Surely these were the ultimate components of the universe.

But then came the discovery of the anti-particles and isotopes— different forms of the same atom. And then again, more complications emerged as muons, mesons, and baryons were identified and, in quark theory, each of these proved to be a unique group of particles in its own right. However, things did not end there. These particles had numerous properties—charge (positive, negative, or neutral), "color," field, "flavor" (up, down, sideways or "strange," charm, top or truth, and bottom or beauty), spin, and "handedness." The "laws of nature" are not necessarily simple (Asimov, 1984, Chapter 7). A Grand Unified Theory (GUT) helps place this complexity into perspective, but even then, the "simplest particle of nature" proves to be amazingly elusive to understand.

So it is with leadership research. Not unlike the bewildering array of subatomic particles and properties, ". . . decades of research on leadership have produced a bewildering mass of findings" (Bass, 1981,

Reprinted from *Papers Dedicated to the Development of Modern Management*, 1986, pp. 12–23, by permission of the authors and the Academy of Management.

p. xvii). Where once we thought of leadership as a relatively simple construct, we now recognize that it is among the more complex social phenomena. We, too, can benefit from a GUT, but it may be some time before our understanding reaches this stage. While recognizing that there are many contributions to our thinking on leadership (see, for example, Barnard, 1938; Fayol, 1949; Follett in Metcalf and Urwick, 1940; and McGregor, 1960), this paper concentrates on the stream of empirical research which extends our understanding by building upon previous research.

The Early Views

One hundred years ago Social Darwinism dominated social science. Perhaps this was a scholarly manifestation of American individualism which held that "anyone can become president." But if so, it was not without careful scrutiny and much discussion. The view, which prevailed in much of the world, that leaders are born was not popular in America where it was felt that the leader was the product of the situation rather than a "blood relative" or descendent of a previous leader (Stogdill, 1975). Whether or not Social Darwinism had merit, it was clear that hereditary monarchies were not inevitable (Commons, 1899–1900). The rise of business leaders "from the ranks" was an important issue, and "science" was seen as an "eminently 'practical'" means of settling the issue (Henderson, 1896, p. 396).

Mumford (1906–1907) provided evidence that while leadership in primitive societies might be instinctive, it is less so in more advanced societies. The group was fundamental—". . . every individual that attains a position of leadership in the group must do so by the performance of some function which the group considers of importance" (Mumford, 1906–1907, p. 522). Leadership was constant in that it existed in all human groups, but the specific abilities vary across both time and circumstances, so that what is needed at one time or in one situation may not be needed at another time or situation (Mumford, 1909). Further, leader ability ". . . is as likely to rise in the ranks of the most lowly as from those of the so-called better class" (Kelsey, 1907, p. 711).

While not identical with more recent contingency views, this early emphasis on the group and the situation continues to be important in leadership theory (Van Fleet, 1977 and 1975). Yet, if the leader did not inherit personal characteristics which led to leadership, personal characteristics still seemed important (Schenck, 1928).

Early in this century, the situational emphasis gave way to universal approaches with a trait focus (this "approach" and "focus" typology is that of Jago, 1982). Generally, personal characteristics (intelligence, values, appearance, etc.) were found to have only weak relations with leadership (see, for example, Kohs and Irle, 1920; Page, 1935). Jenkins (1947) reviewed 74 military studies and concluded that leadership was situationally specific [and] that one could not generalize across different settings.

Other trait research reviews seemed to suggest that, while leaders might have different traits than nonleaders, no replicable set of traits was related consistently to leader effectiveness (Jennings, 1944; Stogdill, 1948; Gibb, 1954; and Mann, 1959). These reviews also suggested that the importance of traits was situationally specific rather than general across situations (Carter, 1953; Shartle, 1956). While a recent review (Stogdill, 1974) does not appear as damning, clearly the view that "leaders are born" has been rejected. Equally clear is that certain characteristics improve a leader's chances of success. Nevertheless, the particular combination of characteristics varies with the situation in ways still not clearly specified or understood (House and Baetz, 1979). What seems to be most important is not traits but rather how they are expressed in the behavior of the leader. Thus, behavioral research has come to dominate the field although personal characteristics may still be involved.

Major Research Problems

Three major research programs have contributed substantially to our knowledge of leader behavior. While all three had a behavioral focus, they continued to employ a relatively universal approach. The earliest of those was a series of studies at the State University of Iowa (Lewin, 1939; Lewin, Lippitt, and White, 1939). The second program was at Ohio State University (Schriesheim and Bird, 1979; Shartle, 1979; Stogdill and Shartle, 1948), and the third was at the University of Michigan (Likert, 1979).

Iowa Studies

The Iowa studies used preteenaged boys in clubs with adult leaders to investigate two styles of leader behavior: democratic and autocratic (Lewin and Lippitt, 1938). The democratic leader coordinated the group's activities and conducted majority-rule voting on major decisions. The autocratic leader directed activities and unilaterally made all decisions. To assure that the leader's behavior and not his personality was the major determinant of results, the roles, including non-verbal behavior and status cues, were carefully controlled. In addition, each of the leaders enacted each role with different groups, and the leader for each group was changed during the course of the study (White and Lippitt, 1960).

During the study, however, one of the leaders got stagefright and failed to enact his role, doing nothing instead. Rather than lose the research, Lewin termed this laissez-faire leadership and incorporated it into the study (Wolf, 1979).

The group's performance and attitudes under the three styles were compared. Both criteria were worst with the laissez-faire leader. Attitudes were best with the democratic leader and performance seemed better with the autocratic leader. Then another research question was asked: "What would happen if the leader left the room?" Little change was observed when the laissez-faire leader left the room. Likewise, the performance and attitudes remained virtually unchanged when the democratic leader left the room; the group went right on working and making decisions on their own. But under the autocratic leader, a radical change occurred. Constructive activity came to a halt and was replaced by horseplay and/or bickering. The evidence was clear—majority-rule decision making and other participative techniques train and involve group members so that they perform well and continue to perform well even in the absence of their leader.

Ohio State Studies

Initially, the effort at Ohio State was to identify leader behaviors and to develop questionnaires to measure them. The two major behaviors identified were: (1) task-oriented behavior ("initiating structure") which included many well established managerial behaviors, such as planning, coordinating, and directing, and (2) maintenance behavior ("consideration") which included friendliness, openness of communication, and participation. Although other, more specific dimensions of leader behavior were also identified, much of the research evolving from these studies has focused on only the two more abstract and general sets of behaviors—consideration and initiating structure. It usually was assumed that a high degree of both types of behavior ("high-high style") would be the best style for a leader. Static correlational studies tended to support such a view, but field experiments (e.g., Fleishman and Harris, 1962; and Skinner, 1969) show that the effects of leader behavior depends on the situation so that a "high-high" style is not universally optimal (Larson, Hunt, and Osborn, 1976, and Nystrom, 1978).

In many studies based on the two broad Ohio State categories (Christner and Hemphill, 1955; Fleishman, 1956; Halpin, 1954 and 1957; and Rush, 1957), consideration was significantly and positively related to subordinate and peer ratings but was not related to or was negatively related to ratings by superiors. Initiating structure, on the other hand, had a more mixed pattern although it tended to be positively related to all of the different ratings. However, few of these studies used objective criteria. One study might find that effectiveness was unrelated to consideration but positively related to initiating structure, but another would seem to find the reverse (compare Halpin, 1957, with Christner and Hemphill, 1955). These sorts of mixed and/or conflicting findings are typical of much of the research which is based on such extremely broad categories of leader behavior.

Michigan Studies

The studies of Likert and his associates at Michigan compared managerial behavior of effective and ineffective supervisors. Effective supervisors were found to be those who focus on the human aspects of their subordinates' problems and "build effective work groups with high performance goals." Supportive behavior and high performance standards, then, were keys to effective leadership. Later research suggested that group methods of supervision including, where appropriate, participation and linking pin or representative behavior were also part of effective leadership. It is unfortunate that many casual readers of Likert's work saw his label of "subordinate centered leadership" and mistakenly thought that it meant only "being nice to workers." It obviously meant more than just that.

These studies demonstrated that there is a time lag between what the leader does and the results of that action. Intervening variables exist between leadership and outcomes, and the time it takes to get results may be lengthy—a year or more in some cases. Evaluations of leader performance should take into account the lagged effects of leader behavior because behavior most likely to achieve long-term effects differs somewhat from the behavior pattern likely to maximize short-term effects (Likert, 1967).

Both of these research programs indicated that leader behavior is more complex than the simple dichotomy of task- and maintenance-behavior. Recent field studies of practicing managers confirm that complexity (Boyatzis, 1982; Kotter, 1982; Bennis and Nanus, 1985). Yet, some evidence suggests that the dichotomy may retain utility in establishing a phenomenologically based leadership morphology (Misumi, 1985; Misumi and Peterson, 1985).

Both the Ohio State and Michigan programs suggested that effective leaders focus on performance (production emphasis at Ohio State and goal emphasis or high performance standards at Michigan) and employ other behaviors as well. Further, both programs found that the pattern of effective behavior varies with the situation (including the goal or objective) just as had been theorized early in this century, so universal approaches gave way to contingency approaches. For these reasons, then, the universal or "one best way" approach, which had dominated leadership research, was largely displaced by contingency approaches.

Contingency Approaches to Leadership

Gradually the universal approach has given way to contingency approaches. In contingency approaches, situational variables moderate the relationship between the leader's behavior or traits and effectiveness criteria. Several major contingency approaches exist. The earliest of these—the LPC Model—has a trait focus; the latter ones—path-goal theory and the work on subordinate participation—have a behavioral focus.

LPC Model

An early effort to integrate selected components of the situation into a comprehensive theory of leadership is that of Fiedler and his associates (1954, 1958, 1967). The basic idea is to match the leader's personality with the situation most favorable for his or her success (Fiedler, 1965, and Fiedler, Chemers, and Mahar, 1976). According to Fiedler, a leader has a relatively permanent personality trait that is very important to leader effectiveness. While not precisely defined, it is measured by the LPC (Least Preferred Co-Worker) Scale and has been described as a tendency to be motivated primarily toward either task accomplishment or personal relationships. If a leader uses relatively positive concepts to describe the person with whom he or she can work least well, the leader is people-motivated; if the leader uses relatively negative concepts, the leader is task-motivated.

The favorableness of the situation for the leader is described in terms of three aspects of the situation: leader-member relations; task structure; and position power (Fiedler and Chemers, 1974). The most favorable situation is one in which the leader possesses considerable powers. The most unfavorable situation is the reverse. Task-motivated leaders are more likely to be effective in favorable and very unfavorable situations. Relations-motivated leaders are more likely to be effective in moderately favorable situations.

This approach stresses the importance of the interaction between leader characteristics, follower characteristics, and the task. It also argues against the simplistic notion that there is "one best way" to lead regardless of the situation. There are, however, problems with the approach and it has been strongly criticized (Ashour, 1973; Hosking, 1981; McMahon, 1972; Schriesheim and Kerr, 1977; and Vecchio, 1977). The notion that leadership effectiveness can be explained by a unidimensional leadership dimension based on personality is questionable, since other research posits leadership as a multidimensional construct.

Fiedler's theory stresses the importance of the situation in determining leader effectivess, yet some aspects of the situation have not been adequately dealt with. Studies with task versus training groups and laboratory and field studies have suggested different patterns of leadership (see tables in Chapter 5 of Fiedler and Chemers, 1974); yet the situational factors accounting for these discrepant results have not been explained fully nor incorporated into later revisions of the model. Further, while evidence exists that business/industrial and military situations are not completely comparable (Yukl and Van Fleet, 1982; Van Fleet and Yukl, 1986), no effort has been made to examine such differences despite the fact that both types of leaders have been studied in research on the LPC.

Path-Goal Theory

Path-goal theory's origins are almost as old as LPC theory (Georgopoulos et al., 1957), but the specific leadership application is more recent (Evans, 1970a and 1970b). Using the expectancy theory of motivation (Vroom, 1964), path-goal theory is an exchange theory (House, 1986). Again, the basic idea is relatively simple. If a group member perceives high productivity to be an easy "path" to attain personal goals, then he or she will tend to be a high producer. On the other hand, if personal goals are obtainable in other ways, then the group member will not likely be a high producer (House, 1971). The task of the group leader is, then, to increase the personal rewards to subordinates for performance in order to make the paths to their goals clearer and easier (Evans, 1974).

Path-goal theory uses two important contingency variables: (1) the personal characteristics of group members; and (2) the work environment. Personal characteristics of group members include their skills, needs, and motives. The work environment includes the degree of task structure, the nature of the formal authority system of the organization, and the work group itself. Task structure is defined in the same way as in Fiedler's theory. The formal authority system refers to the extent to which rules, procedures, and policies both constrain and clarify the task and subordinate behavior. The situational variables are hypothesized to moderate the effects of the leader's behavior on the motivation of group members. Motivation, in turn, is presumed to influence satisfaction and/ or performance. The leader's influence on subordinate motivation is described as a process involving subordinate expectations and perceived valences of work outcomes.

Individual expectations are subjective probability estimates known as path instrumentalities. The first is referred to as the path instrumentality of work behavior for goal accomplishment—the probability that work behavior will lead to goal accomplishment. The second is termed the path instrumentality of work-goal accomplishment for desired consequences—the probability that goal accomplishment will lead to what the subordinate wants. Integrating these probability estimates and the valence associated with both intrinsic and extrinsic consequences enables the path-goal approach to suggest the leader's role in influencing the behavior of group members. Some leaders have considerable influence over the extrinsic consequences of task accomplishment. By doing such things as allowing group members the opportunity to exercise self-control over their own tasks, leaders may also partially determine the intrinsic consequences of accomplishments. By assisting group members in their efforts to achieve task goals, leaders may influence their estimates of the path instrumentality of work behavior for goal accomplishment. In the like manner, consistent and systematic performance appraisals with rewards tied to performance can increase the estimate of path instrumentality of work-goal accomplishment for desired consequences.

Path-goal theory is complex. Indeed, even though much of the research on it has been encouraging, the very complexity of the approach suggests a major problem with it (Schriesheim and von Glinow, 1977, and Greene, 1979). The exact relationships and predictions of path-goal theory are not clear enough to permit as careful testing as, say, those of Fiedler. Further, just as issues exist about Fiedler's measuring instruments, the measurement of the components of path-goal theory is also in need of refinement.

Participation in Decision Making

As noted earlier, among the earliest behavioral research was that of Lewin and his associates which suggested that the use of majority rule decision making and other participative techniques by the leader serve to train and involve group members so that they perform well and continue to perform well even in the absence of the leader (White and Lippitt, 1960). These laboratory results may not generalize to field settings very well, however, due to the complexity of the phenomena under study (Schweiger and Leana, 1986). A mistaken assumption was that leaders were either participative or they were not (Locke and Schweiger, 1979). Tannenbaum and Schmidt (1958) showed that participation takes many forms and is a continuum rather than a dichotomy. They also proposed that the appropriate degree of participation depends upon "forces" in the leader, the led, and the situation; however, they did not say specifically how the situation determines the degree of participation.

A descriptive approach was developed by Heller and Yukl (1969) and later extended by Heller (1971, 1973). Some of the hypotheses which have been supported include the following: (1) the amount of time needed for subordinates to learn how to make decisions is perceived to be longer by leaders than by subordinates; (2) leaders are more autocratic when they perceive that a large difference exists between subordinate skills and the leader's skills; and (3) the organizational level of the manager will influence the choice of how much participation to use. While this research is a considerable improvement on the ideas of Tannenbaum and Schmidt, it still provides little guidance to practicing leaders.

Vroom and Yetton (1973) developed a normative model of participation in decision making to provide just such guidance. Their approach helps the leader identify the most appropriate degree of participation given the quality and acceptance requirements of a decision. Thus, the model is based on two basic criteria of decision effectiveness: (1) the quality of the decisions and (2) the acceptance of those decisions by followers.

The model uses a decision tree to analyze the implications of a series of situational attributes, expressed as a series of questions which separate and identify numerous situations. Then, the degree (feasible set) of participation which could be used in each of those situations is specified. Finally, the model uses choice rules to identify which degree of partic-ipation is most appropriate. The choice depends upon whether short term pressures such as speed (favoring more autocratic decisions) or longer term pressures such as follower development (favoring participative decisions) are most important.

This model seems useful to leaders, and, while criticisms have appeared (Field, 1979 and 1982; Heilman, Hornstein, Cage, and Herschlag, 1984), there is a growing body of supportive research (Schweiger and Leana, 1986; Vroom and Jago, 1974, 1978; and Jago and Vroom, 1980). One element absent from the Vroom-Yetton-Jago model is the existence of crisis or emergency conditions. Some research suggests that more au-tocratic approaches are appropriate in such conditions (Bates, 1953), while only in non-emergency conditions can the leader select from among a greater variety of approaches.

While this model deals with only one aspect of leader behavior— the degree of subordinate participation in decision making—that aspect is so crucial that the model is widely taught and utilized. The rigorous development of the model and the continuing careful testing of it assure that we will continue to learn more about it over time. Like the LPC and path-goal models, however, the Vroom-Yetton model clearly illustrates the shift to contingency approaches which has occurred in the leadership research field.

Other Leadership Research

Other research efforts that contribute to our understanding of leadership include: leaderless group discussion; charismatic leadership; mutual or reciprocal influence views; perceptual leadership theories; reinforcement–social learning views; and a control theory view.

Leaderless Group Discussion

Another relatively early and yet continuing stream of research concerns leaderless group discussion (LGD) as used in assessment centers like those developed for AT&T by Bray and his associates (Bray, Campbell, and Grant, 1974). In the 1940s, the British also were using the technique in the assessment of managerial potential, and, when a Proctor and Gamble industrial psychologist gave a seminar about it at Ohio State University, a doctoral student determined to replace the subjectivity of the technique with objective measurement (Bass, 1981).

Essentially the result was a strikingly high correlation in initially leaderless group discussions between the amount of time a person spent talking and the person's influence as rated by peers and observers (Bass, 1949 and 1954). Sometimes cynically referred to as the "Babble Hypothesis," this result has been one of the more interesting and replicable findings in leadership research. While the simplistic statement, "whoever talks the most becomes the leader," is probably incorrect, the power of oral communication skills and some degree of assertiveness has been aptly demonstrated through this line of research. Recent evidence suggests that, while perceived influence results from the quantity of talking, actual influence is more a function of expertise or what is said (Bottger, 1984).

Charismatic Leadership

The interpersonal influence process involved in charisma has been mysterious; the term itself originally referred to a gift from God or to supernatural powers. The power aspect of charisma is so clear that it has been referred to not as a form of leadership but rather as a form of power, referent/personal power, the power of personality (French and Raven, 1960). House (1977) presented a theory of charismatic leadership and indicated that charismatic leaders have a high need to influence people, a high degree of self-confidence, and strong convictions in their own beliefs and ideals. His work also suggests that their followers share these latter two feelings, that is, the followers trust the correctness of the leader's beliefs, share those beliefs, accept and obey the leader, feel affection toward the leader, and are emotionally involved with the broad goals of the organization.

Yet it has been only recently that much research has been completed on charisma. House (1985) has presented research on charismatic leadership which appears to go far to remove the mystery that has so long been associated with it. Personal characteristics are certainly part of the charismatic process, but selected leader behaviors and, perhaps even more interestingly, non-verbal communication are also critical to charisma (Smith, 1982). Research has tentatively shown that it is possible to train leaders to bring about charismatic effects (Howell, 1985).

A related concept, transformational leadership, has also emerged as an area of interest. Burns (1978) discussed transformative leadership as distinct from transactional leadership with the former dealing with major organizational change processes. While a lot of attention is being paid to this concept (Schein, 1985; Bass, 1985a and 1985b; Bennis and Nanus, 1985), little systematic research has yet to be conducted.

Mutual or Reciprocal Influence Theory

Leadership is an influence or social exchange process. The usual approach is to study only the influence of the leader on followers, but another perspective is that followers influence their leaders just as they are influenced by those leaders (Sims and Manz, 1984). Within the past ten years, this mutual or reciprocal influence view of the leadership process has been developed in three distinct forms: the interactive view profferred by Greene (1975); the vertical-dyad linkage work of Graen and his associates (1970); and the transactional approach of Hollander (1978 and 1979).

The Interactive View. Leadership is a two-way process of leader-follower interaction—a reciprocal or mutual influence process between the leader and the group (Fulk and Wendler, 1982). Specifically, Greene (1975) suggests that the broad Ohio State categories of leader behavior, initiating structure and consideration, seemed linked through a feedback look over time. If followers performed well, the leader displayed more consideration behavior which then led to increased follower satisfaction; if the followers did not perform well, the leader displayed more structuring behavior and there was no increase in satisfaction. It is too early to speculate on the impact of this view as little research has been conducted on this.

Vertical-Dyad Linkage. The vertical-dyad linkage version of mutual influence theory stresses the relationship between the leader and individual followers, rather than between the leader and the group as a whole. Graen and Schiemann (1978) assume that the leader behaves differently toward each follower and that these differences must be analyzed separately. In contrast, most earlier theories assume that the leader behaves much the same toward all group members, and that behavior descriptions from group members can be averaged to accurately describe general leader behavior.

Graen's view suggests that early in the dealings between leaders and followers, leaders somehow categorize followers as belonging to an in-group or an out-group. The leader behaves differently toward members of these two groups. In-group members get more autonomy, more attention from the leader, and may also receive more of other rewards. Naturally enough, in-group members out perform and are more satisfied than out-group members. While some research confirms vertical-dyad linkage theory, there are some problems with the model and its normative implications (Vecchio and Gobdel, 1984).

The Transactional Approach. The transactional approach is a general theoretical treatment of leadership (Hollander, 1978 and 1979). Stemming partly from idiosyncrasy credit theory (Hollander, 1958), it holds that leaders provide benefits for and receive benefits from followers in a social exchange called a "transaction." Idiosyncrasy credit theory indicates how and why a leader both conforms to group norms and is influential in introducing innovation into the group. As the leader contributes to task accomplishment and conforms to the norms of the group, he or she "earns credits." These credits are then spent to introduce innovation or wield power. Experts and high ranking officials can validate the leader's credits and add to the leader's influence or they can invalidate the credits, diminishing that influence. A popular expression of the idiosyncrasy credit concept is that a person "chooses battles carefully," which simply means that the leader chooses carefully in spending credits.

More than just idiosyncrasy credit is involved in the transactional approach. The leader, the followers, and the situation are all involved. A distinction is drawn between attaining and maintaining leadership; attaining is associated with earning credits, while maintaining with both spending and earning credits (Hollander, 1974). Trust, fairness, and two-way sharing of information are critical elements. This means that the approach is dynamic and not precisely specifiable. However, competence—"getting results"—is regarded as the "most important single factor." This view, like that of Bowers and Seashore (1966), suggests that leadership involves a complex role which can be performed by one or more persons. If one person dominates, a conventional view of leadership exists, but dual leadership is readily recognizable as well. If every member of the group shares equally (or nearly so) in the process, then consensus or collegial leadership exists. The failure of some research to account for much variance in group performance may be in part because the behavior of a single person was examined rather than studying the full complexity of the leadership process.

Perceptual Leadership Theories

Perceptual leadership theories (Lord, 1985) are those theories in which leadership is perceived to be implicit in the situation. There are two basic forms of such theories: (1) inferential/attribution theories and (2) recognition/information processing theories. Attribution theory (Kelley, 1971) suggests that we observe the behavior of others and then attribute causes to it. Applied to leadership this suggests that the leaders would respond to their own attributions about subordinate behavior (Calder, 1977). If a subordinate's poor performance is seen (attributed) by the leader to be "caused by" laziness, the leader may engage in criticizing and disciplining behavior; if it is seen as caused by inability, the leader may instead display training behavior; or if it is seen as caused by a lack of resources, the leader may engage in facilitating and representing behavior (Green and Mitchell, 1979; Mitchell and Wood, 1979). The ultimate application of attribution theory is that leadership researchers have attributed more to the leader role than really exists (Meindl, Ehrlich, and Dukerich, 1985).

Information processing theory, as applied to leadership, has much in common with attribution theory (Lord, 1985) since both are theories based on perceptual processes. The information processing approach, however, stresses three major subprocesses. Those subprocesses are: (1) selective attention and encoding, (2) storage and retention, and (3) retrieval and judgment. Social cues and the role of symbols are thus part of this approach to the study of leadership. While interesting, more research needs to be conducted on perceptual leadership theories to establish their validity.

One cannot help but wonder about combining this view with the others to increase our understanding of the leadership process. For instance, if attribution theory is combined with the mutual influence view, we would see that the process involved not just the leader's attributions about followers but also the attributions which followers make about leaders. Further, those attributions could be at the group, subgroup, or individual level.

Reinforcement/Social Learning Views

Yet another recent perspective on leadership is to view it in terms of reinforcement and/or social learning theory. Followers learn their behavior either in a social learning context (Luthans, 1979) or through reinforcement of behaviors (Sims, 1977). The behavioral and cognitive approaches which were long seen as in conflict now appear to have compatible leadership implications (Davis and Luthans, 1979 and 1980). This view suggests that leaders should or at least can influence follower behavior by making consequences contingent upon behavior (Podsakoff, Totor, and Skov, 1982). Structuring reward contingencies is seen, then, as a significant form of leader behavior. Social learning expands upon reinforcement views by recognizing the role of cognitive mediating processes in the relationships between antecedent conditions, behavior, and consequences. To date research in this area is relatively scarce and given the complexity of the concepts, more research is needed before firm conclusions can be reached.

Control Theory

Most recently, Jones (1983), beginning with a macro emphasis and drawing upon the literature on organizational control, reexamined the leadership process. Using multidimensional scaling, he identified four dimensions of leader behavior based on control—unobtrusive versus obtrusive; situational versus personal; process versus output; and paternalistic versus professional. These results suggest that many existing leadership taxonomies may not capture sufficient relevant behavior and need to be expanded. This approach may also help account for some findings which suggest a low or negative correlation between satisfaction and performance (Yukl and Van Fleet, 1982). Further, this approach may help clarify the findings of the substitutes for the leadership view just discussed; "the control of the work flow through task structure or role formalization may be as much a positive leader choice as the decision to control through the use of explicit rewards and punishments or through output control" (Jones, 1983, pp. 169–170).

Other Influences on Leader Behavior

The leader influences followers; but the leader is influenced by followers and by other aspects of the situation as well. Another relatively recent development in the study of leadership is to shift the analysis from a micro level (personal, interpersonal, group) to a macro level (the group's environment). At the macro level, leader behavior is viewed as a dependent variable affected by organizational factors. Role theory, "multiple-influence" theory, and the "substitutes for leadership" theory are three approaches which reflect this development.

Role Theory

The oldest of these views, role theory, says that the behavior of leaders is partly a function of their role perceptions—what is expected of them or what they are supposed to do. Role perception is influenced by documents (rules, regulations, policies, procedures, and job descriptions), oral communication (from superiors, peers, subordinates, and others), and the environment (past experience, feedback, etc.). In addition, the leader's own needs and values influence his or her role perceptions and manner of reacting to feedback (Burke, 1965, and Kahn and Quinn, 1970). Among the most influential of those forces are the leader's superiors in the organization and, indeed, the organization itself. Research indicates that, when faced with conflicting role demands, leaders are more responsive to their superiors than they are to their subordinates (Kahn et al., 1964). Other research suggests that leader task behavior is more responsive to influence by superiors while relationship oriented behavior is more responsive to influences from subordinates (Pfeffer and Salancik, 1975). Thus, a leader's behavior is determined by the leader's perceptions about the role as well as by subordinate performance.

Multiple Influence Theory

More recently, multiple influence theory (initially called adaptive-reactive theory) goes further than role theory by postulating that leader behavior is influenced more by macro variables than by micro ones (Osborn and Hunt, 1975). The theory suggests that leader behavior beyond that prescribed by the leader's role, termed discretionary leadership, will adjust to changing conditions in the environment, context, and structure of the leader's situation (Hunt and Osborn, 1982). For example, the greater the environmental uncertainity or the greater the degree of organizational centralization, the less discretion the leader will have, and the less the leader can do to correct problems or achieve goals. In this case, the leader is, to a large degree, "at the mercy" of the situation.

Substitutes for Leadership

The most recent approach goes beyond the others in that the macro variables are so powerful that they actually substitute for or neutralize leadership (Kerr and Jermier, 1978). Substitutes make leadership unnecessary or redundant; neutralizers counteract leadership or constrain the leader from displaying certain behaviors. Under circumstances where either of these is present, leadership will have a substantially reduced impact on outcomes. For example, highly experienced subordinates would know how to do their tasks and would not need and might even resent a leader who attempts to tell them what to do. The experience of the subordinates substitutes for leader task behavior. If the task is intrinsically satisfying, the leader may not need to "pat the subordinate on the back" for a job well done; here, the intrinsic satisfaction of the task substitutes for leader maintenance behavior. In yet another example, if the leader has no position power, efforts to affect performance may not work because the leader has no control over the necessary contingencies of reinforcement; low position power neutralizes leadership.

An Integrating Framework

Yukl (1981) has suggested an integrating framework for leadership research (Yukl, 1981, pp. 269–273). Yukl (1970) originally proposed a multiple linkage model which suggested that subordinate effort and task skill, the leader role, the amount of resources and support available from the organization, and the cohesiveness and teamwork of the group are all intervening variables between leader behavior and group outcomes. Research on that model also clearly indicated that the pattern of relations significant for one criterion might not be the same as that for another criterion. For instance, the pattern of effective behavior related to subordinate satisfaction (subordinate ratings of superiors) has been shown to be markedly different from the pattern related to performance data such as profits and costs (Yukl and Kanuk, 1979).

Much like the substitutes/neutralizers for leadership work, Yukl suggested that situational variables can be divided into three basic categories. The first category directly affects intervening variables. If a task includes high levels of skill variety, task identity, task significance, and so on, subordinates may tend to be intrinsically motivated by the work itself regardless of the leader's actions. The second and third categories are exogenous situational variables. The second includes variables acting as constraints on the leader's behavior. Schedules may be determined by a central staff unit instead of by the leader, for instance. The third type of situational variable influences the relative importance of the intervening variables. For example, the relative importance of subordinate effort is reduced in situations where automation reduces the need for human energy. These three categories, then, underscore the significance of the linkages between and among situational variables— hence the label, multiple linkages, used to describe this conceptual scheme.

Yukl (1981) changed the basic model to a research framework which included factors that influence leader behavior itself, such as leader traits and skills, power, and role expectations from superiors, peers, and subordinates. Much (but not all) other work and path-goal theory are subsumed by this framework so that it is more complex and less precisely specified than most others; nevertheless it is quite useful as a step toward an integrated theory.

Modifying this framework somewhat, we can see that clearly the universal approach has given way to the contingency approach, and equally clear is the dominance of the behavioral focus over the trait focus. However, if one expands the notion of traits to encompass personal characteristics (which would include traits, physical characteristics, skills, abilities, and competencies), then an integrated theory will recognize the importance of both personal characteristics and behavior of leaders. It is also apparent that influence runs in many directions—from the leader to the followers, individually and as a group, and from the followers to the leader, but the situation also has an influence on and is influenced by the leader. Further, such situational influences may also moderate relationships among the variables, particularly the relation between leader behavior and end-results. It is also reasonable to expect that intervening variables exist between leader behavior and end-results. Finally, the pattern of influence of particular categories of leader behavior will vary according to which end-results are desired—the criterion problem.

This integrating framework is not a complete theory or model; it is merely a way of integrating most of the research which has been done. As such it is, nevertheless, a significant and substantial contribution and should aid others in understanding the sometimes bewildering array of research efforts being conducted in the leadership field. Table 1 indicates the behavior categories used in this framework (Yukl, 1985).

Summary

Despite early theory suggesting the importance of the situation, most of the early research of the past century dealt with personal characteristics. Then there was a gradual shift toward behavioral studies. Although organizational factors such as social distance were still playing a predominant role, the situation was being taken into account as well. Most of the early research programs included large numbers of both business and military samples as well as smatterings of samples from educational and other settings, so that many situational distinctions tended to be obscured.

Research over this past century clearly demonstrates that leadership is not a simple, indivisible construct. It, like the atom, consists of a multitude of components each of which may have multiple characteristics. To some extent the answers we find depend upon the question we ask

TABLE 1
Categories of Managerial Behavior

Informing: disseminating relevant information about decisions, plans, and events that affect the work

Consulting and Delegating: encouraging participation in decision making, and delegating authority and responsibility

Planning and Organizing: determining long-term objectives and strategies, and determining how to use personnel and resources efficiently to accomplish a task or project

Problem Solving and Crisis Management: identifying and analyzing the cause of work-related problems, and acting decisively to deal with a problem or crisis

Clarifying Roles and Objectives: communicating a clear understanding of job responsibilities, task objectives, and performance expectations

Monitoring Operations: gathering information about work activities, and checking on the progress and quality of the work

Motivating Task Commitment: using influence techniques to generate enthusiasm for the work and commitment to task objectives

Recognizing and Rewarding: providing praise, recognition, and rewards for effective performance

Supporting: acting friendly and considerate, and being patient and helpful

Developing: counseling a person about inadequate performance, and providing coaching and career counseling

Harmonizing and Team Building: facilitating the constructive resolution of conflicts, and developing cooperation and teamwork

Representing: acquiring necessary resources and support for the work unit or team, and prompting and defending its interests

Interfacing: developing contacts with other managers and outsiders to gather information, improve coordination with them, and facilitate adaptation to a changing environment

Source: Yukl, 1985.

(Wheeler, 1977), but equally important, we are finding answers. Assuming that there is "truth" in each answer, we, like physicists, need a Grand Unified Theory; unlike physicists, however, we may not have sufficient methodological rigor to expect a GUT approach soon.

It is reasonable to expect that a GUT will emerge over the next century, but not until even more "splintering" in our research occurs. What will the future bring in terms of leadership research? One might expect the near future would include (to name just a few):

1. research on transformational leadership (Burns, 1978; Bennis and Nanus, 1985) which is that "special branch of leadership" (Tichy and Ulrich, 1984) dealing with organizational transition from one state or culture to another (Schein, 1985);
2. related to the above, research on charismatic leadership particularly as it connects to non-verbal communication and symbolic leadership (Bass, 1954) as well as to transformational leadership (Bass, 1985a and 1985b);
3. more research on reinforcement/social learning approaches;
4. more research on social information processing approaches;
5. research integrating mutual influence and information processing approaches—symbolic interactional leadership;
6. research comparing conversion theory (Moscovici, 1976 and 1980) to idiosyncrasy or credit building theory; and
7. research on the role of non-verbal communication and symbols in the leadership process.

There will, of course, continue to be research continuing the dominant behavior/contingency paradigm, but increasingly it will be extended and modified by new and different concepts and approaches.

Acknowledgments

The authors wish to thank Gerald R. Ferris, Ricky W. Griffin, Tim O. Peterson, and David Rubinstein, who read and commented on an earlier draft of this paper.

References

Ashour, A.S. "The Contingency Model of Leadership Effectiveness: An Evaluation," *Organizational Behavior and Human Performance,* Vol. 9, 1973, pp. 339–376.

Asimov, I. *Asimov's New Guide to Science* (New York: Basic Books, 1984).

Barnard, C.I. *The Functions of the Executive* (Cambridge, Mass.: Harvard University Press, 1938).

Bass, B.M. "An Analysis of the Leaderless Group Discussion," *Journal of Applied Psychology,* Vol. 33, 1949, pp. 527–533.

Bass, B.M. "The Leaderless Group Discussion," *Pyschological Bulletin,* Vol. 51, 1954, pp. 465–492.

Bass, B.M. "From Leaderless Group Discussion to the Cross-National Assessment of Managers," *Journal of Management,* Vol. 7, 1981, pp. xvii, 63–76.

Bass, B.M. "Leadership: Good, Better, Best," *Organizational Dynamics,* Vol. 13, 1985a, pp. 26–40.

Bass, B.M. *Leadership and Performance Beyond Expectations* (New York: Free Press, 1985b).

Bates, F.L. "The Coordination of Maintenance Activities in Bomb Wings: Synchronization and Performance." Chapel Hill, North Carolina: University of North Carolina, Institute for Research in Social Science, 1953.

Bennis, W., and Nanus, B. *Leaders: The Strategies for Taking Charge* (New York: Harper & Row, 1985).

Bottger, P.D. "Expertise and Air Time as Vases of Actual and Perceived Influence in Problem-Solving Groups," *Journal of Applied Psychology*, Vol. 69, 1984, pp. 214–221.

Bowers, D.G., and Seashore, S.E. "Predicting Organizational Effectiveness with a Four-Factor Theory of Leadership," *Administrative Science Quarterly*, Vol. 11, 1966, pp. 238–263.

Boyatzis, R.E. *The Competent Manager* (New York: John Wiley & Sons, 1982).

Bray, D.W., Campbell, R.J., and Grant, D.C. *Formative Years in Business: A Long-Term AT&T Study of Managerial Lives* (New York: Wiley, 1974).

Burke, W.W. "Leadership Behavior as a Function of the Leader, the Followers, and the Situation," *Journal of Personality*, Vol. 33, 1965, pp. 60–81.

Burns, J.M. *Leadership* (New York: Harper & Row, 1978).

Calder, B.F. "An Attribution Theory of Leadership." In B.M. Staw and G.R. Salancik (eds.), *New Directions in Organizational Behavior* (Chicago: St. Clair Press, 1977).

Carter, L.F. "Leadership and Small Group Behavior." In M. Sherif and M.O. Lindzey (eds.), *Group Relations at the Crossroads* (New York: Harper, 1953).

Christner, C.A., and Hemphill, J.K. "Leader Behavior of B-29 Commanders and Changes in Crew Members' Attitudes Toward the Crew," *Sociometry*, Vol. 18, 1955, pp. 82–87.

Commons, J.R. "Sociological View of Sovereignty: I–VII," *American Journal of Sociology*, Vols. 5–6, 1899–1900, pp. 1–5 & 67–89 & 155–171 & 347–366 & 544–552 & 683–695 & 814–825.

Davis, T.R.V., and Luthans, F. "Leadership Re-Examined: A Behavioral Approach," *Academy of Management Review*, Vol. 4, 1979, pp. 237–248.

Davis, T.R.V., and Luthans, F. "A Social Learning Approach to Organizational Behavior," *Academy of Management Review*, Vol. 5, 1980, pp. 281–290.

Evans, M.G. "The Effects of Supervisory Behavior on the Path-Goal Relationship." *Organizational Behavior and Human Performance*, Vol. 5, 1970a, pp. 277–298.

Evans, M.G. "Leadership and Motivation: A Core Concept," *Academy of Management Journal*, Vol. 13, 1970b, pp. 91–102.

Evans, M.G. "Leadership." In S. Kerr (ed.), *Organizational Behavior* (Columbus, Ohio: Grid Publishing, 1974), pp. 230–233.

Fayol, H. *General and Industrial Management* (London: Pitman, 1949).

Fiedler, F.E. "Assumed Similarity Measures as Predictors of Team Effectiveness," *Journal of Abnormal and Social Psychology*, Vol. 49, 1954, pp. 381–388.

Fiedler, F.E. *Leader Attitudes and Group Effectiveness* (Urbana, Illinois: University of Illinois Press, 1958).

Fiedler, F.E. "Engineer the Job to Fit the Manager," *Harvard Business Review*, Vol. 43, 1965, pp. 115–122.

Fiedler, F.E. *A Theory of Leadership Effectiveness.* (New York: McGraw-Hill, 1967).

Fiedler, F.E., and Chemers, M.M. *Leadership and Effective Management* (Glenview, Illinois: Scott, Foresman, 1974).

Fiedler, F.E., Chemers, M.M., and Mahar, L. *Improving Leadership Effectiveness: The Leader Match Concept* (New York: Wiley, 1976).

Field, R.H.G. "A Critique of the Vroom-Yetton Contingency Model of Leadership Behavior," *Academy of Management Review,* Vol. 4, 1979, pp. 249–257.

Field, R.H.G. "A Test of the Vroom-Yetton Normative Model of Leadership," *Journal of Applied Psychology,* Vol. 67, 1982, pp. 523–532.

Fleishman, E.A. "Differences Between Military and Industrial Organizations." In R.M. Stogdill and A.E. Coons (eds.), *Leader Behavior: Its Description and Measurement* (Columbus, Ohio: Ohio State University, Bureau of Business Research, 1956).

Fleishman, E.A., and Harris, E.F. "Patterns of Leadership Behavior Related to Employee Grievances and Turnover," *Personnel Psychology,* Vol. 15, 1962, pp. 43–56.

French, J.R., Jr., and Raven, B.H. "The Bases of Social Power." In D. Cartwright and A.F. Zander (eds.), *Group Dynamics* (Evanston, Illinois: Row, Peterson, 1960), pp. 607–623.

Fulk, J., and Wendler, E. "Dimensionality of Leader-Subordinate Interactions: A Path-Goal Investigation," *Organizational Behavior and Human Performance,* Vol. 17, 1982, pp. 241–264.

Georgopoulos, B.S., Mahoney, G.M., and Jones, N.W. "A Path-Goal Approach to Productivity," *Journal of Applied Psychology,* Vol. 41, 1957, pp. 345–353.

Gibb, C.A. "Leadership." In G. Lindzey (ed.), *Handbook of Social Psychology* (Cambridge, Massachusetts: Addison-Wesley, 1954).

Graen, G., Avares, K.M., Orris, J.B., and Martella, J.A. "Contingency Model of Leadership Effectiveness: Antecedent and Evidential Results," *Psychological Bulletin,* Vol. 74, 1970, pp. 285–296.

Graen, G., and Schiemann, W. "Leader-Member Agreement: A Vertical Dyad Linkage Approach," *Journal of Applied Psychology,* Vol. 63, 1978, pp. 206–212.

Green, S.G., and Mitchell, T.R. "Attributional Processes of Leaders in Leader-Member Interactions," *Organizational Behavior and Human Performance,* Vol. 23, 1979, pp. 429–458.

Greene, C.N. "The Reciprocal Nature of Influence Between Leader and Subordinate," *Journal of Applied Psychology,* Vol. 60, 1975, pp. 187–193.

Greene, C.M. "Questions of Causation in the Path-Goal Theory of Leadership," *Academy of Management Journal,* Vol. 22, 1979, pp. 22–41.

Halpin, A.W. "The Leadership Behavior and Combat Performance of Airplane Commanders," *Journal of Abnormal and Social Psychology,* Vol. 39, 1954, pp. 82–84.

Halpin, A.W. "The Leader Behavior and Effectiveness of Aircraft Commanders." In R.M. Stogdill and A.E. Coons (eds.), *Leader Behavior: Its Description and Measurement* (Columbus, Ohio: Ohio State University, Bureau of Business Research, 1957).

Heilman, M.E., Hornstein, H.A., Cage, J.H., and Herschlag, J.K. "Reactions to Prescribed Leader Behavior as a Function of Role Perspective: The Case of the Vroom-Yetton Model," *Journal of Applied Psychology,* Vol. 69, 1984, pp. 50–60.

Heller, F.A. *Managerial Decision-Making: A Study of Leadership Styles and Power-Sharing Among Senior Managers* (London: Tavistock, 1971).

Heller, F.A. "Leadership, Decision Making, and Contingency Theory," *Industrial Relations,* Vol. 12, 1973, pp. 183–199.

Heller, F.A., and Yukl, G.A. "Participation, Managerial Decision-Making and Situational Variables," *Organizational Behavior and Human Performance,* Vol. 4, 1969, pp. 227–241.

Henderson, C.R. "Business Men and Social Theorists," *American Journal of Sociology,* Vol. 1, 1896, pp. 385–397.

Hollander, E.A. "Conformity, Status and Idiosyncrasy Credit," *Psychological Review,* Vol. 65, 1958, pp. 117–127.

Hollander, E.A. "Processes of Leadership Emergence," *Journal of Contemporary Business,* Vol. 3, 1974, pp. 19–33.

Hollander, E.A. *Leadership Dynamics: A Practical Guide to Effective Relationships* (New York: The Free Press, 1978).

Hollander, E.A. "The Impact of Ralph M. Stogdill and the Ohio State Leadership Studies on a Transactional Approach to Leadership," *Journal of Management,* Vol. 5, 1979, pp. 157–165.

Hosking, D. "A Critical Evaluation of Fiedler's Contingency Hypothesis," *Progress in Applied Psychology,* Vol. 1, 1981, pp. 103–154.

House, R.J. "A Path-Goal Theory of Leader Effectiveness," *Administrative Science Quarterly,* Vol. 16, 1971, pp. 321–338.

House, R.J. "A 1976 Theory of Charismatic Leadership." In J.G. Hunt and L.L. Larson (eds.), *Leadership: The Cutting Edge* (Carbondale, Illinois: Southern Illinois University Press, 1977), pp. 189–207.

House, R.J. "Research Contrasting the Behavior and Effects of Reputed Charismatic vs. Reputed Non-Charismatic Leaders." Paper presented as part of a symposium, "Charismatic Leadership: Theory and Evidence." Academy of Management, San Diego, California, 1985.

House, R.J. "Exchange and Charismatic Theories of Leadership." Unpublished working paper, University of Toronto, 1986.

House, R.J., and Baetz, M.L. "Leadership: Some Empirical Generalizations and New Research Directions." In B.M. Staw (ed.), *Research in Organizational Behavior,* Vol. 1 (Greenwich, Connecticut: JAI Press, 1979), pp. 341–423.

Howell, J.M. "An Experimental Test of the Theory of Charismatic Leadership." Paper presented as part of a symposium, "Charismatic Leadership: Theory and Evidence." Academy of Management, San Diego, California, 1985.

Hunt, J.G., and Osborn, R.N. "Toward a Macro-Oriented Model of Leadership: An Odessy." In J.G. Hunt, U. Sekaran, and C.A. Schriesheim (eds.), *Leadership: Beyond Establishment Views* (Carbondale, Illinois: Southern Illinois University Press, 1982), pp. 196–221.

Jago, A.G. "Leadership Perspectives in Theory and Research," *Management Science,* Vol. 28, 1982, pp. 315–336.

Jago, A.G., and Vroom, V.H. "An Evaluation of Two Alternatives to the Vroom-Yetton Normative Model," *Academy of Management Journal*, Vol. 23, 1980, pp. 347–355.

Jenkins, W.O. "A Review of Leadership Studies with Particular Reference to Military Problems," *Psychological Bulletin*, Vol. 44, 1947, pp. 54–79.

Jennings, H.H. "Leadership: A Dynamic Redefinition," *Journal of Educational Sociology*, Vol. 17, 1944, pp. 431–433.

Jones, G.R. "Forms of Control of Leader Behavior," *Journal of Management*, Vol. 9, 1983, pp. 159–172.

Kahn, R.L., and Quinn, R.P. "Role Stress: A Framework for Analysis." In A. McLean (ed.), *Mental Health and Work Organizations* (Chicago: Rand McNally, 1970).

Kahn, R.L., et al. *Organizational Stress: Studies in Role Conflict and Ambiguity* (New York: Wiley, 1964).

Kelley, H.H. *Attribution in Social Interaction* (Morristown, New Jersey: General Learning Press, 1971).

Kelsey, C. "Social Darwinism," *American Journal of Sociology*, Vol. 12, 1907, pp. 711.

Kerr, S., and Jermier, J.M. "Substitutes for Leadership: Their Meaning and Measurement," *Organizational Behavior and Human Performance*, Vol. 22, 1978, pp. 375–403.

Kohs, S.C., and Irle, K.W. "Prophesying Army Promotion," *Journal of Applied Psychology*, Vol. 4, 1920, pp. 73–87.

Kotter, J.P. *The General Managers* (New York: The Free Press, 1982).

Larson, L.L., Hunt, J.G., and Osborn, R.N. "The Great Hi-Hi Leader Behavior Myth: A Lesson from Occam's Razor," *Academy of Management Journal*, Vol. 19, 1979, pp. 628–641.

Lewin, K., "Field Theory and Experiment in Social Psychology: Concepts and Methods," *American Journal of Sociology*, Vol. 44, 1939, pp. 868–896.

Lewin, K., and Lippitt, R. "An Experimental Approach to the Study of Autocracy and Democracy: A Preliminary Note," *Sociometry*, Vol. 1, 1938, pp. 292–300.

Lewin, K., Lippitt, R., and White, R.K. "Patterns of Aggressive Behavior in Experimentally Created Social Climates," *Journal of Social Psychology*, Vol. 10, 1939, pp. 271–301.

Likert, R. *Human Organization* (New York: McGraw-Hill, 1967).

Likert, R. "From Production- and Employee-Centeredness to Systems 1–4," *Journal of Management*, Vol. 5, 1979, pp. 147–156.

Locke, E.A., and Schweiger, D.M. "Participation in Decision-Making: One More Look." In B.M. Staw (ed.), *Research in Organizational Behavior*, Vol. 1 (Greenwich, Connecticut: JAI Press, 1979), pp. 265–339.

Lord, R.G. "An Information Processing Approach to Social Perceptions." In L.L. Cummings and B.M. Staw (eds.), *Research in Organizational Behavior*, Vol. 7 (Greenwich, Connecticut: JAI Press, 1985).

Luthans, F. "A Proposal for a Social Learning Theory Base and Observational and Functional Analysis Techniques to Measure Leader Behavior." In J.G. Hunt and L.L. Larson (eds.), *Crosscurrents in Leadership* (Carbondale, Illinois: Southern Illinois University Press, 1979), pp. 201–208.

Mann, R.D. "A Review of the Relationship Between Personality and Performance in Small Groups," *Psychological Bulletin*, Vol. 56, 1959, pp. 241–270.

McGregor, D. *The Human Side of Enterprise* (New York: McGraw-Hill, 1960).

McMahon, J.T. "The Contingency Theory: Logic and Method Revisited," *Personnel Psychology*, Vol. 25, 1972, pp. 697–710.

Meindl, J.R., Ehrlich, S.B., and Dukerich, J.M. "The Romance of Leadership," *Administrative Science Quarterly*, Vol. 30, 1985, pp. 78–102.

Metcalf, H.C., and Urwick, L. (eds.), *Dynamic Administration: The Collected Papers of Mary Parker Follett* (New York: Harper & Row, 1940).

Misumi, J. *The Behavioral Science of Leadership* (Ann Arbor: University of Michigan Press, 1985).

Misumi, J., and Peterson, M.F. "The Performance-Maintenance (PM) Theory of Leadership: Review of a Japanese Research Program," *Administrative Science Quarterly*, Vol. 30, 1985, pp. 198–223.

Mitchell, T.R., and Wood, R.E. "An Empirical Test of an Attributional Model of Leaders' Responses to Poor Performance." Symposium on Leadership, Duke University (North Carolina), April 1979.

Moscovici, S. *Social Influence and Social Change* (New York: Academic Press, 1976).

Moscovici, S. "Toward a Theory of Conversion Behavior." In L. Berkowitz (ed.), *Advances in Experimental Social Psychology*, Vol. 13 (New York: Academic Press, 1980).

Mumford, E. "Origins of Leadership," *American Journal of Sociology*, Vol. 12, 1906–7, pp. 216–240 & 367–397 & 500–531.

Mumford, E. *Origins of Leadership* (Chicago: University of Chicago Press, 1909).

Nystrom, P.C. "Managers and the Hi-Hi Leader Myth," *Academy of Management Journal*, Vol. 21, 1978, pp. 325–331.

Osborn, R.N., and Hunt, J.G. "An Adaptive-Reactive Theory of Leadership: The Role of Macro Variables in Leadership Research." In J.G. Hunt and L.L. Larson (eds.), *Leadership Frontiers* (Carbondale, Illinois University Press, 1975).

Page, D.P. "Measurement and Prediction of Leadership," *American Journal of Sociology*, Vol. 41, 1935, pp. 31–43.

Pfeffer, J., and Salancik, G.R. "Determinants of Supervisory Behavior: A Role Set Analysis," *Human Relations*, Vol. 28, 1975, pp. 139–153.

Podsakoff, P., Totor, W., and Skov, R. "Effect of Leader Contingent and Non-Contingent Reward and Punishment Behavior on Subordinate Performance and Satisfaction," *Academy of Management Journal*, Vol. 25, 1982, pp. 810–821.

Rush, C.H. "Leader Behavior and Group Characteristics." In R.M. Stogdill and A.E. Coons (eds), *Leader Behavior: Its Description and Measurement* (Columbus, Ohio: Ohio State University, Bureau of Business Research, 1957).

Schein, E.H. *Organizational Culture and Leadership* (San Francisco: Jossey-Bass, 1985).

Schenck, C. "Leadership," *Infantry Journal*, Vol. 33, 1928, pp. 111–122.

Schriesheim, C.A., and Bird, B.J. "Contributions of the Ohio State Studies to the Field of Leadership," *Journal of Management*, Vol. 5, 1979, pp. 135–145.

Schreisheim, C.A., and Kerr, S. "Theories and Measures in Leadership: A Critical Appraisal of Current and Future Directions." In J.G. Hunt and L.L. Larson (eds.), *Leadership: The Cutting Edge* (Carbondale, Illinois: Southern Illinois University Press, 1977), pp. 9–45.

Schriesheim, C.A., and von Glinow, M.A. "The Path-Goal Theory of Leadership: A Theoretical and Empirical Analysis, *Academy of Management Journal,* Vol. 20, 1977, pp. 398–405.

Schweiger, D.M., and Leana, C.R. "Participation in Decision Making." In E.A. Locke (ed.), *Generalizing from Laboratory to Field Settings* (Lexington, Massachusetts: Lexington Books, 1986), pp. 148–166.

Shartle, C.L. *Executive Performance and Leadership* (Englewood Cliffs, New Jersey: Prentice-Hall, 1956).

Shartle, C.L. "Early Years of the Ohio State University Leadership Studies," *Journal of Management,* Vol. 5, 1979, pp. 127–134.

Sims, H.P., Jr. "The Leader as Manager of Reinforcement Contingencies: An Empirical Example and a Model." In J.G. Hunt and L.L. Larson (eds.), *Leadership: The Cutting Edge* (Carbondale, Illinois: Southern Illinois University Press, 1977), pp. 121–137.

Sims, H.P., Jr., and Manz, C.C. "Observing Leader Verbal Behavior: Toward Reciprocal Determinism in Leadership Theory," *Journal of Applied Psychology,* Vol. 69, 1984, pp. 222–232.

Skinner, E.W. "Relationships Between Leadership Behavior Patterns and Organizational-Situational Variables," *Personnel Psychology,* Vol. 22, 1969, pp. 489–494.

Smith, B.J. "An Initial Test of a Theory of Charisma: Leadership Based on the Responses of Subordinates." Unpublished doctoral dissertation, University of Toronto, 1982.

Stogdill, R.M. "Personal Factors Associated with Leadership: A Survey of the Literature," *Journal of Psychology,* Vol. 25, 1948, pp. 35–71.

Stogdill, R.M. *Handbook of Leadership: A Survey of Theory and Research* (New York: The Free Press, 1974).

Stogdill, R.M. "The Evolution of Leadership Theory," *Proceedings of the Academy of Management,* 1975, pp. 4–6.

Stogdill, R.M., and Shartle, C.L. "Methods for Determining Patterns of Leadership Behavior in Relation to Organization Structure and Objectives," *Journal of Applied Psychology,* Vol. 32, 1948, pp. 286–291.

Tannenbaum, R., and Schmidt, W.H. "How to Choose a Leadership Pattern," *Harvard Business Review,* Vol. 36, 1958, pp. 95–101.

Tichy, N., and Ulrich, D. "Revitalizing Organizations: The Leadership Role." In J.R. Kimberly and R.E. Quinn (eds.), *New Frontiers: The Challenge of Managing Corporate Transitions* (Homewood, Illinois: Dow Jones–Irwin, 1984), pp. 240–264.

Van Fleet, D.D. "Changing Patterns of Significant Authors on Leadership and Managerial Effectiveness," *Journal of Management,* Vol. 1, 1975, pp. 39–44.

Van Fleet, D.D. "Academic Disciplines in Leadership Research." Paper presented to the Management History Division, Academy of Management, Orlando, Florida, August 1977.

Van Fleet, D.D., and Yukl, G.A. *Military Leadership: An Organizational Behavior Perspective* (Greenwich, Connecticut: JAI Press, 1986).

Vecchio, R.P. "An Empirical Examination of the Validity of Fiedler's Model of Leadership Effectiveness," *Organizational Behavior and Human Performance,* Vol. 19, 1977, pp. 180–206.

Vecchio, R.P., and Gobdel, B.C. "The Vertical Dyad Linkage Model of Leadership: Problems and Prospects," *Organizational Behavior and Human Performance,* Vol. 20, 1984, p. 520.

Vroom, V.H. *Work and Motivation* (New York: John Wiley and Sons, 1964).

Vroom, V.H., and Jago, A.G. "Decision Making as a Social Process: Normative and Descriptive Models of Leader Behavior," *Decision Sciences,* Vol. 5, 1974, pp. 743–769.

Vroom, V.H., and Jago, A.G. "On the Validity of the Vroom-Yetton Model," *Journal of Applied Psychology,* Vol. 63, 1978, pp. 151–162.

Vroom, V.H., and Yetton, P.W. *Leadership and Decision-Making* (Pittsburgh, Pennsylvania: University of Pittsburgh Press, 1973).

Wheeler, J.A. "Genesis and Observership." In Butts and Hintikka (eds.), *Foundational Problems in the Social Sciences* (Dordrecht, Holland: D. Reidel Publishing Company, 1977), pp. 3–33.

White, R.K., and Lippitt, R. *Autocracy and Democracy: An Experimental Inquiry* (New York: Harper, 1960).

Wolf, W.B. Tape recordings of Mrs. K. Lewin and of R. Lippitt played at the "Ralph M. Stogdill Memorial Symposium: Reflections on the Origins of Leadership Models, Concepts, and Approaches," Management History Division of the Academy of Management meetings, August, 1979.

Yukl, G.A. "Toward a Behavioral Theory of Leadership," *Organizational Behavior and Human Performance,* Vol. 6, 1970, pp. 414–440.

Yukl, G.A. *Leadership in Organizations* (Englewood Cliffs, New Jersey: Prentice-Hall, 1981).

Yukl, G.A. "Categories of Managerial Behavior: An Integrating Middle Range Taxonomy." Paper presented to the Society for Organizational Behavior, Pittsburgh, Pennsylvania, October 1985.

Yukl, G.A., and Kanuk, I. "Leadership Behavior and Effectiveness of Beauty Salon Managers," *Personnel Psychology,* Vol. 32, 1979, pp. 663–675.

Yukl, G.A., and Van Fleet, D.D. "Cross-Situational, Multimethod Research on Military Leader Effectiveness," *Organizational Behavior and Human Performance,* Vol. 30, 1982, pp. 87–108.

PART TWO

PEOPLE AND
PERSONALITIES

Peter Drucker, perhaps the world's most renowned management philosopher, argues that although leadership does matter, it has little to do with "leadership qualities and traits" and even less to do with "charisma." We believe that the importance of leader traits and qualities should not be understated, but we realize that the significance of those qualities is dependent upon the situation and the people involved. Personality issues are important elements of our lives whether we are followers or leaders.

Differences between individuals—those characteristics that make us unique—are important to consider when attempting to link motivation, values, and competencies to successful leadership. Specific attributes of leadership will vary from circumstance to circumstance. In a few cases, technical knowledge and technical skills may be more important than the ability to influence a group. We believe that qualities such as personal integrity, inspiration, creativity, charisma, loyalty, and courage are necessary elements for effective leadership, but we are not sure exactly how they interact and why they sometimes seem to conflict with each other. Whatever the qualities may be that are associated with good leadership, there are some cautions about accepting appealing but simplistic approaches.

First, the "one best way" generic solutions are inappropriate as well as improbable. Second, where one person succeeds as a leader, others may fail, even though their backgrounds and life experiences are similar. Third, timing, or knowing when to act, is as important as possessing success-linked traits; being in the right place at the right time can be a matter of luck, or it can be the result of careful planning and preparation. Fourth, the qualities we admire most in people may or may not be factors in their success as leaders.

Earlier, leadership was defined as an influence process dependent upon the relationship between leader and followers. But the gap between leaders and followers has narrowed—to paraphrase Gertrude Stein, a leader is a follower is a leader. It is often taken for granted that followers give legitimacy to the leadership role, and the failure to recognize interdependencies between leader and followers can have grave consequences. These interdependencies are critical to a leader's success, and they ensure an ongoing pattern of leadership development.

In addition, followers' expectations are changing. Social, economic, and technological environments have created a better educated and more sophisticated constituency. Similarly, superior education, technical skill, and access to information are no longer solely within the purview of the leader. As a result leaders are feeling the effects of a narrowing gap between their followers' competencies and their own abilities. Increasingly, leaders must actively involve followers in organizational processes.

The dynamics of the leader-follower relationship revolve more around the group than the leader. Yet leaders come from the ranks of the followers. We wonder whether leaders can be successful without first having learned the skills of following. Aristotle's *Politics*, Plato's *Republic*, Homer's *Odyssey*, and Hegel's *Phenomenology of Mind* affirm the mastery of followership as the sine qua non of leadership. Hence the contemporary study of leadership must include the dimension of followership and leader development, as it affects organizational success and serves as a prerequisite for effective leadership.

Leadership Perspectives

In "Charismatic and Consensus Leaders: A Psychological Comparison" (Chapter 6), Abraham Zaleznik distinguishes between the charismatic leader, who generates strong feelings and appears as a distinctive personality, and the consensus leader, who is an outgrowth of bureaucracy and is difficult to distinguish clearly as a person. Zaleznik believes that the personality traits of both types of leaders are too often disregarded and that those who argue that a leader's role is defined by the situation ignore the significance of personality characteristics that determine how an individual will respond to that situation. According to Zaleznik, many leaders find themselves in trouble when shifting events demand modes of action that lie outside their normal personal style. This view adds credence to the theory that successful leader traits are indeed a function of the situation.

A personal quality most often found in successful leaders is creativity. Morgan McCall, Jr., conjectures about creative leaders in Chapter 7. He lists some hypothetical descriptions of creative leaders: crafty, grouchy, dangerous, feisty, contrary, evangelistic, prejudiced, and spineless. He goes on to suggest that despite these "horrible" characteristics, creative leaders have a great sense of "play." "Playfulness," according to McCall, "does not necessarily lead to creativity," but people in creative organizations "have a great deal of fun because there is nothing more exciting than to succeed at what you are doing." This is an interesting view of leader behavior that seems to be characteristic of entrepreneurial organizations. But we all know that for many of us, work is not all "fun." Hard work is a quality more often rewarded, particularly in bureaucratic organizations. McCall presents an interesting challenge.

In "When Leadership Collides with Loyalty" (Chapter 8), James Kouzes describes the results of the study he did with Barry Posner, which indicate that leaders are expected to be forward-looking and inspiring. Leaders and followers alike each want the other to be capable and effective; they need to be able to depend on and trust one another, and to set aside their own agendas for that of the organization. Yet being forward-looking and inspiring is often incompatible with being cooperative and dependable, which presents another dilemma. The leader who usually is both must make an "either-or" choice between "Do I lead?" and "Do I follow?"

Chapter 9, "In Praise of Followers," by Robert Kelley, centers on the human qualities that allow effective followership to occur. So that we do not lose sight of those people whom leaders will lead, Kelley examines the role of the follower and the relationship necessary to create an environment of successful leadership. He stresses that skilled leaders must also be skilled followers and that by doing so, they set an example for others. Effective followership involves (1) redefining followership and leadership, (2) honing followership skills, (3) performance evaluation and feedback, and (4) conducive organizational structures. Today's organizations need people who are comfortable in supporting as well as leading roles.

David Nadler and Michael Tushman, in "What Makes for Magic Leadership?" (Chapter 10), ask why some charismatic leaders work magic while others fail. They contrast framebreaking and framebending organizational change and explain that successful leaders are most often associated with framebending. In either case, success requires strong leadership.

Finally, in "Mentoring: A Gateway to Leader Development," William Rosenbach (Chapter 11) reviews the literature on mentorship and its consequences for the mentor, protégé, and organization. Informal mentoring relationships have been very successful in the past, but with the realization that one of the leaders' most important responsibilities is development of their subordinates, formal mentorship programs may be characteristic of organizations in the future.

The Issues

It is difficult to make value judgments about leader effectiveness because of the complex interaction among leaders, followers, and their various circumstances. A person may be an effective lay leader in the church but relatively ineffective in a formal organization. The personality is the same; only the participants and situation are different. We may find creativity and innovation encouraged and valued in some settings and threatening and discouraged in others. Mentoring is seen as a valuable form of leader development in some organizations but as a form of politicking and unfair favoritism in others. Just as individuals differ in terms of their characteristics and qualities, so do organizations. Hence leadership becomes a complex interaction of personalities, people, and situations.

Knowing yourself is, then, the prime ingredient in effective leadership. This knowledge is the unique quality each person brings to the situation. One cannot perform effectively unless one has confidence and self-knowledge. Whether the attributes each contributor describes have meaning will depend upon the willingness and ability of the leader to accept who he or she is when relating to others. These six chapters provide a spectrum of opportunity.

6

Charismatic and Consensus Leaders: A Psychological Comparison

ABRAHAM ZALEZNIK

One of the outgrowths of industrialization and the development of bureaucracy is the consensus leader. Unlike his opposite, the charismatic leader who generates strong feelings and appears as a distinctive personality, the consensus leader is difficult to distinguish clearly as a person.

The consensus leader would seem to fit the outlines of the antihero who, while a "common man" figuratively speaking, does have the distinction of being able to survive the rigors of institutional politics. The questions for psychoanalysts, historians, and political scientists interested in the relationship between personality and politics center on understanding the character structure of the survivor who becomes leader through the control of consensus mechanisms. What manner of man is the consensus leader? How do the charismatic and consensus leaders differ in personality structure and dynamics? To what types of pathology are charismatic and consensus leaders vulnerable; and if these pathologies differ, how can the underlying patterns of conflict and defense be explained? How do pathological manifestations affect the pattern of leadership and do these manifestations have consequences for the decisions made by these two types of leaders?

Sociologist David Riesman *et al.* in *The Lonely Crowd: A Study of the Changing American Character* (1950) found two types of national character they called the "inner-directed" and the "other-directed." Briefly, the inner-directed person relies on his own beliefs and ideas to guide his thoughts and actions. The other-directed personality depends on the views of others to determine his response. This distinction can be taken

Reprinted from *Bulletin of the Menniger Clinic*, 38:3 (May 1974), pp. 222–238, by permission of the author and publisher.

as a point of departure for examining and comparing charismatic and consensus leaders in an effort to answer the questions I have posed.

The Charismatic Leader

The psychoanalytic study of charismatic leadership began with Freud's (1895) early work on hysteria and the nature of the influence one person can have on another, especially when deep emotional attachments are unilateral. At the root of hysterical symptoms is the unconscious love an individual feels for another—a love that can progress from fantasy to idealization of the object. All children pass through such phases in their love of their parents in which fantasy compels the child to center his emotional ties on the loved parent. These ties are the basis for influence on thoughts and feelings, intimately affecting character through the mechanisms of incorporation, identification, and imitation. If one cannot have the loved object, one will try to be like him, to gain his approval, and in all respects meet his standards and expectations. To be sure, maturation modifies and transforms an individual's attachments; therefore, the leader and the led experience many different types of relationships, ranging from the deep and sometimes pathological to the purely objective and rational.

The concept of chrisma and its applications to leadership and authority were originated by the German sociologist Max Weber (Parsons 1947). He used charisma in the religious sense as a spiritual quality, an inner light, which resulted from divine revelation and conversion. As applied to leadership, "it is the charismatically qualified leader as such who is obeyed by virtue of personal trust in him and his revelation, his heroism or his exemplary qualities so far as they fall within the scope of the individual's belief in his charisma." In its more general application, charisma refers to any combination of unusual qualities in an individual which are attractive to others and result in special attachments, if not devotion, to his leadership. John F. Kennedy had such qualities, as illustrated by his ability to attract crowds during his presidential campaign, and as especially evidenced in the "jumping" phenomenon demonstrated by young girls in the crowd who would jump up and down and squeal with delight over his appearance, much like the crowd response to a "teen-age rock idol." Certainly, Kennedy's appeal grew substantially during and following his performance in the famous debates with Nixon. Although it is not clear what unconscious and preconscious imagery the debates evoked in the minds of the electorate, it does seem clear that they petrified Mr. Nixon. The legend grew into the imagery of Camelot, with the brave and fearless band of brothers kept together by the youthful leader, ready to take on all challengers and overcome all obstacles in "getting America moving again."

A somewhat different quality of charisma appeared in the person or the image of Charles de Gaulle (Hoffmann & Hoffmann 1968). France in defeat was an aberration awaiting a leader to restore her to her proper place in the constellation of nations. De Gaulle was aloof and distant, yet heroic in the depth of his conviction that France must not only be served but must also follow the path of greatness.

Franklin D. Roosevelt presented still another type of charismatic leader. Instead of aloofness and elitism, this patrician conveyed a sense of pragmatism in facing the terrifying effort to overcome economic paralysis at home and a new kind of tyranny abroad. With a voice which evoked symbols to which individuals from diverse groups and backgrounds could relate, Franklin Roosevelt forged a new coalition in American politics, drawing together the liberal/intellectual, the blue collar worker, the farmer, and the ethnic minorities. Studies of his presidency have yet to grasp how he elicited loyalty from such diverse groups and from whence came the wellspring within his personality which fed his capacity for communication.

The list of illustrations of charismatic leaders could easily be expanded to include individuals with other types of personalities; yet, all had the capacity to secure the emotional ties of others to themselves. Gandhi, for example, embodied both the earlier conception of charisma as a spiritual quality and the modern preoccupation with the revolutionary personality. The study of developing nations suggests, as in the case of India, that the transition from the tribal feelings and the orientation to village and clan on the one hand to the attitudes of nationhood on the other frequently turns on the presence of a charismatic individual. The list of such personalities is long and includes Sukarno in Indonesia, Nkrumah in Ghana, Nasser in Egypt, and, of course, Mao Tse-tung in China.

To discover what makes for the successful emergence of such charismatic leaders, one must look at the interface of psychology and history. Erik Erikson (1958, 1969) is pioneering in the new field of psychohistory with his inquiry into Martin Luther's late adolescent identity crisis and with his more recent study of the emergence of Gandhi's *satayagraha*, or passive resistance, in leading the workers of the Ahmadabad textile mills out on strike.

Those generalizations that can be made from the psychohistorical study of these great leaders seem to center on the fusion of great personal and historical conflicts. For Martin Luther, the personal issue was loyalty to his father and obedience to authority. His father, knowing the new secular careers offered possibilities for upward mobility, wanted his gifted son to study law. Yet, because of deep oedipal conflicts, young Luther could neither accede to his father's wishes nor rebel in an outright way. Rebellion against his father became possible when he entered a monastery to follow the priesthood, for he could then submit to the overriding code of obedience of another authority figure. However, such a compromise could not stabilize the conflict for long, and the issue of rebellion or submission escalated from the authorities in the monastery to the Pope and ultimately to God. Erikson says this crisis resulted in a series of transformations which cannot be easily explained by sublimation or the neutralization of energy. Instead, the nature of the transformations can only be understood by a close look at the individual's endowments, the demands of narcissism, and, above all, the nature of historical change, where personal conflicts provide the media for communication between leader and led. Luther was not alone in his doubts about obedience, particularly in accepting intermediaries in man's relationship with God. The emergence of strong princes and the resulting conflict between secular and religious authority gave Luther some powerful allies in his struggle to which he attracted the masses through his personal eloquence and the message that good works are a sign of predestined salvation.

As mentioned earlier and as alluded to in the previous example, the study of charismatic leadership must start with the origins of influence and the forms of psychic disequilibria which arise in early object ties. Here, Riesman's (1950) designation of the "inner-directed" personality may be applied to the charismatic leader. Such a leader has a highly developed and well populated inner life as a result of introjecting early objects and later identifying with objects, symbols, and ideals which have some connection to the introjects. The imagos, or internal audience, exert a powerful influence on the leader and form the basis for the ties he establishes with the masses.

The study of Charles de Gaulle illustrates how introjects work in the development of a charismatic leadership style. Stanley and Inge Hoffmann in their paper "The Will to Grandeur: de Gaulle as Political Artist" (1968) correlate de Gaulle's majestic sense with the quality of his internal audience which he projected upon France. De Gaulle's introjects established his sense of independence which he manifested in school and later in his career; but his independence did not involve rebellion against his parents. As the Hoffmans show, de Gaulle remained deeply attached to his parents; even so, he was able to transform this attachment into an idealized relationship with France. To de Gaulle, authority transcended men and ordinary human relationships so that when an individual submitted, it was to ideals. Therefore, he avoided conventional compliance, as demonstrated in his dealings with Pétain, and later with Churchill and Roosevelt. For these latter two, de Gaulle remained a perplexing and vexing figure, seemingly without power but enormously absorbed in and directed toward one overriding goal—restoring France to her rightful place in the constellation of nations. De Gaulle was able to bide his time in England during the war, personifying France in waiting. He was also able to withdraw, accept defeat, and sustain himself through his imagos, awaiting the call to power in 1958. Once in power, he acted decisively to extricate France from Algeria without waiting to test for consensus and acceptance.

This capacity to wait and accept passivity, then to act and move assetively would seem to depend upon the sustaining effects of benevolent introjects, for such self-assurance must come from being at one with these inner images. From this integration, the charismatic leader secures his sense of being special, and here the relationship to mother appears significant. In Freud's words, "A man who has been the indisputable favorite of his mother keeps for life the feeling of a conqueror, that confidence of success that often induces real success [Jones 1953, p. 5]." However, this statement does not completely explain how introjects function for creative individuals in all fields. Some transformations take place in which the sense of being special and the attachment to early objects as introjects are related to social and historical reality with both a past and a future.

To understand this transformation requires a look at the types of psychopathology manifested in the lives and works of charismatic leaders. The psychopathology of the charismatic leader is straight out of Shakespeare. Megalomania, paranoia, all the massive psychic upheavals fit for a King Lear are still valid indicators of how great men fall ill. Although the examples are many, there are still too few good analytic studies.

Studies of Adolph Hitler (Erikson 1950; Langer 1972) serve as counterpoints to studies of charismatic leaders who secure and communicate visions of the future—visions which mobilize and focus the forces of change in society. In contrast, Hitler's life and work exemplify the return to primitive modes of thinking and acting. Only a charismatic leader of this kind could link his own primitive fantasies to a nation's potential for regression, with history as witness to the almost unbelievable outcomes. For a partial explanation, we must again look at the nature of the introjects and their origins in personal history and development.

Hitler was possessed by an internalized audience which mirrored unsettled yet intense attachments to his parents. To begin with, Hitler had doubts about his own origin and legitimacy, and there was also some question about whether his father was born of an illegitimate relationship—both of which found expression in his obsession with a pure race. Hitler's father, who died when the boy was 13 years old, was 23 years older than his mother. Hitler had either witnessed or was obsessed by fantasies that his father beat his mother. In any case, Hitler's relationship to his father was distant, which left him not only with a hatred for his father but with an insecure feeling about what it means to be a man. This hatred became the basis for his hatred of the Jews; he projected upon the Jews what he hated in himself, and he set out to destroy them.

Hitler's incestuous love for his mother, who also died during his adolescence, provided the emotional reservoir which fed his desire for a "pure" reconstructed and unravished German nation. This love of mother and nation remained deeply erotic—untransformed sexuality and aggression—and became the motive power for his sadism. However, Hitler retained a two-sided view of his mother—the earthly, warm, seductive side and the powerful "iron virgin" (to use Erikson's term). The latter became his, and ultimately Germany's, ideal for the nation. The quality of these introjects and the inability to fuse the contrasting images of his parents led to his intense, hysterical love affair with the German people—an affair conducted at the expense of humanity and perpetuated by an inability to tame impulses which once unleashed only destroyed.

Although it is seemingly a long journey from the nature of influence in the parent-child relationship to the structure of power relations in political life, the conceptual links—love and sexuality on the one hand and aggression on the other—are reasonably clear as illustrated in the previous examples. In the cohesive political structure, the direction of love toward a leader or some representation, such as an ideology or a totem, serves to bind members to each other (Freud 1921). If, at the same time, the group's aggression is dampened or is directed toward some external object (e.g., toward tasks to be achieved or toward the representation of some common enemy who in real or mythological terms threatens the group's survival), then the structure is preserved. This classic model of group cohesion may also describe a condition of object surrender, where the followers hand over their egos to the leader and remain susceptible to his commands and directives. They submit in order to preserve their love of the leader, and whatever esteem they experience comes from the sense of devotion to the ideals and causes established in the leader's image.

The study of charismatic leaders invariably is a study of change, specifically the relationship between personal and historical change. Undoubtedly in all generations there are potential charismatic figures who never appear on the stage of history. Individual conflicts and attempts at their resolution remain purely personal events until great historical crises call forth new definitions of self-interest. When established authority structures begin to crumble, seldom is only one segment of society affected; the effects are visible in the family, community, religious institutions, universities, and, of course, government. Therefore, more than one charismatic leader appears at one time. The great depression of the 1930s and World War II pushed many great men forward to both generate and resolve crises. Similarly, the demise of these great men brought about a new era. There has been no genuinely charismatic leader in the United States since Franklin Roosevelt (although John Kennedy had some attributes of such a leader). Likewise, in Great Britain after Winston Churchill, the succession of leaders has been a product of close political infighting, reflecting the problems of alliance (rather than crisis) politics. Even in the great dictatorships, the mantle has not been passed to another individual as often as to a coalitional or bipartite leadership structure. When the last of the charismatic leaders of World War II, Charles de Gaulle, relinquished power, his successor, Georges Pompidou, exemplified the type of leader who arises from the anonymity of bureaucratic function to the top position as a result of consensus politics.

The Consensus Leader

The consensus form of leadership has deep roots in the American national character, for Americans seem to have a basic distrust of charismatic leaders. The nation which began with the overthrow of authority had to establish a legacy in which authority of all kinds (not the least of which is paternal) was suspect. In addition, the experience of overpowering nature with technology has produced a sense of optimism which is peculiarly American—an optimism which produced a system in which a man is judged by *what* he does rather than *who* he is. Status by achievement rather than ascription, furthermore, supports a peer group culture built on the dual images of pragmatism and egalitarianism.

With this foundation which rejects the paternal image and charisma, the question of leadership is ambiguous. The types of leaders (political as well as institutional) who have gained power in the United States present a new personality configuration in which the idealized image, as well as the problematic image, is that of brother and peer rather than father. The philosophical basis for this new personality configuration can be found in the works of George Herbert Mead (1934) and Charles Horton Cooley (1956). In their theory and philosophy, they based the formation of the American character on the conscious assessments and acceptances of others. In other words, character is defined by an individual's memberships and roles. That group formations occur within the fabric of society and that there is an interrelationship between groups and institutions led these theorists to conclude that the American ego belongs to society. Because control of aggression is central to the types of constraints groups exert upon individuals, the taming of destructive impulses is assured by the individual's unwillingness to risk the impoverishment and possible ostracism which would be his lot if he violated group codes. Libido is less troublesome since group relationships have absorbed and ritualized unconscious homosexual impulses; yet, overt aggression, such as competitiveness, status striving, and outright attempts to secure dominance and control, runs counter to the ideology of primary group ties among brothers.

On the whole, our understanding of the psychology of the consensus leader is limited. Such leaders do not generate much interest among psychobiographers; besides, anonymity is a characterological trait of consensus leaders and accounts in no small measure for their successful rise to power. The consensus leader's classical tactic is to establish his position in the center of the political spectrum and gradually to widen the power base, isolating the opposition outside the consensus structure. Centrists tend to be followers rather than leaders of opinion. They avoid sustantive positions for as long as possible and, instead, concentrate their energies on procedure.

One of the striking characteristics of consensus leadership is the relative absence of strong emotional bonds between leader and follower. The leader is the first among equals; and calculated self and group interests are the ties that bind men to the structure. However, men are willing to compromise in order to reach some satisfactory consensus in which interest groups neither win nor lose. Therefore, in a sense, dependency in consensus structures is masked, for the polity is mutually dependent; and the leader, if anything, is more dependent on his followers than they on him. This reversal of the usual dependency pattern is especially marked in complex bureaucracies where the leader knows less about any particular issue than selected subordinates. What a chief executive brings to policy making is more a sense of timing than expertise.

As a case example, let us look at Lyndon Baines Johnson as senate majority leader and as president of the United States (Geyelin 1966). Although there is little doubt that history will judge him brilliant as majority leader and more equivocally as president, Johnson exemplified the consensus style of leadership in his ability to bring together diverse points of view and personalities in the Senate even (or perhaps especially) under a president from the opposing party. Johnson liked to quote the prophet Isaiah, "Come, let us reason together," condensing the complex of calculated interests of senators and their constituencies. He could reason, mediate, and persuade more adroitly when his own position was either unformed or genuinely neutral. He also functioned for consensus when he brought forth the political IOUs which he amassed by doing things for others. Given the tradition of compromise and the avoidance of win-lose tactics in the Senate, many senators found Johnson's actions in keeping with thier own desires to avoid polarization and exaggerated contentions.

That Johnson performed so brilliantly as majority leader suggests that he experienced the self-enhancement which occurs when the demands of a job and the psychological dynamics of the individual are in almost perfect harmony. In his early years as president, Johnson turned the grief of the nation into a national sentiment to fulfill a program in civil rights and domestic reform which the fallen hero had been unable to accomplish. However, Johnson's decisive victory in the 1964 election gave him power in his own name, providing a mandate for his style of leadership while, at the same time, signifying rejection of his opponent who seemed to evoke extremist images (particularly on issues of war and peace). Yet, what occurred over the next four years prompts a number of questions: Did Johnson's personality change, and did he abandon the consensus style for an arbitrary and autocratic position which was out of keeping with national sentiment? Or, did his problems as president reflect the limitations of the consensus style of leadership?

The Vietnam War was a product of consensus politics and does not reflect a change in either Johnson's style of leadership or his personality (Halberstam 1972). The choices were to stay out and let the fate of the Indochina peninsula go its way or to launch an all-out military operation to secure the existence of South Vietnam. Although the American people were not prepared for the second course, the first course of action, to stay out, aroused fears about the domino effect in Southeast Asia. The Washington bureaucracy and the power structure were fearful about the public reaction to the fall of a new territory to a communist government, for they were still sensitized by public reaction to the events in China in 1949. Therefore, the compromise, or the consensus position, was to respond with enough force to tip the balance in favor of South Vietnam while, at the same time, avoiding not only the classical economic argument of guns versus butter but also the decisions accompanying mobilization for warfare. Events largely have indicated that these decisions reached through consensus were unwise; and the military operations of 1972 suggest that our government under President Nixon was still entrapped by the consensus approach. Therefore, one of the limitations of the consensus approach to leadership is that the accumulation of individual compromises in decision making can and often does result in a rigid, extremist position.

In its most highly developed form, consensus leadership is a product of large-scale corporations and works especially well when goals are explicit and measurement of outcomes is equally clear-cut. To a striking degree, policy initiatives come from below and are debated and modified long before they reach the attention of or become identified with a consensus leader.

An extreme example of consensus as a mechanism and style of leadership is the Japanese style of *ringisei.* Policy proposals are debated at lower levels of management and only move to higher levels of authority when a consensus has been reached with each participant signifying his agreement by initialing the policy documents. When the policy initiatives finally reach the chief executive, his role is purely symbolic— attesting to the consensus. The consensus leader in Japan, a position usually reserved for elder statesmen, is like a grandfather (to use the analogy of kinship structures); in less extreme cases, the consensus leader functions as an older brother, in contrast to the charismatic leader as a parental figure.

The particular strengths of the consensus style are in the individual's capacity to form alliances initially with a small number of individuals and then progressively to gain wider participation in decision making by distributing power throughout the hierarchy and by encouraging initiatives from below. Such alliances and participative structures would be impossible to sustain without the consensus leader's orientation to peers and his sensitivity to their motives and interests. These characteristics were outstanding features in the personality of one of American industry's great corporate innovators.

A recent history of Pierre Du Pont's corporate leadership (Chandler & Salisbury 1971) traces the evolution of the Du Pont Corporation and General Motors as a product of consensus leadership. Pierre Du Pont came to power with two cousins, Coleman and Alfred, who collectively succeeded the older generation of Du Ponts. When Coleman, the older cousin, lost interest in the corporation, Pierre and Alfred became contenders for leadership. Pierre's strategic position in dealing with the financial affairs of the corporation placed him in the best spot for assuming leadership, in contrast to Alfred's narrow specialization in the manufacture of gunpowder. Given his position and personality, Pierre found it congenial to encourage initiative from below and to solidify a coalition with suborbinates by appealing to their interests and motives. Alfred, on the other hand, experienced his isolation as somewhat consistent with his defenses and could not put together a workable coalition to counter Pierre.

Among the personality attributes which suited Pierre for consensus leadership were a sense of attachment and responsibility to subordinates. This trait he developed early in life, perhaps as a result of his father's premature death. Pierre became a surrogate father to his younger siblings;

in fact, they called him "Dad." However, as surrogate, he avoided the emotional and behavioral characteristics of the strong and even autocratic father. He was truly an older brother. His attachment to peers both in his family and in the Du Pont corporation probably accounts for the fact that he did not marry until late in life and that he never had children.

To maintain a consistent attitude of caring, responsibility, and attachment to peers the consensus leader must moderate both libido and aggression. If the libidinal charge is too intense or insufficiently disguised, excessive anxiety would be roused in others and would result in the dissolution of group formations. Perhaps more significant in understanding the consensus leader's character structure is the fate of aggression. The aggression must be low-key, directed outside the group (if manifested at all), and, in general, limited in the degree to which aggression is actually experienced by both the consensus leader and his group. Understanding of the vicissitudes of aggression suggests that the consensus leader apparently experiences excessive guilt in containing, if not resolving, the oedipus complex and must maintain reaction formation as an ego defense. Although both guilt and reaction formation sustain the consensus leader's intense sense of responsibility toward his group, these affective repressors account for the frequency with which such leaders appear bland, opaque, and gray in demeanor and personality. However, those individuals for whom reaction formation and guilt are such prominent aspects of their psychic experience occasionally lose control and often react with anger that is disproportionate to the provocation. On the other hand, when anger may be genuinely used in the service of action, it seems to them that such an expression is beyond the range of permissible behavior.

All of these formulations concerning the consensus leader are familiar in relation to the outcomes of the infantile oedipus complex. Although these formulations are valid, I believe they are somehow incomplete. Therefore, a more specific look at the nature of psychopathology in consensus leaders must be taken.

Those who opt for corporate and political leadership are very bright people, ambitious, upwardly mobile; yet, with all their intellectual gifts, they persist in magical beliefs about performance and accomplishment. These fantasies begin the person's sense of having *been* special, of winning the oedipal struggle. As long as one maintains the sense of being special, he will not fall into the predepressive or detached and affectively isolated state so aptly presented in Albert Camus' *The Stranger* (1964). The loss of this sense of being special occurs when there is some setback which causes a leak in the narcissistic reservoir. The disruptions in self-esteem may also occur in what Elliott Jacques (1965) described as the "mid-life crisis." Individuals who have achieved substantial success are beset with the disappointments associated with the failure of reality to live up to expectations; this condition leads to regressive longings and the wish to return to the idyllic states encapsulated in preoedipal fantasies. The defense against these longings is built into adaptation to reality. These individuals owe their success to their capacity to establish a fit with some social reality and, in this sense, function through hyperadaptation and excessive activity.

Consensus leaders seem to lack stable, benevolent, and well-integrated introjects. The explanation for this inner impovershment in personality is that in early development the individual experienced disruption in object ties, particularly in separation from mother and in his reactions to the birth of younger siblings. When such disruptions occur, there may be a precipitous and premature reach for new objects, bypassing the mental process of turning inward to fantasy and recovering the object through internalization and identification. The consequences of such a pattern of develoment can be found in cognitive and affective modes—the "radar effect" of turning outward, or field dependency.

Subject and Audience: The Theater of Leadership

I want to engage in one further comparison of charismatic and consensus leaders—one that is particularly appropriate during a season of political campaigning. During a campaign, we become exquisitely attuned to and consequently manipulated by the stagecraft of politics. Both the consensus and the charismatic leader employ a form of theatrics in the way they present themselves to an audience and in evoking the actions and reactions they seek. However, this similarity is superficial and misleading. The consensus leader's performance tends to utilize role playing as a form of acting, while the charismatic leader's performance is a renewed dramatization, merging (if only momentarily) the internalized audience and the real audience.

The charismatic leader has a continuous dialogue with his internal images which are joined episodically with the external audience. For this reason, the observer in initially observing charismatic figures has the experience of standing outside a dramatization. The appeal is voyeuristic; the fascination is being a witness to the unfolding of a personality which occurs as though the actor were performing unobserved. This feeling of watching from the outside permits both the performer and the audience to relax their defenses, to "suspend disbelief," and to allow their emotions to surge and to join with those of others. Once joined, the distance between performer and audience suddenly disappears. The audience is on the inside, having lost the separation of self and objects which characterizes rational thought in which intellect and emotion are split off. Within the audience, the images of parents as protectors and love objects surface in a collapse of time—a merging of past and present. The orator now has a hold on his audience. If he is a demagogue, he can seduce them into ignoring reality; and, instead of creating a future, he re-creates a past in a mythological form in which scapegoats are presented to focus hatred and to mislead. If the charismatic leader is in communication with benevolent images, he appeals to a future—a new reality that is an unexpected combination of intellect and emotion which transcends the limits of narrow rationality. (After all, it was narrow rationality that led the United States into Vietnam and later sought to extricate us with our original purpose intact and the rules of power unchanged.)

The Hoffmanns (1968) further explain the charismatic leader's dramatizations in terms of the warmth the leader seeks. For the charismatic leader, as in the case of de Gaulle,

> The warmth he needs is not the intimacy of equals, but the support and sympathy of the led. The "melancholy" that is the accepted price of domination, that willing sacrifice of ordinary human relations, becomes intolerable and leads to "ill-explained retreats" only when the *leader's* soul becomes engulfed by what Clemenceau . . . called its worst pain: cold— the indifference or hostility of the led. The warmth he needs is public. [p. 854]

For the consensus leader, the mass audience provides little warmth and, in fact, is an object of mistrust, a feeling which parallels his reaction to his internal audience. His inner images are vague, illusory, and contradictory. Consequently, they provide little warmth and support for the consensus leader's sense of self-esteem, and even less substance for projecting a collective belief or idea onto the public. The consensus leader in politics, therefore, uses a type of role playing rather than dramatization.

Role playing is a very calculating method of communicating ideas to an audience and requires a structure made up of three parts: a stereotyped image, an audience of one, and the player. The stereotype must be easily recognized and simply presented, e.g., Mr. Nixon's famous "Checkers" speech in which he evoked the stereotype of the naive but honest son who is the victim of oppression at the hands of a powerful aggressor. The audience of one and the player both accept the stereotype but maintain it as an object outside of themselves. They avoid close identification with the stereotype, since otherwise it would arouse too much emotion which is unacceptable both in the psychology of consensus and in role playing. The emotional level can also be kept down by preventing the audience of one from merging with a collective audience— "playing it cool" is the key.

Of course, television is ideally suited for role playing. Besides being a "cool medium," it prevents the audience from forming bonds with one another or directly with the player. Technically, television maintains distance between the sterotype, the audience of one, and the player.

When this structure is established with a low-keyed emotional tone, the role play can be brought to its conclusion. Here the player tries to present himself as a peacemaker, a preserver of law and order, a reformer, a protector of property, a friend of the disadvantaged, or any of the other political images. It is even possible in concluding the role play to disguise a policy or decision by presenting the opposite image. If the president is about to undertake major air bombardment in Indochina, then the conclusion of the role play is to present hmself as a peacemaker and negotiator, which may have been the purpose behind Mr. Nixon's decision to "blow the cover" on Dr. Kissinger's secret negotiations with the North Vietnamese. If he is about to take action which will probably displease the right wing of his consensus position, then predictably it is timely for a role play to evoke recognizable stereotypes and self-presentations in line with conservative choices.

The consensus leader through indirectness and the capacity to manipulate through role playing seeks to enlarge and control the center of the political spectrum and to prevent it from fragmenting into many interest groups. While this capacity may be successful in being elected to office, the cost for the consensus leader and consequently his constituents is potentially high. He seldom experiences the peace of mind which comes from the security of purpose, the commitment to deeply held convictions, the realization that he is master of his own house. For too long he has sought to control the insecurities of the sibling and the competition of peer relationships through maneuvering and adjustment to the outside world.

Conclusion

The personality traits of both charismatic and consensus leaders have been too often disregarded. It has been argued that a leader's role is defined by the situation. However, this argument ignores the significance of personality characteristics which determine how an individual will respond. Any leader will act or react in ways consistent with his personal style and will resort to his habitual modes of managing internal and external conflict. I cannot offer a definitive answer to the relative weight of situational and personal factors in determining decisions. However,

I believe the personality factors have been underestimated in their capacity to determine how a chief executive acts upon the constraints and opportunities available to him. In fact, many leaders discover themselves in trouble when shifting events place a burden on their defensive apparatus because these events demand modes of action which lie beyond the leader's personal style.

For example, many of the problems Woodrow Wilson experienced in his relationship with the Senate after the negotiation of the peace treaty resulted from a shift in group psychology—from attachment to the strong leader to the urge to equalize power consistent with peer group attitudes. Had Wilson been able to adapt to the requirements of this new consensus psychology, he might have salvaged the treaty and the League of Nations. But Wilson reacted like the father under attack from rebellious sons. Under these conditions of stress, he resorted to his appeal to the masses, his favored coalition, and bypassed leaders in the Senate for whom consultation was both necessary and desirable in their quest for a new distribution of power. The appeal to the masses failed, and Wilson was unable to shift his presidential style, a fact that contributed (at least in part) to his subsequent stroke and incapacitation (George & George 1956).

In the various phases of a lifetime, in the progression from infancy to old age, the decisive event in adulthood, for which the early years are preparation, is the change from being the son and peer to being the father and leader (at least in the family if not in organizational or elective politics). However, this progression seems to have been interrupted culturally as well as politically. The emergence of the fraternal ideal as the substitute for the heroic father has created a standard which only adds to the anxieties under which the transition from son to father takes place. But there is a limit to how effective cleverness, adroitness, and flexibility can be in circumventing reality and anxiety. When this limit is reached in the cyclical currents of group psychology, the turn may well be toward the leadership of a charismatic man who knows how to wait.

References

Camus, Albert: *The Stranger*, Stuart Gilbert, trans. New York: Knopf, 1946.

Chandler, A. D., Jr., & Salisbury, Stephen: *Pierre S. Du Pont and the Making of the Modern Corporation*. New York: Harper & Row, 1971.

Cooley, C. H.: *Social Organization*. Glencoe, Ill.: Free Press, 1956.

Erikson, E. H.: *Childhood and Society*. New York: Norton, 1950.

————: *Young Man Luther: A Study in Psychoanalysis and History*. New York: Norton, 1958.

———— : *Gandhi's Truth on the Origins of Militant Nonviolence.* New York: Norton, 1969.

Freud, Sigmund (1895): The Psychotherapy of Hysteria. *Standard Edition* 2:255–305, 1955.

———— (1921): Group Psychology and the Analysis of the Ego. *Standard Edition* 18:69–143, 1955.

George, Alexander, & George, Juliette: *Woodrow Wilson and Colonel House: A Personality Study.* New York: Day, 1956.

Geyelin, Philip: *Lyndon B. Johnson and the World.* New York: Praeger, 1966.

Halberstam, David: *The Best and the Brightest.* New York: Random House, 1972.

Hoffmann, Stanley, & Hoffmann, Inge: The Will to Grandeur: de Gaulle as Political Artist, *Daedulus* 97(3):829–87, Summer 1968.

Jacques, Elliott: Death and the Mid-Life Crisis. *Int. J. Psycho-Anal.* 46(4):502–14, 1965.

Jones, Ernest: *The Life and Work of Sigmund Freud,* Vol. 1, New York: Basic Books, 1953.

Langer, W. C.: *The Mind of Adolph Hitler: The Secret Wartime Report.* New York: Basic Books, 1972.

Mead, G. H.: *Mind, Self and Society from the Standpoint of a Social Behaviorist,* C. W. Morris, ed. Chicago: University of Chicago Press, 1934.

Parsons, Talcott, ed.: *Max Weber: The Theory of Social and Economic Organization.* New York: Oxford University Press, 1947.

Riesman, David, *et al.: The Lonely Crowd: A Study of the Changing American Character.* New Haven: Yale University Press, 1950.

7

Conjecturing About Creative Leaders

MORGAN W. McCALL, JR.

I will frankly admit to you that both the terms creative and leadership confuse me. I have learned to be relatively comfortable with some of the ambiguities and outrages of leadership research, but I have always been afraid to confront the nebulousness of creativity, much less to try to put creativity and leadership together. So it is my hope to share a few thoughts with you, not based in science. Abraham Maslow once said that "science is a means whereby noncreative people can create." So I will avoid data. My intention here is to stir up some controversy, and I think that is almost assured. I am certainly not giving prescriptions; in fact, maybe you should do the opposite of what I suggest if you want to be a creative leader.

In preparing for this talk, I drew heavily on Karl Weick (1974, 1976, 1978) and Michael Cohen and Jim March (1974), who to me are among the most creative of the social scientists writing today. I'll try to give them credit where it is due. I also drew on John Steinbeck (1962) who is one of the most creative persons whom I have ever encountered in print. And finally, I drew on David Ogilvy (1965) who is the head of a major advertising firm and has written some very interesting things.

What I am going to be talking about is leaders in organizations. I am going to be talking about managers, administrators, presidents, foremen, supervisors; I am not going to be talking about the research and development types, or isolated staff specialists, or independent creative people. What I am going to do is to try to reflect on what creative leadership might be in a nonreflective, fast-paced, constrained, goal-oriented system. In a real-life organization what can creative leadership possibly mean?

Reprinted by permission from *The Journal of Creative Behavior*, 14:4 (1979), pp. 225–234.

I think one way to start is with the Second Law of Thermodynamics. Entropy is a natural law that things tend to run down, fly apart, return to their natural disorganized state. One way to look at managers is as manifestations of negative entropy, because managers are the glue that keeps systems from flying apart, running down, and disorganizing.

Cohen and March studied the presidents of 42 universities. What they had to say about the lives of those people is relevant to other managers as well. They described them as reactive, parochial, conventional, and living an illusion (Cohen & March, 1974). By reactive, Cohen and March could be talking about Warren Bennis (he was then President of the University of Cincinnati) who described some 500 interest groups with which he had to deal. Most of his job was reacting to the demands and concerns of other people. By parochial, they mean that if you look at where college presidents come from, you discover that they have similar backgrounds, similar experiences, and relatively narrow views of the world. If you look at upwardly mobile corporate managers, some of those same characteristics apply. They mean conventional in the sense that many people have expectations about what a president, or manager, or chief executive officer will do; people have certain expectations of what leaders will do and they tend to be conventional expectations. Leaders will handle the budget, will administer, will be fair, and so forth. Finally, the illusion Cohen and March write about is that presidents think they have a lot of control, when the reality is that presidents have only modest control over events. The main things affecting universities are far beyond the power of any individual to do much about. They may be things as esoteric as the birthrate 20 years ago. And the same thing is true for leaders of corporations, and particularly for the President of the United States.

Leaders work in an environment that sees creativity as a threat, especially creativity defined as a deviant response. The deviant response is something that could ruin an organization as easily as it could move it forward. So organizations tend to be designed for survival, not for creativity. And managers are imbedded in an organization that runs contrary to most of the things that we know about creativity. In fact, most organizations might have a sign that says "stamp out creativity." Many organizations deal with creativity by isolating it, controlling it, judging it, and, at times, even eliminating it.

What is a creative leader in this kind of environment, and what is that creative leader trying to do? It is probably useful to describe a simple series of steps that creative leaders are involved with. One thing that they are trying to do is generate, or stimulate others to generate, original, creative ideas, and so come up with new processes, new ways of doing things. The second thing that they have to do as managers is to find out somehow what all these ideas are, collect them in some way, and then evaluate them, because in an on-going organization you can't just let ideas float around indefinitely. Then, having evaluated and picked a few of them, creative leaders have to convince the organization that an idea is worth the investment and worth the trouble to implement. Now that is a very simple model, not profound; but I would suggest to you, for the sake of heresy, that there are already so many ideas, and so much information, and so many different opinions running around in organizations that the real challenge of creative leadership is in the last two steps. Nonetheless, there is some value in trying to produce more ideas; so how might we describe one of these creative leaders in an ongoing organization? I am going to describe creative leaders as being crafty, grouchy, dangerous, feisty, contrary, inconsistent, evangelistic, prejudiced, and spineless. (I'm indebted to Karl Weick [1976] who used a similar series of adjectives to describe organizations.) Let me try to justify these descriptions one at a time.

Crafty

My feeling is that creativity itself, and certainly the evaluation of whether something is good or bad, involves a value judgment. If I were to put up six pieces of modern art and ask you which were creative and which were good, I would get a lot of differences of opinion. So the first thing about creativity is that, because value judgments are involved, people will disagree about whether an idea is good or bad, or whether it is even creative. The second aspect is that organizations are political systems. The evidence is overwhelming; all of you live in organizations, and you see the political activities all around you. So you put those two together, and you have a value judgment being made in a political system. That is why I suggest to you that creative leaders are crafty. There is a good deal of cunning involved, first in helping others to create something, and, second, in being able to create something oneself in a political environment. This means that leaders out there who are creative are, in fact, able to negotiate very well; they are able to circumvent constraints; they are very sensitive to the tactical issues involved in the use of power. Although power is a different topic, I don't think you can talk about creative leadership in organizations without talking about power, because power is unevenly distributed; and whether or not the people who are trying to push through a creative idea have power is going to make a lot of difference in their effectiveness. The literature on power includes a variety of tactics, some subtle, some blatant—and I suspect that creative leaders are well versed in how to use the power that they have.

Another interesting aspect of craftiness is that, in organizations, managers have to survive failures. We have interviewed a lot of managers, and we have discovered that a manager is usually permitted one or two boners. After that he or she is in trouble. The nature of creativity requires taking a series of half-baked ideas, pushing for them, and getting them implemented. Because of power structures, if creative leaders are to survive, they have to be able to disassociate with failures and associate with successes. Thus, creative leaders are probably manipulative, even Machiavellian. They probably use structure, create structure, disband structure, and change structure. They probably also use people; in short, they are probably extremely political.

Grouchy

I suspect that complacency is the enemy of creativity. There has been a lot of research done on the issue of satisfaction, and some people have claimed that if your employees are satisfied, your employees will be more productive. The accumulated research evidence is heavily against that. There are few consistent relationships between the satisfaction of individual employees and their productivity. Sometimes the relationship is negative, sometimes it is positive, but most of the time there is no relationship at all. In fact, when there is a causal relationship between employee satisfaction and performance, it usually goes the other way: high performing employees are more satisfied; more satisfied employees are not necessarily more productive. So I would suspect that our grouchy, creative leader can be quite demanding and controlling, and may, in fact, have exorbitant standards.

This brings us to the issue of complaints. One of Maslow's interesting suggestions is that the number of complaints in an organization is relatively constant; that no matter how good you are to people, the number of complaints will remain the same. What happens is that complaints will change in level. Karl Weick elaborated on this idea when he suggested that we consider the level of complaint in an organization. If people are complaining about conditions of work and job security, you have a relatively low level of complaint going on in your organization. However, if people are complaining about not getting praised, or about threats to their self-esteem, then you have a higher level of complaint. It means you have evolved as an organization. Weick goes on to say that in the effective organization, a large number of complaints focus on perfection, truth, beauty, and other higher ideals. To give you an example of what I mean, I'll quote from Maslow (cited by Weick, 1976):

To complain about the garden programs in the city where I live, to have committees heatedly coming in and saying that the rose gardens in the parks are not sufficiently cared for, is in itself a wonderful thing; because it indicates the height of life at which the complainers are living. To complain about rose gardens means that your belly is full, that you have a good roof over your head, that your furnace is working, that you are not afraid of bubonic plague, that you are not afraid of assassination, that the police and fire departments work well and many other pre-conditions are already satisfied. This is the point, the high level complaint is not to be taken simply like any other complaint. It must be used to indicate all the pre-conditions which have been satisfied in order to make the height of his complaint theoretically possible.

So we may have some grouches out there who are trying to keep people from being complacent by moving them to a different level of noncomplacency, if such a thing is possible.

We have done some research using Mintzberg's ten managerial roles. One, leadership, concerns what is called "consideration and initiating structure" in our jargon, and means creating a warm, supportive climate for subordinates, structuring their work, and setting goals. This is the only one of the ten roles negatively related to both level in the organization and promotion rate within the organization in a sample of 2,700 managers. I suspect that creative leaders are, in fact, a bit grouchy, that they do prod people, and that they probably won't worry as much about the satisfaction of their people as might be suspected.

Dangerous

From an organizational perspective, creative leaders are indeed dangerous. As I said before, creative ideas are something new, something untried, something different that a leader is going to get implemented. In most organizations implementing a major new idea means millions of dollars, new plants, commitments for years ahead. So new ideas represent a threat to organization survival. Take, for example, a new technology. An organization taking advantage of new technology may have to build a plant before it even knows if the new product will sell. Failure might sink the organization; success could make it great. Maybe that is why research and development tends to be isolated on a hill somewhere. In most companies they do that; they build a little cage and put all their creative people in it, and then when an idea comes out they take it back to the management committee and evaluate it in the cold light of day-to-day realities. But creative leaders can be dangerous because they tend to take risks first and ask questions later. From an organizational point of view, the unpredictability of this can be disturbing.

Feisty

I suspect that creative leaders deliberately create conflict—not to increase competition necessarily but to create sparks that contain ideas. If you have ever read Oliver Wendell Holmes, you may remember the notion of the dice and marbles (Weick, 1974). You can take two positions and visualize them as dice. They have sharp corners and they are very distinct. The noncreative leader takes a rasp and files all the sharp corners off so that they roll around, and anybody who wants to can roll them. In fact, some people have argued that compromise is the worst possible strategy because the result is the most inane parts of two ideas—the parts that everybody can agree on; you lose what was really dramatically different about them. I suspect that creative leaders, rather than trying to suppress conflict, sometimes generate it and often try to control and direct it. The real challenge is to make that conflict useful.

Another reason that creative leaders may be feisty is that in an organization, it is tough to get resources, so they are fighting for resources and the power to implement ideas. To protect people out there having weird ideas takes a lot of work—it takes some fighting. Some of the managers that we talked to, the ones that struck us as creative, markedly loved to straighten out messes, to get involved in conflicts, and make conflicts productive.

Contrary

By contrary I simply mean that some of the creative leaders out there must be contrary to our laws of human nature. Let me give you five of these contradictions out of Cohen and March (1974). Creative leaders might treat:

1. goals as hypotheses;
2. intuition as reality;
3. hypocrisy as transition;
4. memory as an enemy; and
5. experience as theory.

Most of us like to have a concrete goal, something that we are working for; but apparently some people, who are a little bit more creative than most of us, treat goals as hypotheses. They are not wedded to a particular point of view, a particular thing that they are after.

As for treating intuition as reality—intuition can be viewed as an excuse for doing something you can't justify. However, creative leaders see it as a real factor and will go on a hunch. As I said before, they will take a risk and see what happens: they'll learn by experience.

Creative leaders treat hypocrisy as transition. Now there is a thought-provoking idea. Most of us in our lives try to balance our attitudes and values with what we do. We are uncomfortable when we believe one thing and do a different thing. We try to balance. It is called "cognitive balance" in the jargon. If I like Mary, and Mary likes John, then I want to like John—because if I don't I have an imbalance. Cohen and March argue that when people behave differently than they believe, they are ripe for change. And there is good research evidence to say that behavior creates attitudes, not the reverse. What you think is a poor predictor of what you do, but what you do is an excellent predictor of what you will eventually think. So creative leaders may be out there trying to get people to behave differently and, in so doing, may be creating new values.

Memory is treated as an enemy. Habit, folklore, and myth are as prevalent in organizations as anywhere else, so creative leaders try not to be susceptible to them. And finally, creative leaders treat experience as a theory. They act before thinking rather than think before acting. So there are five ways in which creative leaders may be contrary.

Inconsistent

We envision managers having things highly integrated, with lots of rules, processes, and control. The survival of the organization depends on its different pieces being interdependent and being controlled and being watched. However, creative leaders may try to keep the system flexible so the different pieces can do different things. John Steinbeck (1962) has talked about that, and he puts it in terms of integration. As we integrate organizations—make them more interdependent, more controlled—we drive out the possibility that different parts of the organization can do things differently. Steinbeck says:

> We thought that perhaps our species thrives best and most creatively in a state of semi-anarchy, governed by loose rules and half-practiced mores. To this we added the premise that overintegration in human groups might parallel the law in paleontology that over-armor or over-ornamentation are symptoms of decay and disappearance. Indeed, we thought, over-integration *might be* the symptom of human decay. We thought: there is no creative unit in the human save the individual working alone. In pure creativeness, in art, in music, in mathematics, there are no true collaborations. The creative principle is a lonely and an individual matter. Groups can correlate, investigate, and build, but we could not think of any group

that has ever created or invented anything. Indeed, the first impulse of the group seems to be to destroy the creation and the creator. But integration, or the designed group, seems to be highly vulnerable.

He then goes on to give some examples which suggest that we don't want integrated systems, and then says:

Consider the blundering anarchic system of the United States; the stupidity of some of its lawmakers, the violent reaction, the slowness of its ability to change. Twenty-five key men destroyed could make the Soviet Union stagger, but we could lose our Congress, our President, and our general staff and nothing much would have happened. We could go right on. In fact we might be better for it.

In any case I suspect that creative leaders might have to fight the urge to integrate, to solidify, to make everything interdependent. They want to keep the pieces loose enough so that they could lose a few and the organization would still survive.

Evangelistic

Karl Weick once said, "Leaders are evangelists, not accountants." By that he meant that creative leaders manipulate symbols for the rest of the organization. If you walk into an organization that is bottom-line oriented, what you are walking into is a symbol; this is the way we punctuate reality in this organization, this is the reality we strive for. Creative leaders create the myths and symbols by which other people operate. In that sense, they are evangelists, preaching a cause, saying it is alright to be creative, saying that the organization prefers this to that, using a reward system to make people who do something bizarre-but-effective a symbol for the whole organization. It is the suggestion box raised to a level at which it becomes a symbolic part of the people in the organization.

Prejudiced

When I suggest that creative leaders are prejudiced, I don't mean sex bias or race bias; they may or may not be prejudiced in those ways. I do suspect, though, that creative leaders are prejudiced about competence. They use it and discriminate with it. If they have different kinds of people, they match them to jobs so that the creative ones are not mixed in with the Philistines. There is some evidence in the leadership research that leaders rarely treat all of their subordinates the same way. They have in-groups and out-groups, and when you look at their relationships with individual subordinates, they are, in fact, discriminating. There is a quote from Ogilvy that I want to share with you. At one time he worked in a French kitchen and apparently the head chef was a real tyrant. Ogilvy (1965) said this about him:

> M. Pitard did not tolerate incompetence. He knew that it is demoralizing for professionals to work alongside incompetent amateurs. I saw him fire three pastry cooks in a month for the same crime: They could not make the caps on their brioches rise evenly. Mr. Gladstone would have applauded such ruthlessness; he held that the first essential for a prime minister is to be a good butcher. M. Pitard taught me exorbitant standards of service.

While creative leaders are prejudiced, they are not at all egalitarian. This idea has been expanded on by Craig Lundberg (1978) who has talked about Lieutenants, about how effective leaders in organizations find an ally with whom they work closely. They may exclude others; they may fight the selection system. So I suggest that any creative leaders out there would be far from egalitarian or participative in the way they make decisions.

Spineless

One of the crucial things about living in a complex organizational environment and being able to deal with it is to be a listener, an absorber, a monitor. The data we have indicate a positive correlation between monitoring information and promotion rate in the organization. In a recent essay, Karl Weick (1978) makes a point about managers being a media. To demonstrate this point, he uses a contour gauge. You can set it down on a corner, press on it, and you'll come away with a precise image of the corner. Weick elaborates on this analogy by pointing out that each one of the little spines in the contour gauge operates independently of the others. In much the same way, he says, creative leaders are out there absorbing all kinds of different things, but not necessarily connecting them. The interesting irony of all this is that creative leaders are also able to act. They can turn their absorbing, monitoring functions around and use all that differentiation to make something happen. It is almost like being on the other side of the contour gauge when you push it down.

So, these are some hypothetical characteristics of creative leaders: they may be crafty, grouchy, dangerous, feisty, contrary, evangelistic, prejudiced, and spineless.

I suspect that some of the creative leaders in organizations would appear two-faced to an outsider, because on the one hand, they are playing the traditional organizational game so that they can stay in the system and continue to do something with it, while on the other hand they are moving ahead, gaining credits, and being generally outrageous.

Finally, I believe that people have fun in organizations in spite of these "horrible" characteristics of creative leaders. My proposition would be that success is the fun. Playfulness does not necessarily lead to creativity, but successfully creative organizations have a great deal of fun because there is nothing more exciting than to succeed at what you are doing.

Let me close by reminding you that I started out with Cohen and March describing managers as reactive, parochial, conventional, and living an illusion. Because I think there are many oxymorons in creative leadership, and because the nature of creativity is making opposites fit and frames of reference clash, what we really may be talking about is reactive reflection, broad parochialism, unorthodox conventionalism, and solid illusions.

References

Cohen, M. D., & March, J. G. *Leadership and ambiguity*. NYC: McGraw-Hill, 1974.

Lundberg, C. The unreported leadership research of Dr. G. Hypothetical. In McCall, M., & Lombardo, M. (eds.), *Leadership: where else can we go?* Durham, NC: Duke University Press, 1978.

Ogilvy, D. M. The creative chef. In Steiner, G. A. (ed.), *The creative organization*. Chicago: University of Chicago Press, 1965.

Steinbeck, J. *The log from the sea of Cortez*. NYC: Viking, 1962.

Weick, K. E. Reward concepts: dice or marbles. Presented at the School of Industrial and Labor Relations, Cornell University, Ithaca, NY, 1974.

Weick, K. E. On re-punctuating the problem of organizational effectiveness. Paper presented at a conference on organizational effectiveness at Carnegie-Mellon University, Pittsburgh, 1976.

Weick, K. E. The spines of leaders. In McCall, M. & Lombardo, M. (eds.), *Leadership: where else can we go?* Durham, NC: Duke University Press, 1978.

8

When Leadership
Collides with Loyalty

JAMES M. KOUZES

Despite our cry for more effective leadership, I've become convinced that we are quite satisfied to do without it. We would much rather have loyalty than leadership. Recall the fight between former General Motors board member H. Ross Perot and G.M.'s chairman, Roger B. Smith, that erupted when someone other than the official leader of the corporation began to articulate a strategic vision for the company.

Or take the case of a friend of mine, a former senior vice president of a large packaged goods company. A few years ago he faced a critical leadership challenge. New technology made it possible to introduce a substitute for his company's food product. His market studies clearly indicated that the future of the industry lay in the new substitute product. He was convinced that his company had to revise its long-range plans and develop its own entry into the market or suffer disastrous consequences.

But the board did not share his point of view. It authorized its own independent studies by two prestigious management consulting firms, which to the board's surprise supported the senior vice president's sense of the market. Still unconvinced, the board asked two law firms to determine whether entry into the new market would pose any antitrust issues. Both sets of lawyers agreed there would be no problem.

Despite the overwhelming evidence, the board then sought the opinion of yet a third law firm. This one gave it the answer it was looking for and it abandoned the new product.

The senior vice president would not be false to his beliefs and subsequently left the company. He has since successfully applied his leadership talents to dramatically improve the performance of a business he now owns in another industry. And he was right about the future of his former company. It experienced serious financial losses, went through a dramatic downsizing, and has yet to recover fully from its myopic strategy.

This critical incident illustrates an extraordinarily difficult choice executives must often make: Do I lead or do I follow? While one is frequently a leader and a follower in the same organization, there are times in executive careers when the choice is either-or. That is because there are distinct differences [in] what we expect of followers. These expectations are in dramatic conflict.

During the course of doing research for a book, my co-author, Barry Posner, and I asked top-level managers to complete a checklist of the characteristics they look for and admire most in a leader. According to our study, the majority of senior managers admire leaders who are: honest, competent, forward-looking and inspiring.

In a separate study, we asked a similar group of executives about what qualities they value in a follower. The majority of executives in our study said they admire honesty, competency, dependability and cooperation.

In every survey we conducted in the United States, honesty and competency ranked first and second in our expectations of what we want from our leaders and our followers. If we are to follow someone willingly, we first want to know that the person is worthy of our trust. Similarly, when a leader inquires into the status of a project he wants to know that the information is completely accurate.

We also want leaders and followers alike to be capable and effective. When a leader delegates a task he naturally wants assurance that it will be carried out with skill and precision.

But we also expect our leaders to have a sense of direction and a concern for the future of the organization. Leaders must know where they are going. We expect them to be enthusiastic, energetic and positive about the future. It is not enough for a leader to have a dream—he must be able to communicate his vision in ways that uplift and encourage people to go along with it.

Leaders want to know they can count on people to be team players. They want to know they will work together willingly and will be able to compromise and subordinate individual needs to the common purpose.

These qualities are absolutely essential for even the most mundane tasks in organizations. We must be able to rely on each other, to trust each other, and to set aside our own agendas for that of the organization. Without dependability and cooperation, nothing would get done, and politics would be rampant.

Yet being forward-looking and inspiring—two essential leadership qualities—is often not harmonious with being cooperative and dependable. That is what happened in the case of the senior vice president of the packaged goods company. His integrity demanded that he stand up for his point of view. The result was that he was perceived not to be a team player.

If an individual's vision of the future is opposed to that of his superiors, he may be perceived as uncooperative and disloyal even if his point of view is correct. Persistently selling a point of view only reinforces this perception and may diminish support within the organization. It may even lead to being branded a renegade, and result in being fired, transferred, or to a "voluntary" departure.

As essential as cooperativeness and dependability are, they can be inhibitors of organizational change. If they are too rigidly adhered to, they can result in faithful allegiance to the status quo and unquestioning loyalty to the party line. They also can inhibit the development of the leadership skills we so need in business today.

There is another crucial difference between a pioneering leader and a dependable follower. While success in both is founded on personal credibility, leadership requires the realization of a unique and ideal vision of the future. Following requires cooperative and reliable adherence to that common vision. When an individual's vision is in conflict with the existing strategic vision of an organization, he may have to make a choice: do I lead or do I follow?

There is no easy path. If organizations inhibit the honest articulation of fresh strategic visions of the future, they will never grow and improve. They will never create a climate that fosters leadership. On the other hand, if individuals cannot learn to subordinate themselves to a shared purpose, then anarchy will rule.

In these times of business transformation, it is wise for executives to encourage and tolerate more internal conflict than we have allowed in the past. If we expect people to show initiative in meeting today's serious business challenges, then we have to relax our expectations of abiding devotion. Instead, we must support the efforts of honest and competent people to find solutions to the problems that are confronting our companies. In short, we must develop the leader in everyone.

9

In Praise of Followers

ROBERT E. KELLEY

We are convinced that corporations succeed or fail, compete or crumble, on the basis of how well they are led. So we study great leaders of the past and present and spend vast quantities of time and money looking for leaders to hire and trying to cultivate leadership in the employees we already have.

I have no argument with this enthusiasm. Leaders matter greatly. But in searching so zealously for better leaders we tend to lose sight of the people these leaders will lead. Without his armies, after all, Napoleon was just a man with grandiose ambitions. Organizations stand or fall partly on the basis of how well their leaders lead, but partly also on the basis of how well their followers follow.

In 1987, declining profitability and intensified competition for corporate clients forced a large commercial bank on the east coast to reorganize its operations and cut its work force. Its most seasoned managers had to spend most of their time in the field working with corporate customers. Time and energies were stretched so thin that one department head decided he had no choice but to delegate the responsibility for reorganization to his staff people, who had recently had training in self-management.

Despite grave doubts, the department head set them up as a unit without a leader, responsible to one another and to the bank as a whole for writing their own job descriptions, designing a training program,

Reprinted by permission of the *Harvard Business Review.* "In Praise of Followers" by Robert E. Kelley (Nov.-Dec. 1988). Copyright © 1988 by the President and Fellows of Harvard College; all rights reserved.

Author's note: I am indebted to Pat Chew for her contributions to this article. I also want to thank Janet Nordin, Howard Seckler, Paul Brophy, Stuart Mechlin, Ellen Mechlin, and Syed Shariq for their critical input.

determining criteria for performance evaluations, planning for operational needs, and helping to achieve overall organizational objectives.

They pulled it off. The bank's officers were delighted and frankly amazed that rank-and-file employees could assume so much responsibility so successfully. In fact, the department's capacity to control and direct itself virtually without leadership saved the organization months of turmoil, and as the bank struggled to remain a major player in its region, valuable management time was freed up to put out other fires.

What was it these singular employees did? Given a goal and parameters, they went where most departments could only have gone under the hands-on guidance of an effective leader. But these employees accepted the delegation of authority and went there alone. They thought for themselves, sharpened their skills, focused their efforts, put on a fine display of grit and spunk and self-control. They followed effectively.

To encourage this kind of effective following in other organizations, we need to understand the nature of the follower's role. To cultivate good followers, we need to understand the human qualities that allow effective followership to occur.

The Role of Follower

Bosses are not necessarily good leaders; subordinates are not necessarily effective followers. Many bosses couldn't lead a horse to water. Many subordinates couldn't follow a parade. Some people avoid either role. Others accept the role thrust upon them and perform it badly.

At different points in their careers, even at different times of the working day, most managers play both roles, though seldom equally well. After all, the leadership role has the glamour and attention. We take courses to learn it, and when we play it well we get applause and recognition. But the reality is that most of us are more often followers than leaders. Even when we have subordinates, we still have bosses. For every committee we chair, we sit as a member on several others.

So followership dominates our lives and organizations, but not our thinking, because our preoccupation with leadership keeps us from considering the nature and the importance of the follower.

What distinguishes an effective from an ineffective follower is enthusiastic, intelligent, and self-reliant participation—without star billing—in the pursuit of an organizational goal. Effective followers differ in their motivations for following and in their perceptions of the role. Some choose followership as their primary role at work and serve as team players who take satisfaction in helping to further a cause, an idea, a product, a service, or, more rarely, a person. Others are leaders in some situations but choose the follower role in a particular context. Both these

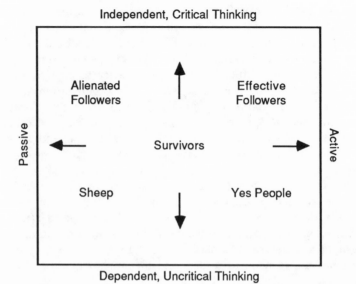

Independent, Critical Thinking

Alienated
Followers

Effective
Followers

Passive

Active

Survivors

Sheep

Yes People

Dependent, Uncritical Thinking

groups view the role of follower as legitimate, inherently valuable, even virtuous.

Some potentially effective followers derive motivation from ambition. By proving themselves in the follower's role, they hope to win the confidence of peers and superiors and move up the corporate ladder. These people do not see followership as attractive in itself. All the same, they can become good followers if they accept the value of learning the role, studying leaders from a subordinate's perspective, and polishing the followership skills that will always stand them in good stead.

Understanding motivations and perceptions is not enough, however. Since followers with different motivations can perform equally well, I examined the behavior that leads to effective and less effective following among people committed to the organization and came up with two underlying behavioral dimensions that help to explain the difference.

One dimension measures to what degree followers exercise independent, critical thinking. The other ranks them on a passive/active scale. The resulting diagram identifies five followership patterns.

Sheep are passive and uncritical, lacking in initiative and sense of responsibility. They perform the tasks given them and stop. Yes People are a livelier but equally unenterprising group. Dependent on a leader for inspiration, they can be aggressively deferential, even servile. Bosses weak in judgment and self-confidence tend to like them and to form alliances with them that can stultify the organization.

Alienated Followers are critical and independent in their thinking but passive in carrying out their role. Somehow, sometime, something turned them off. Often cynical, they tend to sink gradually into disgruntled acquiescence, seldom openly opposing a leader's efforts. In the very center of the diagram we have Survivors, who perpetually sample the wind and live by the slogan "better safe than sorry." They are adept at surviving change.

In the upper right-hand corner, finally, we have Effective Followers, who think for themselves and carry out their duties and assignments with energy and assertiveness. Because they are risk takers, self-starters, and independent problem solvers, they get consistently high ratings from peers and many superiors. Followership of this kind can be a positive and acceptable choice for parts or all of our lives—a source of pride and fulfillment.

Effective followers are well-balanced and responsible adults who can succeed without strong leadership. Many followers believe they offer as much value to the organization as leaders do, especially in project or task-force situations. In an organization of effective followers, a leader tends to be more an overseer of change and progress than a hero. As organizational structures flatten, the quality of those who follow will become more and more important. As Chester I. Barnard wrote 50 years ago in *The Functions of the Executive*, "The decision as to whether an order has authority or not lies with the person to whom it is addressed, and does not reside in 'persons of authority' or those who issue orders."

The Qualities of Followers

Effective followers share a number of essential qualities:

1. They manage themselves well.
2. They are committed to the organization and to a purpose, principle, or person outside themselves.
3. They build their competence and focus their efforts for maximum impact.
4. They are courageous, honest, and credible.

Self-Management. Paradoxically, the key to being an effective follower is the ability to think for oneself—to exercise control and independence and to work without close supervision. Good followers are people to whom a leader can safely delegate responsibility, people who anticipate needs at their own level of competence and authority.

Another aspect of this paradox is that effective followers see themselves—except in terms of line responsibility—as the equals of the leaders they follow. They are more apt to openly and unapologetically disagree with leadership and less likely to be intimidated by hierarchy and organizational structure. At the same time, they can see that the people they follow are, in turn, following the lead of others, and they try to appreciate the goals and needs of the team and the organization. Ineffective followers, on the other hand, buy into the hierarchy and, seeing themselves as subservient, vacillate between despair over their seeming powerlessness and attempts to manipulate leaders for their own purposes. Either their fear of powerlessness becomes a self-fulfilling prophecy—for themselves and often for their work units as well—or their resentment leads them to undermine the team's goals.

Self-managed followers give their organizations a significant cost advantage because they eliminate much of the need for elaborate supervisory control systems that, in any case, often lower morale. In 1985, a large midwestern bank redesigned its personnel selection system to attract self-managed workers. Those conducting interviews began to look for particular types of experience and capacities—initiative, teamwork, independent thinking of all kinds—and the bank revamped its orientation program to emphasize self-management. At the executive level, role playing was introduced into the interview process: how you disagree with your boss, how you prioritize your in-basket after a vacation. In the three years since, employee turnover has dropped dramatically, the need for supervisors has decreased, and administrative costs have gone down.

Of course not all leaders and managers like having self-managing subordinates. Some would rather have sheep or yes people. The best that good followers can do in this situation is to protect themselves with a little career self-management—that is, to stay attractive in the marketplace. The qualities that make a good follower are too much in demand to go begging for long.

Commitment. Effective followers are committed to something—a cause, a product, an organization, an idea—in addition to the care of their own lives and careers. Some leaders misinterpret this commitment. Seeing their authority acknowledged, they mistake loyalty to a goal for loyalty to themselves. But the fact is that many effective followers see leaders merely as coadventurers on a worthy crusade, and if they suspect their leader of flagging commitment or conflicting motives they may just withdraw their support, either by changing jobs or by contriving to change leaders.

The opportunities and the dangers posed by this kind of commitment are not hard to see. On the one hand, commitment is contagious. Most people like working with colleagues whose hearts are in their work. Morale stays high. Workers who begin to wander from their purpose are jostled back into line. Projects stay on track and on time. In addition, an appreciation of commitment and the way it works can give managers an extra tool with which to understand and channel the energies and loyalties of their subordinates.

On the other hand, followers who are strongly committed to goals not consistent with the goals of their companies can produce destructive results. Leaders having such followers can even lose control of their organizations.

A scientist at a computer company cared deeply about making computer technology available to the masses, and her work was outstanding. Since her goal was in line with the company's goals, she had few problems with top management. Yet she saw her department leaders essentially as facilitators of her dream, and when managers worked at cross-purposes to that vision, she exercised all of her considerable political skills to their detriment. Her immediate supervisors saw her as a thorn in the side, but she was quite effective in furthering her cause because she saw eye to eye with company leaders. But what if her vision and the company's vision had differed?

Effective followers temper their loyalites to satisfy organizational needs—or they find new organizations. Effective leaders know how to channel the energies of strong commitment in ways that will satisfy corporate goals as well as a follower's personal needs.

Competence and Focus. On the grounds that committed incompetence is still incompetence, effective followers master skills that will be useful to their organizations. They generally hold higher performance standards than the work environment requires, and continuing education is second nature to them, a staple in their professional development.

Less effective followers expect training and development to come to them. The only education they acquire is force-fed. If not sent to a seminar, they don't go. Their competence deteriorates unless some leader gives them parental care and attention.

Good followers take on extra work gladly, but first they do a superb job on their core responsibilities. They are good judges of their own strengths and weaknesses, and they contribute well to teams. Asked to perform in areas where they are poorly qualified, they speak up. Like athletes stretching their capacities, they don't mind chancing failure if they know they can succeed, but they are careful to spare the company wasted energy, lost time, and poor performance by accepting challenges that coworkers are better prepared to meet. Good followers see coworkers as colleagues rather than competitors.

At the same time, effective followers often search for overlooked problems. A woman on a new product development team discovered that no one was responsible for coordinating engineering, marketing, and manufacturing. She worked out an interdepartmental review schedule that identified the people who should be involved at each stage of development. Instead of burdening her boss with yet another problem, this woman took the initiative to present the issue along with a solution.

Another woman I interviewed described her efforts to fill a dangerous void in the company she cared about. Young managerial talent in this manufacturing corporation had traditionally made careers in production. Convinced that foreign competition would alter the shape of the industry, she realized that marketing was a neglected area. She took classes, attended seminars, and read widely. More important, she visited customers to get feedback about her company's and competitors' products, and she soon knew more about the product's customer appeal and market position than any of her peers. The extra competence did wonders for her own career, but it also helped her company weather a storm it had not seen coming.

Courage. Effective followers are credible, honest, and courageous. They establish themselves as independent, critical thinkers whose knowledge and judgment can be trusted. They give credit where credit is due, admitting mistakes and sharing successes. They form their own views and ethical standards and stand up for what they believe in.

Insightful, candid, and fearless, they can keep leaders and colleagues honest and informed. The other side of the coin of course is that they can also cause great trouble for a leader with questionable ethics.

Jerome LiCari, the former R&D director at Beech-Nut, suspected for several years that the apple concentrate Beech-Nut was buying from a new supplier at 20% below market price was adulterated. His department suggested switching suppliers, but top management at the financially strapped company put the burden of proof on R&D.

By 1981, LiCari had accumulated strong evidence of adulteration and issued a memo recommending a change of supplier. When he got no response, he went to see his boss, the head of operations. According to LiCari, he was threatened with dismissal for lack of team spirit. LiCari then went to the president of Beech-Nut, and when that, too, produced no results, he gave up his three-year good-soldier effort, followed his conscience, and resigned. His last performance evaluation praised his expertise and loyalty, but said his judgment was "colored by naiveté and impractical ideals."

In 1986, Beech-Nut and LiCari's two bosses were indicted on several hundred counts of conspiracy to commit fraud by distributing adulterated apple juice. In November 1987, the company pleaded guilty and agreed to a fine of $2 million. In February of this year [1988], the two executives were found guilty on a majority of the charges. The episode cost Beech-Nut an estimated $25 million and a 20% loss of market share. Asked during the trial if he had been naive, LiCari said, "I guess I was. I thought apple juice should be made from apples."

Is LiCari a good follower? Well, no, not to his dishonest bosses. But yes, he is almost certainly the kind of employee most companies want to have: loyal, honest, candid with his superiors, and thoroughly credible. In an ethical company involved unintentionally in questionable practices, this kind of follower can head off embarrassment, expense, and litigation.

Cultivating Effective Followers

You may have noticed by now that the qualities that make effective followers are, confusingly enough, pretty much the same qualities found in some effective leaders. This is no mere coincidence, of course. But the confusion underscores an important point. If a person has initiative, self-control, commitment, talent, honesty, credibility, and courage, we say, "Here is a leader!" By definition, a follower cannot exhibit the qualities of leadership. It violates our stereotype.

But our stereotype is ungenerous and wrong. Followership is not a person but a role, and what distinguishes followers from leaders is not intelligence or character but the role they play. As I pointed out at the beginning of this article, effective followers and effective leaders are often the same people playing different parts at different hours of the day.

In many companies, the leadership track is the only road to career success. In almost all companies, leadership is taught and encouraged while followership is not. Yet effective followership is a prerequisite for organizational success. Your organization can take four steps to cultivate effective followers in your work force.

1. *Redefining Followership and Leadership.* Our stereotyped but unarticulated definitions of leadership and followership shape our expectations when we occupy either position. If a leader is defined as responsible for motivating followers, he or she will likely act toward followers as if they needed motivation. If we agree that a leader's job is to transform followers, then it must be a follower's job to provide the clay. If followers fail to need transformation, the leader looks ineffective. The way we define the roles clearly influences the outcome of the interaction.

Instead of seeing the leadership role as superior to and more active than the role of the follower, we can think of them as equal but different activities. The operative definitions are roughly these: people who are effective in the leader role have the vision to set corporate goals and strategies, the interpersonal skills to achieve consensus, the verbal capacity to communicate enthusiasm to large and diverse groups of individuals, the organizational talent to coordinate disparate efforts, and, above all, the desire to lead.

People who are effective in the follower role have the vision to see both the forest and the trees, the social capacity to work well with others, the strength of character to flourish without heroic status, the moral and psychological balance to pursue personal and corporate goals at no cost to either, and, above all, the desire to participate in a team effort for the accomplishment of some greater common purpose.

This view of leadership and followership can be conveyed to employees directly and indirectly—in training and by example. The qualities that make good followers and the value the company places on effective followership can be articulated in explicit follower training. Perhaps the best way to convey this message, however, is by example. Since each of us plays a follower's part at least from time to time, it is essential that we play it well, that we contribute our competence to the achievement of team goals, that we support the team leader with candor and self-control, that we do our best to appreciate and enjoy the role of quiet contribution to a larger, common cause.

2. *Honing Followership Skills.* Most organizations assume that leadership has to be taught but that everyone knows how to follow. This assumption is based on three faulty premises: (1) that leaders are more important than followers, (2) that following is simply doing what you are told to do, and (3) that followers inevitably draw their energy and aims, even their talent, from the leader. A program of follower training can correct this misapprehension by focusing on topics like:

Improving independent, critical thinking
Self-management
Disagreeing agreeably
Building credibility
Aligning personal and organizational goals and commitments
Acting responsibly toward the organization, the leader, coworkers, and oneself
Similarities and differences between leadership and followership roles
Moving between the two roles with ease

3. *Performance Evaluation and Feedback.* Most performance evaluations include a section on leadership skills. Followership evaluation would include items like the ones I have discussed. Instead of rating employees on leadership qualities such as self-management, independent thinking, originality, courage, competence, and credibility, we can rate them on these same qualities in both the leadership and followership roles and then evaluate each individual's ability to shift easily from the one role

to the other. A variety of performance perspectives will help most people understand better how well they play their various organizational roles.

Moreover, evaluations can come from peers, subordinates, and self as well as from supervisors. The process is simple enough: peers and subordinates who come into regular or significant contact with another employee fill in brief, periodic questionnaires where they rate the individual on followership qualities. Findings are then summarized and given to the employee being rated.

4. *Organizational Structures That Encourage Followership.* Unless the value of good following is somehow built into the fabric of the organization, it is likely to remain a pleasant conceit to which everyone pays occasional lip service but no dues. Here are four good ways to incorporate the concept into your corporate culture:

• In leaderless groups, all members assume equal responsibility for achieving goals. These are usually small task forces of people who can work together under their own supervision. However hard it is to imagine a group with more than one leader, groups with none at all can be highly productive if their members have the qualities of effective followers.

• Groups with temporary and rotating leadership are another possibility. Again, such groups are probably best kept small and the rotation fairly frequent, although the notion might certainly be extended to include the administration of a small department for, say, six-month terms. Some of these temporary leaders will be less effective than others, of course, and some may be weak indeed, which is why critics maintain that this structure is inefficient. Why not let the best leader lead? Why suffer through the tenure of less effective leaders? There are two reasons. First, experience of the leadership role is essential to the education of effective followers. Second, followers learn that they must compensate for ineffective leadership by exercising their skill as good followers. Rotating leader or not, they are bound to be faced with ineffective leadership more than once in their careers.

• Delegation to the lowest level is a third technique for cultivating good followers. Nordstrom's, the Seattle-based department store chain, gives each sales clerk responsibility for servicing and satisfying the customer, including the authority to make refunds without supervisory approval. This kind of delegation makes even people at the lowest levels responsible for their own decisions and for thinking independently about their work.

• Finally, companies can use rewards to underline the importance of good followership. This is not as easy as it sounds. Managers dependent on yes people and sheep for ego gratification will not leap at the idea of extra rewards for the people who make them most uncomfortable. In my research, I have found that effective followers get mixed treatment.

About half the time, their contributions lead to substantial rewards. The other half of the time they are punished by their superiors for exercising judgment, taking risks, and failing to conform. Many managers insist that they want independent subordinates who can think for themselves. In practice, followers who challenge their bosses run the risk of getting fired.

In today's flatter, leaner organization, companies will not succeed without the kind of people who take pride and satisfaction in the role of supporting player, doing the less glorious work without fanfare. Organizations that want the benefits of effective followers must find ways of rewarding them, ways of bringing them into full partnership in the enterprise. Think of the thousands of companies that achieve adequate performance and lackluster profits with employees they treat like second-class citizens. Then imagine for a moment the power of an organization blessed with fully engaged, fully energized, fully appreciated followers.

10

What Makes for
Magic Leadership?

DAVID A. NADLER
MICHAEL L. TUSHMAN

True, it takes a hero to turn around an organization in trouble. But the hero can't do the job all alone.

In the emerging folklore of corporate leadership, larger-than-life characters transform or save major American companies single-handedly. The current literature is rife with references to such figures as Lee Iacocca, John Sculley, Jack Welch, and others whose exploits assume mythic proportions.

Magic leaders, we call these heroes, and clearly they play a central role in revitalizing organizations. Our studies of 285 companies during the past 15 years show that forceful, visible leadership at the top is essential to successful change. But the story is more complicated than the myth makers would have us believe. The ghosts of would-be-heroes stalk the corridors of executive suites throughout America. For every Lee Iacocca, there are many more like Don Burr of People Express and Steve Jobs of Apple Computer—charismatic leaders who failed to guide their organizations through the traumas of critical change.

How is it that some work magic while others fail? The answer: A heroic aspect is not enough. Unless the magic leader has developed complementary leadership in the ranks below, his efforts to create change may badly disrupt the organization—or even wreck it.

Change is an essential fact of organizational life, but not all change requires extraordinary leadership. Most change is incremental, consisting of the constant fine-tuning that allows an organization to adapt to an environment in flux. Sometimes the organization needs to undertake

Reprinted by permission from *Fortune*, June 6, 1988, pp. 261–262. © 1988 Time Inc. All rights reserved.

strategic change. Management asks basic questions: Who are we, what business are we in, how do we compete, and what values are uppermost? The answers may set the stage for a fundamental recasting of the organization's philosophy and rationale.

When strategic change dramatically severs an organization from its past, we call it framebreaking, because the frames of reference and definition that had long served the organization are ruptured, and a new structure begins to take shape. Framebreaking is usually a response to environmental and competitive upheavals so dramatic that they threaten the organization's survival. Recent examples include the turnabouts of Apple, Navistar (the former International Harvester), and Chrysler.

More often an organization can adapt with less dramatic—though still profound—changes in strategy, structure, people, processes, values, and behavior. Here the changes are relatively gradual and the organization that emerges retains continuity with the past. We refer to such changes as organizational framebending. Xerox, Digital Equipment, Ford, NCR, and Kodak are among the many companies that have completed such changes.

The magic leader turns up more often as a framebender than a framebreaker, largely because senior management rarely survives the corporate meltdown that leads to framebreaking. In our studies we have found no instance of successful framebending without strong and visible leadership. A pattern emerges: A senior manager, usually the CEO, generates a sense of urgency; he acts as the organizational catalyst and establishes a compelling strategic agenda; he builds a bond with large numbers of people in the organization, getting them to "sign up" for meaningful change. The magic in leadership is the mixture of presence and stature that can inspire energy, dedication, and purpose in others. Such a leader can mobilize individuals, groups, and the entire organization to work enthusiastically toward new goals even without a brutally clear threat to survival.

What do these magic leaders do? While their personal styles inevitably differ, they all start by creating a vision and making it clear to others. As they articulate this vision, they set high standards and make their own behavior a model of what's expected from others. They energize everyone through their own excitement and their confidence that the organization can handle the challenge, and they bolster the entire effort by calling attention to particular successes.

The leaders must also invest a great deal in what we call enabling the change—providing broad personal support to members of the organization. They convey the message that they understand the problems, obstacles, and challenges that individuals are facing, and they reaffirm the depth and quality of the contributions of all employees.

This type of leadership is inspiring and compelling. The leader personifies the spirit of the change in an attractive public figure with whom other people in the organization can identify. But it is also risky. The magic leader may become the object of unrealistic expectations, trapped by the obligation to perform one magical feat after another. People may feel betrayed if the organization doesn't change and flourish as promised. The leader frequently ends up disenfranchising the next level of management in the organization because no pronouncement, directive, or initiative is regarded as completely valid unless it has his personal stamp. Finally, there are limits to what one person can accomplish: It is almost impossible to sustain the magic over an extended period.

The leader can often avoid these pitfalls by delegating. In many successful framebending cases the magic leader's complement is the less visible but equally critical operational leader, who is charged with putting the changes into effect. His tasks include structuring, controlling, and rewarding (or punishing) to ensure that people carry out the leader's vision. Operational leadership may lodge in a single person—the chief operating officer, for example—or a group of managers.

But even the best combination of magic leader and operational leader can achieve only so much by itself. The companies most successful at change have developed skilled leaders at all levels. Unless it already exists, such institutional leadership has to be painstakingly developed with the active participation of the magic leader. A good starting point is to assemble a senior team made up of, say, the people who run the major business units. The top leaders meet with them regularly, spending as much time as possible with them, so that they truly become a team with an emotional commitment to the new vision. The idea is to make them owners of the process, rather than management centurions executing a set of orders.

The next step, no less crucial, is to extend the boundaries or definition of senior management, so that the top 30 to 100 managers, depending on the size of the organization, also become owners. Ultimately, organizational change succeeds or fails because of the day-to-day activities of employees and managers beyond the reach of top management.

These principles of leadership are applicable outside the world of business. Jimmy Carter is a good example of a political leader who lacked the magic needed to create a vision and mobilize the country around it. Ronald Reagan and Jesse Jackson, by contrast, have shown that they can identify popular themes, create inspired visions, generate energy, and get people to follow them. But both have fallen short in establishing the operational and institutional leadership essential for achieving thoroughgoing organizational change. Mikhail Gorbachev is another magic leader attempting radical organizational change. Unless he can build a team and establish a broad "senior management" committed to his vision, he too will fail.

So we see the danger in glorifying the leader as savior. Magic leadership is essential for strategic change, but it is likely to fail without complementary operational and institutional leadership. Organizations need to think more strategically about developing leaders at all levels so that executive succession brings the right mix of people to senior management ranks. At best, they will ensure the day-to-day leadership that will keep the institution from crisis in a turbulent environment. At worst, they will provide the magic leader who can pull it through the next wrenching change.

11

Mentoring: A Gateway to Leader Development

WILLIAM E. ROSENBACH

In *The Odyssey*, the Greek poet Homer described the loyal and wise Mentor who was entrusted by Ulysses with the care and education of his son Telemachus. For generations, mentors have provided guidance, counsel, and discipline to young people and helped them become mature and effective leaders. The concept of mentorship has become familiar in academia, the military, the professions, and even in professional sports. Homer's Mentor helped his young protégé understand the world and human nature, learn courage, prudence, honesty, and a commitment to serving others. Mentoring allows protégés to become intimately familiar with a well-developed style of leadership that should enable them to better develop their own style.

Scholars and psychologists who study organizations argue that mentoring is essential for personal and organizational growth and development. At the same time, there are problems and risks associated with mentoring that can have adverse effects on both the individual and organization. But the benefits of mentoring may outweigh the risks in terms of the development of the mentor, protégé, and organization as a whole. If mentoring is to play a crucial role in American organizations, then formal mentoring systems should be expanded.

There are many varying definitions of a mentor. Lasden (1985) defines a mentor as a wise, powerful parental figure who is willing to take a person under his or her wing; someone who will advise, protect, and promote the protégé during the process of achieving organizational and personal goals. Levinson's (1978) definition varies a little; he sees a mentor as a guide, teacher, and sponsor, a mixture of good parent and good friend who invites the young person into the new world. Bowen (1986, p. 61) provides a meaningful definition of the mentorship process when he attempts to capture the essence of the mentor-protégé relationship:

Mentoring occurs when a senior person (mentor) in terms of age and experience undertakes to provide information, advice, and emotional support to a junior person (protege) in a relationship lasting over an extended period of time and marked by substantial emotional commitment by both parties. If opportunity presents itself, the mentor uses both formal and informal forms of influence to further the career of the protege.

The mentor, who can be within the protégé's organization or outside of it, can be a supervisor, company executive, associate, spouse, friend, teacher, or counselor. The mentor opens doors for the protégé and helps that person learn to arrive at decisions through support and feedback. The relationship is based on an intellectual and emotional exchange that offers challenge and excitement.

Mentoring is not only for the benefit of the protégé; the mentor and organization profit as well. Generally, however, the protégé reaps most of the rewards.

Benefits to the Protégé

In a mentor-protégé relationship, the protégé receives such benefits as knowledge, psychological support, organizational intervention, protection, and sponsorship in career development from the mentor. The mentor teaches the protégé the basic skills needed to perform the job as well as the best methods of leading people. In addition, the mentor provides an understanding of the organizational structure, and the protégé learns the less visible aspects of politics and ethics in the organization. Aside from lessons, the mentor also provides career guidance by outlining paths that are available to the protégé, both inside and outside of the organization. Hennefrund (1986) describes mentoring as a highly durable system for passing along basic skills and knowledge from one generation to another.

The mentor also provides personal support to the protégé. This support may be psychological, for example, helping the protégé deal with the pressures of promotion. The mentor may also build the protégé's confidence and self-image by giving him or her "pep talks" when needed. Moreover, the mentor can assist with problems in the protégé's personal life. A young protégé can be faced with many problems outside of the organization; and although learning the skills of a job are important, it is also important for the protégé to learn both how to deal with personal problems and how to keep those problems from affecting his or her job performance. Riech (1985) observes that "a mentor relationship can increase the self-confidence of protégés as they advance to more responsible positions . . . executives who don't have a mentor often stagnate waiting for recognition."

The mentor may also provide protection and assistance with regard to promotions. To provide protection, the mentor intervenes in conflicts and situations that may endanger the protégé's advancement. In addition, the mentor aids in acquiring promotions for the protégé by marketing her or his skills to upper-level management. In a sense, the mentor goes out on a limb for the protégé. Of course, the mentor is only truly effective if he or she is powerful and influential within the organization. And that power and influence can be the deciding factor in whether a protégé gets promoted. Zey (1984, p. 43) summarizes this point:

Obviously the mentor's position in the organization can be an important determinant of the extent of his influence on the protege's career. The protege's career is almost always unmistakenly connected to the career of the mentor, politics playing a very important role in the ultimate progress of the protege.

Benefits to the Mentor

Some feel that mentors take on the sponsor role because they are fulfilling some deep-seated need to teach, assume a parental role, or indulge various altruistic yearnings. Some executives do desire to teach or pass on their knowledge to younger generations. But they may also receive many other career benefits from the mentoring relationship. The protégé helps the mentor with his or her job, serves as a source of organizational information and intelligence, and often becomes a trusted advisor. Jones (1982, p. 50) notes,

Mentoring is a two-way exchange; your mentor will benefit enormously from your relationship—sometimes far more than you do. In fact the rewards can be so great that a full understanding of the dynamics in their favor may even make you feel a little shortchanged.

During the relationship the protégé performs various tasks that benefit the mentor. First, a successful and hard-working protégé enhances the mentor's career by performing job duties well, which, in turn, contributes to the mentor's reputation. If the mentor has a number of successful protégés, he or she can build an empire within the organization; this empire will improve the mentor's reputation as a "starmaker." Not only will promotions be more likely but the mentor will also increase his or her referent power within the organization. Second, by contributing to the stock of knowledge in the group, the protégé can become a trusted advisor to the mentor. Of course, having bright, ambitious young people on his or her team makes the mentor look better. Third, the successful protégé gives the mentor a sense of pride, a sense of contributing to the organization. Mentors derive personal satisfaction by teaching young leaders. According to Riech's study on mentoring, mentors highly value being able to keep exceptional people on their team and thus improve group performance. They also value personal satisfaction, but less so. Intelligent protégés truly enhance their mentors' careers by their contributions.

Although mentors can benefit greatly from the relationship, they also encounter some risks. There is a large amount of ambiguity and uncertainty in the relationship that often is not recognized from the outset. For example, a protégé that does not live up to the mentor's expectations could prove embarrassing to the mentor. During the relationship the mentor may experience stressful situations and risks having potentially embarrassing weaknesses revealed to others in the organization by the protégé. Finally, the mentor's reputation is partially dependent on the protégé and could be severely damaged if the protégé fails. Zey (1984, p. 40) describes the two-way exchange between mentor and protégé:

> In a mentor-protege relationship the benefits for the mentor can be just as striking as those enjoyed by the protege. Indeed, it is this mutuality that makes the relationship work in the first place. However this mutuality is often lost because the mentor-protege alliance is, by design, a relationship between unequals, and hence fraught with ambiguity.

Benefits to the Organization

The benefits of a mentoring relationship are enjoyed not only by the mentor and protégé, but by the organization as well. These benefits include smoothly functioning leadership teams and properly socialized and integrated members. One of the primary outcomes enjoyed by the organization is a clear line of leader succession that will ensure the continuation of organizational values and culture from one generation to another. In addition, the protégé will be more smoothly integrated into the organization, which, in turn, will ensure a continuance of the corporate culture. Myers and Humphreys' (1985) research indicates that many organizations use mentoring to reduce turnover among newly hired recruits and to build protégé loyalty. The relationship helps integrate protégés more smoothly into the organization, so that they do not get lost in the system. The skills that protégés learn from their mentors will ultimately assist in their productivity; as the protégé becomes more productive, so does the organization.

Apart from the benefits that mentoring brings to the organization, there are also risks and problems. Myers and Humphreys divide these problems into three categories. The first involves problems that arise in the selection process of mentors and protégés. Process problems that are encountered during the mentoring process fall into the second category, and the third comprises problems that arise as a result of an intense mentor relationship.

Selection problems include preselection, "old boy" networks, nepotism, and outright discrimination. People qualified to be protégés may be passed over because of race, sex, or lack of contacts within the organization. Some of the discrimination in the protégé selection process is undoubtedly unintentional; nevertheless, discrimination has adversely affected the careers of women and minorities.

Process problems occur when the mentor overburdens the protégé with work and vice versa. Protégés may also experience unwelcome or too much surveillance of their work by their mentors. When protégés make mistakes they may receive unduly harsh treatment or be publicly embarrassed by their mentors. Finally, some protégés feel as if they receive more criticism than is necessary. Blotnick (1984, p. 45) describes the process:

> (1) The mentor likes you and respects you (privately); (2) he or she supports that view publicly; (3) you therefore have to work harder (public performance) so that (4) your boss can work with you more often and talk about you (public praise).

The problem is that public praise may be accompanied by public criticism. The mentor does not want to show that he or she is favoring the protégé and therefore catches the protégé off guard. Process problems can be avoided if the mentor and protégé know what kind of relationship they are getting into beforehand and understand each other's goals.

Outcome problems in mentoring relationships arise when protégés experience guilt and embarrassment because they are associated with a failing mentor. If executives fail or fall out of favor with the organization, then their protégés also fall out of favor. This process, often referred to as the "black halo" effect, can block a protégé's promotion. Fairly or unfairly, the protégé becomes associated with the mentor. One-third of the people Riech (1985) studied reported that others identified them (protégés) too closely with their mentors. Blotnick observes that nearly half the protégés in his 25-year study end up being fired by their mentors. Levinson (1978) warns that mentoring relationships that last two or three years often end in rancor and bitterness. Although these reports appear to be negative, other evidence is more positive. In his book, *The Corporate Steeplechase,* Blotnick (1984) supports mentoring as a risk worth taking. In addition, although Riech's research recognizes some of the risks and problems associated with mentoring, his findings clearly show that the advantages outweigh the disadvantages.

Cross-Gender Mentoring

In *The Odyssey,* Athena, the Greek goddess of wisdom, disguised herself and stood in for Mentor to teach Ulysses' son. This fictionalized account of cross-gender mentoring has real-life counterparts. If it is necessary for a man to have a mentor to be successful, it may be even more essential for a woman. Roche (1979) observes that to reach leadership positions, women without family connections must have fatherlike sponsors. Additionally, it seems necessary that a man stand behind a woman to say, in effect, "She's okay. She can hack it. She belongs."

Riech's 1986 research shows that, like men, women benefit from the mentoring relationship by gaining more leadership skills, joining winning teams, developing useful contacts, and being granted more autonomy in the workplace. In these areas, mentoring gives women the same opportunities as men for upward mobility. In addition to helping women acquire the same skills as men, mentoring relationships also help them with other problems. Women continually face career barriers that men do not. These barriers are the products of perceptual, behavioral, and cultural factors that mentoring can help women overcome. Zey (1984) observes that cross-gender mentoring helps in structural and attitudinal areas. Because mentoring represents the leader's public commitment to a junior member, the organization is brought closer to accepting a woman as a bonafide member of its leadership team. And as more women are given the unique opportunity to succeed that mentoring affords, these accomplishments will further establish their rightful place in leadership roles.

Women are subject to mentor-protégé problems peculiar to the cross-gender mentoring process. Clawson and Kram (1984) categorize these problems into two sets: internal relationships and external relationships. Internal relationships are the levels of intimacy or interaction the cross-gender mentoring subjects experience and the way these levels affect the relationship. External relationships concern the amount of office gossip or innuendo that arises outside of the relationship. When a man and a woman interact in a close setting, they may be attracted to each other. Due to the closeness of the mentor-protégé relationship, it is easy for romance to develop. But romantic or sexual interests confound the mentor relationship and may create conflicts and power struggles. A woman may develop sexual feelings toward a male mentor and he toward her. Too often it is believed that the woman alone should be responsible for professional behavior. Fortunately, some male mentors feel that responsibility should be shared; although the potential for sexual attachment is always present, professional conduct by both people is essential. All things considered, the most common problem is the resentment of co-workers and spouses.

If female employees successfully avoid the sexual trap, they still have to be aware of the servant trap (Josefowitz 1980). Many men are accustomed to having women serve them and, as a result, may ask women to perform chores not appropriate for their position. The thoughtful mentor will avoid these problems. Once cross-gender mentoring becomes more common, and a reasonable number of women have moved through the system, these problems will decrease. People will grow accustomed to the relationships. If they wish, women can mentor women, and the problems of cross-gender mentoring can be avoided altogether. Sexism in the workplace will disappear as leaders learn to work in mixed gender teams and begin to view both sexes as friends and colleagues.

Formal Versus Informal Mentoring

Until recently, mentoring programs in most organizations have been informal. Some suggest that because of the importance of mentoring to organizations, formal systems should be developed. Formal systems may eliminate many of the problems and risks of the mentor-protégé relationship. Riech (1985) notes that one company used a formal system only for women and minorities. But he also found that 83 percent of respondents to his survey recommended against formal programs. Indeed, many feel that the mentoring process should never be made formal. For example, Lasden (1985) argues that the relationship must be spontaneous to ensure the chemistry between the two individuals. Furthermore, others believe that if formal programs are implemented, protégés should not be allowed to choose their own mentors. Mentors chosen through formal programs seldom pull strings for the protégés, protect them, or become involved in the lasting and strong friendships that are characteristic in informal mentoring relationships. In fact, they appear to avoid such entanglements by specifying time limits and emphasizing task orientations.

Keele, Buckner, and Bushnell (1987) find three characteristics common to all successful formal mentoring programs. First, the mentoring activity is only a part of an overall development program for potential leaders. Second, the programs emphasize coaching behaviors directed to job-related activities, and third, the mentoring programs are a part of an organizational culture that supports individual and organizational development and provides rewards for those who participate.

Although formal mentoring has not often been successful in the past, mentoring is such an integral part of human resource development that formal mentoring may eventually become an accepted mechanism for leadership development. Before an organization implements a formal mentoring program, clear goals should be established and communicated to potential participants. The organization's ability to absorb individuals completing the program should be determined, and the cooperation of the entire organization should be encouraged through rewards. The selection process should be as autonomous as possible, and the mentors' commitment should be assured. Withdrawal from the program should be permitted, without prejudice. Finally, and very importantly, the program should be continually evaluated.

Conclusion

Strong leadership that motivates followers to perform beyond expectations is built upon personal identification with the leader, a shared vision of the future, and subordination of self-interests. This transformational form of leadership creates an organizational culture that values renewal and revitalization of the individual.

A culture of transformational leadership stimulates mentoring. Protégés are encouraged to believe in themselves and to achieve their leadership potential. Their success will ensure the continued influence, power, respect, and competitive advantage of the organization. Mentors affirm their self-confidence and view leader development as a part of their job. Mentoring is not appropriate for every individual or organization; it is an opportunity to share talent and prepare leaders. With a supportive environment and the right attitude, mentoring can be a powerful force in leadership development.

References

Blotnick, Srully. *The Corporate Steeplechase: Predictable Crisis in a Business Career.* New York: Facts on File, 1984.

———. "With Friends Like These . . . " *Savvy,* October 1984, pp. 42–52.

Borman, C., and S. Colson. "Mentoring: An Effective Career Guidance Technique." *The Vocational Guidance Journal,* Vol. 3, 1984, pp. 192–197.

Bowen, Donald D. "The Role of Identification in Mentoring Female Proteges." *Group and Organization Studies,* March-June 1986, pp. 61–74.

Clawson, James G. "Is Mentoring Necessary?" *Training and Development Journal,* April 1985, pp. 36–39.

Clawson, James G., and Kathy E. Kram. "Managing Cross Gender Mentoring." *Business Horizons,* May-June 1984, pp. 22–32.

Cook, Mary F. "Is the Mentor Relationship Primarily a Male Experience?" *Personnel Administrator,* November 1979, p. 40.

Cunningham, Mary. *Powerplay: What Really Happened at Bendix.* New York: Simon and Schuster, 1984.

"Everyone Who Makes It Has a Mentor." *Harvard Business Review,* July-August 1978, pp. 81–101.

Farren, Caela, Janet Dreyfus Gray, and Beverly Kaye. "Mentoring: A Boon to Career Development." *Personnel,* November-December 1984, pp. 20–24.

Fitt, Lawton, and Derek Newton. "When the Mentor Is a Man and the Protege a Woman." *Harvard Business Review,* March-April 1981, pp. 56–60.

Halcomb, Ruth. "Mentors and the Successful Woman." *Across the Board,* February 1980, pp. 13–18.

Hennefrund, William. "Taking on the Measure of Mentoring." *Association Management,* January 1986, pp. 78–83.

Hennig, Margaret, and Anne Jardim. *The Managerial Woman.* New York: Doubleday, 1977.

Hunsker, Johanna S. "The Mentor Relationship: Fact or Fiction." Paper presented at the Annual Meeting of the Academy of Management, New York (August 16, 1982).

Johnson, Mary C. "Mentors: The Key to Development and Growth." *Training and Development Journal,* July 1980, pp. 55–57.

Jones, Linda Phillips. *Mentors and Proteges.* New York: Arbor House, 1982.

Josefowitz, Nataska. *Paths to Power: A Woman's Guide from First Job to Executive.* Reading, Mass.: Addison-Wesley, 1980.

Keele, R., K. Buckner, and S. Bushnell. "Formal Mentoring Programs Are No Panacea." *Management Review,* February 1987, pp. 67–68.

Kram, Kathy E. "Improving the Mentoring Process." *Training and Development Journal,* April 1985, pp. 40–42.

Lasden, Martin. "A Mentor Can Be a Milestone." *Computer Decisions,* March 26, 1985, pp. 74–81.

Lean, Elizabeth. "Cross-Gender Mentoring: Downright Upright and Good for Productivity." *Training and Development Journal,* May 1983, pp. 61–65.

Levinson, Daniel J. *The Seasons of Man's Life.* New York: Alfred A. Knopf, 1978.

Myers, Donald W., and Neil J. Humphreys. "The Caveats in Mentorship." *Business Horizon,* July-August 1985, pp. 9–14.

Noe, Raymond A. "Women and Mentoring: A Review and Research Agenda." *Academy of Management Review,* Vol. 13, No. 1, 1988, pp. 65–78.

Odcorne, George S. "Mentoring—An American Management Innovation." *Personnel Administrator,* May 1985, pp. 63–70.

Riech, Muiry H. "Executive Views from Both Sides of Mentoring." *Personnel,* March 1985, pp. 42–46.

———. "The Mentor Connection." *Personnel,* February 1986, pp. 50–56.

Roche, Gerald R. "Much Ado About Mentors." *Harvard Business Review,* January-February 1979, pp. 14–28.

Shapiro, Eileen C., Florence P. Haseltine, and Mary P. Rowe. "Moving Up: Role Models, Mentors, and the Patron System." *Sloan Management Review*, Spring 1978, pp. 51–58.

Sheehy, Gail. *Passages: Predictable Crises of Adult Life*. New York: E. P. Dutton and Company, 1974.

———. "The Mentor Connection: The Secret Link in the Successful Woman's Life." *New York Magazine*, April 1976, p. 90.

Sheeran, L. R., and O. Fenn. "The Mentor System." *Inc.*, June 1987, pp. 138–142.

Warichay, Philomena D. "The Climb to the Top: Is the Network the Route for Women?" *Personnel Administrator*, April 1980, pp. 72–80.

Zey, Michael G. *The Mentor Connection*. Homewood, Ill.: Dow-Jones-Irwin, 1984.

PART THREE

STYLE, SUBSTANCE, AND CIRCUMSTANCE

Issues of Style

Effective leaders, who come in all statures and from all cultures, seem to behave in ways that fit their personalities, the situation, and the needs of the group they are leading. Some leaders take charge; others nurture the group so that everyone accepts responsibility. We know leaders who are great orators; we also know those who are quiet and uninspiring with words but effectively lead by example. Some act decisively, others act with slow deliberation. The key is that effective leaders set the stage with their personalities and expectations and present a consistent image.

What leaders do is important, but how they do it is of equal concern. Style reflects the process by which leaders interact with others to accomplish their objectives. Much of the leadership research has focused on style. But there is not simply one style or personality that is best for all situations. The nature of the task may influence the style; the more ambiguous and complex the task, the greater the need to have broad participation—a collegial style. Relatively simple, routine tasks can often be dealt with by a leader acting alone—an independent style. Style is related not only to task, but also to timing. Participative styles are time consuming. Shared leadership includes subordinates, and the path to consensus decisions is often long and tedious. When decisions must be made quickly, the leader must act alone on available information as well as on intuition. Thus, time is the discriminator.

Issues of Substance

All successful leaders seem to have a broad view of the world. It is helpful to thoroughly understand the microcosm of the organization, but the broad perspective helps put everything in context. To create a vision of the future, leaders must understand the environment in which the organization exists. Studying the classics can provide the foundation for such an understanding. Leaders who have studied the arts and humanities often develop a heightened sensitivity to values and feelings. It is not surprising that we often see successful leadership as a passion, a wellspring of emotion that keeps the leader directed toward the vision. If we imagine the leader as producer-director, the metaphor comes alive. Leaders serve a variety of people in organizations, and they need to relate to them culturally as well as professionally.

Leaders must synthesize many inputs so that the highest common denominator is found. The task of leadership is to find out what the group values. In the productive, successful organization, the leader helps group members to achieve their personal goals as the group members strive to accomplish the organizational goals. How the leader relates to all the members depends upon the leader's understanding of why people do what they do. If, as we believe, leadership is based upon the confidence of self-knowledge and introspection, then a thorough grounding in history, literature, the arts, and language is the best training for leadership.

Issues of Circumstance

There have always been barriers to leadership. Some result from attitudes in society while others are inherent in the nature of organizations. Many critics contend that the barriers are merely perceived, but people act on their perceptions—the barriers are real to the individuals involved.

Leaders must be accepted by those who are to be led, whether that acceptance is determined by law, a form of economic exchange, or moral persuasion. A social exchange takes place between leaders and groups, which legitimizes the leaders in their role. At the same time there are multiple roles for leaders to play. Leaders are often at the head of organizations, formally established and associated with specific responsibilities and authority. Informal leadership may exist independently of organization structure, but in any case, there are standards and expectations for leaders. Some organizations are open to leadership while others restrict access and effectiveness.

The real dilemma is understanding whether one is constrained in exercising leadership because of limited opportunity (organizational) or lack of self-confidence (individual). Do minorities and women have *access* to positions of leadership? Does everyone have the same opportunity for leadership development? Are there issues of gender and race that limit leadership potential? Yes, perhaps, but they are not clear. Our society has gone through a great deal of change in the past ten years. On the one hand, minorities and women are being encouraged to seek leadership positions; they are being nurtured in a variety of ways. On the other hand, we see very few women and minorities in important leadership positions. The numbers are increasing, but they do not reflect our intentions. The situation may be the result of a "pipeline" problem as our organizations catch up with changing attitudes and make a true commitment to equal opportunity, or it may be a manifestation of restricted access.

The Challenge

We believe that everyone has the potential to be a leader. Self-knowledge is a personal endeavor, and we all have the opportunity to explore who we are and what we believe. It is not always easy to ask ourselves the hard questions. Who am I? What are my strengths and weaknesses? Where am I going? What are my values? And the list goes on. . . . These are questions that should not be asked unless we are ready to accept the answers.

We evaluate leaders in terms of their personal effectiveness in achieving organizational goals, which are the intrinsic and extrinsic outcomes of leadership. Apart from the organizational measurement systems, the leader has a personal commitment to accomplishment. Leaders are continually involved in self-evaluation because, to a leader, making a difference is important.

The role that a leader chooses to play (or is expected to play) also relates to his or her effectiveness. As a figurehead or spokesperson, the leader is a communicator who represents the goals and values of the organization to all of its constituencies. Or the leader can choose to focus internally, acting as a buffer against the external environment and concentrating his or her efforts on actions within the organizational boundaries. The leader can also elect to be a storyteller, primarily inspiring members to work toward a common objective. Many leaders lead by example; they are the hardest workers and make sacrifices to create a positive environment for all to contribute to. Effective leaders know their strengths and weaknesses and act accordingly.

Transactional leaders recognize the rewards participants want from their work and try to see that they get them if warranted by their performance—exchanging rewards (and promises of rewards) for effort. The leader recognizes the role the follower must play to attain outcomes desired by the leader. Roles are clarified, giving participants the confidence necessary to achieve the goals. At the same time, the leader recognizes what the participants need, clarifying (for the participants) how those needs can be fulfilled in exchange for satisfactory effort and performance. Properly implemented, transactional leadership is effective and desirable for appropriate situations.

Transformational leadership involves strong personal identification with the leader; group members join in a shared vision of the future— going beyond self-interest and exchange of rewards for compliance. The transformational leader motivates participants to perform beyond expectations by

- creating a shared awareness of the importance and value of designated outcomes,
- influencing followers to transcend their own self-interest, and
- altering or expanding participant motivations to the higher orders of self-esteem and self-actualization.

Through language, transformational leaders enable followers to develop a mental picture of the vision and transform purpose into action. The challenge is to put it all together.

Leadership Perspectives

In "Would Women Lead Differently?" Virginia Schein (Chapter 12) suggests that differences within each sex are often greater than the differences between the sexes and argues that the proponents of androgynous leadership take a narrow, simplistic approach to a broad and complex set of issues. Schein suggests that effective leaders, regardless of gender, strive to implement their visions, vary their behaviors contingent upon the situation; and, in general, grapple successfully with the complex and dynamic needs of their organizations; ineffective leaders, male or female, do not. The appropriate question, she says, is: "How can we restructure work in a society in which work and family no longer are separate, but interface?" According to Schein, attitudes and organizational structures must change if we are to have climates receptive to and supportive of qualified and committed men and women who desire to demonstrate their leadership qualities.

John Heider's "The Leader Who Knows How Things Happen" (Chapter 13) is adapted from a sixth-century B.C. Chinese text, *Tao Te Ching*, by Lao Tzu, on how to rule a kingdom and live wisely. In these selections Lao Tzu addresses himself to the concerned, thoughtful leader, the wise leader who "knows how things happen." This ancient voice provides an interesting counterpoint to the more familiar twentieth-century thinking.

In "Classic Tales of Captains, Castles, . . . and Corporations" (Chapter 14), Beverly Kempton points to very interesting links between the classics and modern leadership. Through the classics, which are nonthreatening, people in responsible positions can consider what is important and not important and ask fundamental questions about themselves and the way they lead.

In Chapter 15, Michael Cohen and James March describe the position of college president as "leadership in an organized anarchy" and posit that the ambiguities college presidents face are the same as those encountered by any formal leader. The authors identify four fundamental areas of ambiguity: purpose, power, experience, and success. The common metaphors of leadership and our tradition of personalizing history tend to confuse the issue by ignoring the basic ambiguities that leaders face, according to the authors. They conclude that the contributions of leaders may often be measured by their capacity for maintaining a creative interaction between foolishness and rationality—an idea that provides an interesting dilemma for those seeking a simple notion of leadership.

Finally, in Chapter 16, Karl Kuhnert and Philip Lewis in "Transactional and Transformational Leadership: A Constructive/Developmental Analysis" describe the transactional and transformational theories of leadership developed by James MacGregor Burns and Bernard Bass. They clarify and extend the concepts by using a constructive and developmental theory to explain how critical personality differences in leaders determine either transactional or transformational leadership styles. They also propose a three-stage developmental model of leadership.

12

Would Women Lead Differently?

VIRGINIA E. SCHEIN

The search for more effective leaders has led many to tout the virtues of the androgynous manager. Such a manager blends the characteristics of dominance, assertiveness, and competitiveness with those of concern for relationships, cooperativeness, and humanitarian values. As the argument goes, the former set of characteristics is too limited to meet the requirements of management and leadership in today's complex and changing environment. Effectiveness requires a broad range of characteristics, one that encompasses competence and compassion, toughness and tenderness.

The androgynous manager possesses both masculine characteristics, those seen as commonly held by men, and feminine characteristics, those viewed as more commonly held by women. The focus on feminine as well as masculine characteristics puts femininity into the leadership effectiveness equation. It highlights gender differences and suggests that, indeed, women would lead differently. Unlike the global warrior or John Wayne manager, a feminine leader would be oriented toward cooperation, teamwork, and concern for others.

That women would lead or govern differently is not a new idea. Women's leadership has been linked with enhancing world peace, reducing corruption, and improving opportunities for the downtrodden. If women, as keepers of the values of social justice, nurturance, and honesty, are put in charge, then the conflicts, corruption, and greed around us will go away—or so say proponents of this view. The maximalist perspective within the now fragmented feminist movement supports this idea. It argues for innate or highly socialized gender differences and views women as more likely to exhibit cooperative, compassionate, and humane types of behaviors than men.

At first glance, the new priority given to femininity and a feminine leadership style would seem to be a boon for women aspiring to leadership positions. The same sex role stereotyping that often excludes women from managerial positions can now be used to enhance their opportunities. Florence Nightingale meets John Wayne, and together they lead us into the sunset of greater leadership effectiveness.

In my opinion, however, this entire line of reasoning is both a foolhardy and dangerous one to pursue. It will not add to our understanding of leadership effectiveness, for it takes a narrow and simplistic approach to what is a broad and complex set of issues and activities. It will not promote equality of opportunity in the workplace because it perpetuates sex role stereotypical thinking that has no basis in reality. The androgynous orientation builds a managerial access bridge for women on a shaky foundation of sand.

The Leadership Labyrinth

Numerous researchers have shown that leadership effectiveness entails far more than a task versus people style or a trait approach. Yukl, for example, had identified more than 13 categories of relevant managerial behaviors, including representation, crisis management, problem solving, operations monitoring, etc. A large-scale study conducted by the American Management Association identified competency clusters such as entrepreneurial abilities, intellectual abilities, and socioemotional maturity, among others. Still other recent research stresses the importance of effective communication.

The view of the organization as a political coalition diverts us from a leader-follower concentration, where the style emphasis originated, and highlights the important role of external relationships. Effective managers need to deal with other groups and departments, form alliances and coalitions, and influence those over whom they have no direct authority in order to get things done. Effectiveness in an organization may be far more related to these behaviors than to leadership style.

Position is also a relevant variable. Dunnette and others have found that supervisory, middle-managerial, and executive positions differ as to the priority and importance of particular behaviors. The nature of the business and the environment in which it operates also determines the type of behaviors that are critical. Finally, as more and more organizations must undergo change in order to survive and compete successfully, transformational leadership has become valued and necessary.

Given the preceding factors, how much variance can specific characteristics, either masculine or feminine ones, account for in leadership effectiveness? Certainly, personality plays a part. But the Great Man (as it was called) trait theory of leadership went out with the buggy whip. Organizational cultures vary as much as the required behaviors within them. One constellation of behaviors may be appropriate within a bureaucratic, rigid structure but quite inappropriate in a loose, entre-preneurial type of organization. Creativity and flexibility may be im-portant for the advertising executive, but stability and follow-through are probably more important for the effective insurance executive. The payoff in pursuing the trait theory is clearly limited.

Male and Female Managers— How Different Are They?

The focus on masculinity and femininity suggests significant innate or ingrained socialized differences between the sexes. Research does show some differences between males and females; however, there are far fewer differences than is commonly believed. Moreover, research indicates that the differences within each sex are greater than the differences between the sexes. That is, the differences among women (or men), considering variations in background, experience, and so on, are greater than the differences between women in general and men in general.

More to the point, the bulk of the evidence on managerial behaviors shows few differences between men and women. A major investigation by researchers at the Center for Creative Leadership, based on their own data as well as other research reports, concludes that "as individuals, executive women and men seem to be virtually identical psychologically, intellectually, and emotionally" (Morrison, White, and Velsor, 1987, p. 18).

Thus, even if the Great Man (or Great Person) trait theory had some validity, seeking those characteristics deemed relevant, such as intui-tiveness or assertiveness, on the basis of the gender of the manager would not produce the desired results. Male and female managers appear to be cut from the same cloth, with some portions of it tattered and inappropriate and other parts of high quality. But gender will not predict the composition of the cloth. From a performance perspective, male and female leadership is more likely to be similar than different.

Within the corporate world, however, there is one glaring difference between the sexes. There are far fewer women in positions of power and influence than men. This is also true in the public sector. Although women have made significant inroads into lower and middle management ranks over the last 15 years, progress into senior ranks has been slow. There is a dearth of women in senior executive positions and among the ranks of the highest paid positions in major corporations. The barrier to the top, termed the "glass ceiling," has led to many female middle managers "bailing out." Some choose to seek power and influence through entrepreneurial channels; others choose to redirect the balance of the motherhood and managerhood juggling act in favor of the former, given the limited payoffs of the latter for women. Of the top 100 corporate women featured in a 1976 *Business Week* cover story, only 5 are working today in positions considered crucial for advancement to a senior executive post.

The Work and Family Interface: Meeting the Challenge

The glass ceiling barrier is both structural and attitudinal in nature. Although the male-female ratio in the work force in general, and in lower managerial ranks in particular, has changed dramatically, the recognition of the need for structural changes in the way work is accomplished as a result of this changed ratio has been much slower in coming. The gender-based division between work and family no longer exists, yet much of the work world is still structured as if there is a full-time spouse/parent at home attending to family responsibilities. Although some structural changes, such as child care benefits and flexible working hours, are being implemented, albeit on a limited basis, they will have little effect on the demands made in the "race for the top." Total attention, time, and energy must still be devoted to the endeavor. It is the woman, by virtue of her biological role as childbearer, who gets squeezed out of the race. Called "super moms," many simply drop from exhaustion in what can only be a no-win contest with their male counterparts.

Asking women to choose between motherhood and career is the wrong question. Few have considered the implications if all of our bright, energetic women chose the latter. More importantly, such a question places a burden of choice on women that is not asked of their male counterparts. Although many men are asked to limit the amount of time they have available to devote to spouse and offspring, few are asked to give up the opportunity for spouse and offspring all together.

The right question is: "How can we restructure work in a society in which work and family no longer are separate, but interface?" This question should be addressed to, and serious responses expected of, our corporate and government leaders. It is when this question comes into play that the possibility emerges that *women would lead differently.* The biological responsibilities of women suggest that women as leaders might be more understanding of and willing to grapple with accommodating this work and family interface.

A case in point is the Norwegian government. Norway's prime minister is a woman and 7 of its 17 Cabinet members are female. Norway's Labor Party members of Parliament include more than 40 percent women as does the party's ruling National Board. Do women govern differently in Norway? Despite falling oil prices and huge spending cuts, the Norwegian government increased its emphasis on women and children. Child care subsidies are up, as are the number of weeks of paid parental leave. In addition, working parents have 10 days each (single parents have 20) to handle the "little crises" of child raising. At a recent Cabinet meeting, which was running overtime, the defense minister was neither uncomfortable nor frowned upon for excusing himself to pick up his son at nursery school.

If Norway is any example, women would indeed lead differently. They would focus on structural changes to facilitate the interface of work and family. This priority would encourage a work climate in which the work-family interface was recognized and accommodated, and its reality was not denied. As leaders, women would be more willing to grapple with the hard questions. These questions include: To what extent are some job expectations, such as last-minute travel demands, simply convenient in a corporate environment in which family responsibilities are handled by others? What work demands are essential and job related? What time frames, such as 7 years until partnership, are convenient only in the old order of a gender-based division of labor, and what career time frames are job related? In a society in which work and family must interface, "what is convenient to the corporation" and "what is job related" must be separated. This is a complex and challenging task.

Women as leaders have an investment in determining viable answers to these questions and restructuring the world of work accordingly. As such, they would foster an organizational climate receptive to and supportive of qualified and hard-working women and men. The race might not get any easier, but at least it would have the same type and number of bumps and hurdles for both sexes.

Attitudinal Barriers Revisited

Ironically, strongly held attitudinal barriers may well be blocking the very increases in the number of women in powerful positions necessary to bring about these vital changes. Although sex role stereotypes have little basis in reality, they can color our evaluations of people. In the early 1970s my research showed that both male and female managers viewed the characteristics required of a successful manager as more likely to be held by a man than a woman. This attitude limits women's opportunities for entry into and promotion within the managerial ranks.

A replication of this work in the mid-1980s reveals that this perception continues to hold true among male managers today. Males, predominant in senior managerial positions, are still more likely to see a man, rather than a woman, as next in line for an executive position. On the other hand, today's female managers no longer share the "think manager–think male" view. They see the characteristics necessary for success as just as likely to be held by a woman as by a man. To the extent women leaders, unlike their male counterparts, are more likely to be gender-blind in their promotional decision making, women leaders would foster more equal access to the race for the top as well as equalize the hurdles for male and female competitors.

The Leadership Difference

Evidence suggests few differences in the actual behaviors of men and women leaders. Effective leaders, male or female, seek to implement their visions, vary their behaviors contingent upon the situational requirements, and in general grapple successfully with the ever-changing and complex internal and external demands upon their organizations. Ineffective leaders, male or female, do not. Effective leadership is difficult. Both corporations and governments admit to a leadership shortage. The ever-increasing attention today on leadership evidences both its importance and the high priority placed on improving the quality of leadership in all of our institutions.

Women's attention to structural changes enhancing the work-family interface and a more gender-blind evaluation of qualifications can open the doors to allow more women entrants into the race for future leadership positions. If we want "the best and the brightest" to lead our major institutions, then the larger the supply of qualified candidates, the more selective we can be. The more rigorous the selection criteria, the better our chances for excellence in leadership in any one organization and in the number of organizations with such quality leadership.

This perspective need not be, and in many individual cases is not, "for women only." Although women leaders may be more instrumental in enhancing women's advancement opportunities, the real focus should be on erasing this difference between the sexes as well. Both men and women need to grapple seriously with the impact of a changing society on our organizations and to provide opportunities for the most qualified of either sex to apply their talents and energies to the leadership of our public and private institutions.

Selected References

Brenner, O. C., J. Tomkiewicz, and V. E. Schein. 1989. The relationship between sex role stereotypes and requisite management characteristics revisited. *Academy of Management Journal* (in press).

The Corporate Woman—A Special Report. 1986. *Wall Street Journal*, March 24.

Council on Economic Priorities Survey. 1987. 20 corporations that listen to women. *Ms.*, November, 45–52.

DeGeorge, G. 1988. Where are they now? *Business Week*'s leading corporate women of 1976. In *Corporate strategies*, edited by J. Pearce and R. Robinson. New York: McGraw-Hill.

Dunnette, M. D. 1986. Describing the role of the middle manager. Symposium paper presented at the 94th Annual Meeting of the American Psychological Association, Washington, D.C.

Maccoby, E., and C. N. Jacklin. 1974. *The psychology of sex differences*. Stanford, Calif.: Stanford University Press.

Morrison, A., R. White, and E. Velsor. 1987. Executive women: substance plus style. *Psychology Today*, August, 18–21.

Overholser, G. 1987. Would women govern differently? *New York Times*, June 15, A16.

Schein, V. E. 1973. The relationship between sex role stereotypes and requisite managerial characteristics. *Journal of Applied Psychology*, 57:95–100.

———. 1975. The relationship between sex role stereotypes and requisite managerial characteristics among female managers. *Journal of Applied Psychology*, 60:340–344.

Yukl, G. A. 1985. Categories of managerial behavior: An integrating middle range taxonomy. Paper presented to the Society for Organizational Behavior, Pittsburgh, Pa.

13

The Leader Who Knows
How Things Happen

JOHN HEIDER

This article consists of twelve chapters of Lao Tzu's *Tao Te Ching*. I have adapted these chapters for group leaders, psychotherapists, and other human-potential educators.

According to tradition, *Tao Te Ching* was written in sixth century B.C. China by Lao Tzu, a state librarian and sage. Myth and history mingle in this tradition.

Tao Te Ching is very short: eighty-one chapters, each no longer than a single page. There are many translations of *Tao Te Ching*. I have included in this article an annotated list of six translations for the reader who wishes to compare my interpretation of Lao Tzu with more literal versions of the same chapters.

I have selected twelve of the original eighty-one chapters of *Tao Te Ching* in order to focus on Lao Tzu's approach to leadership. Other chapters, not presented here, deal with metaphysics (how things happen) and ethics (how to live in accordance with how things happen).

Lao Tzu addressed himself to the sage or to the wise ruler. Here his words are for the wise leader, the leader who knows how things happen.

John Heider, "The Leader Who Knows How Things Happen," *Journal of Humanistic Psychology,* 27:3 (Summer 1982), pp. 33–39. Copyright © 1982 by the Association for Humanistic Psychology. Reprinted by permission of Sage Publications, Inc.

Author's note: Chapter numbers and titles: The chapter *numbers* used here are the same as those generally used in other versions of *Tao Te Ching*. The reader can compare this rendition of Chapter 9 with Chapter 9 in any of the translations listed in the reference section. The chapter *titles* are my own: not every version of *Tao Te Ching* uses titles for individual chapters.

Chapter 9: A Good Group

A good group is better than a spectacular group.

When leaders become superstars, the teacher outshines the teaching.

Also, very few superstars are down-to-earth. Fame breeds fame. Before long they get carried away with themselves. They then fly off center and crash.

The wise leader settles for good work and then lets others have the floor. The leader does not take all the credit for what happens and has no need for fame.

A moderate ego demonstrates wisdom.

Chapter 11: The Group Field

Pay attention to silence. What is happening when nothing is happening in the group? That is the group field.

Thirteen people sit in a circle, but it is the climate or the spirit in the center of the circle, where nothing is happening, that determines the nature of the group field.

Learn to see emptiness. When you enter an empty house, can you feel the mood of the place? It is the same with a vase or pot; learn to see the emptiness inside, which is the usefulness of it.

People's speech and actions are figural events. They give the group form and content.

The silences and empty spaces, on the other hand, reveal the group's essential mood, the context for everything that happens. That is the group field.

Chapter 17: Like a Midwife

The wise leader does not intervene unnecessarily. The leader's presence is felt, but often the group runs itself.

Lesser leaders do a lot, say a lot, have followers, and form cults.

Even worse ones use fear to energize the group and force to overcome resistance.

Only the most dreadful leaders have bad reputations.

Remember that you are facilitating another person's process. It is not your process. Do not intrude. Do not control. Do not force your own needs and insights into the foreground.

If you do not trust a person's process, that person will not trust you.

Imagine that you are a midwife. You are assisting at someone else's birth. Do good without show or fuss. Facilitate what is happening rather than what you think ought to be happening. If you must take the lead, lead so that the mother is helped, yet still free and in charge.

When the baby is born, the mother will say: we did it ourselves.

Chapter 26: Center and Ground

The leader who is centered and grounded can work with erratic people and critical group situations without harm.

Being centered means having the ability to recover one's balance, even in the midst of action. A centered person is not subject to passing whims or sudden excitements.

Being grounded means being down-to-earth, having gravity or weight. I know where I stand, and I know what I stand for: that is ground.

The centered and grounded leader has stability and a sense of self.

One who is not stable can easily get carried away by the intensity of leadership and make mistakes of judgment or even become ill.

Chapter 31: Harsh Interventions

There are times when it seems as if one must intervene powerfully, suddenly, and even harshly. The wise leader does this only when all else fails.

As a rule, the leader feels more wholesome when the group process is flowing freely and unfolding naturally, when delicate facilitations far outnumber harsh interventions.

Harsh interventions are a warning that the leader may be uncentered or have an emotional attachment to whatever is happening. A special awareness is called for.

Even if harsh interventions succeed brilliantly, there is no cause for celebration. There has been injury. Someone's process has been violated.

Later on, the person whose process has been violated may well become less open and more defended. There will be a deeper resistance and possibly even resentment.

Making people do what you think they ought to do does not lead toward clarity and consciousness. While they may do what you tell them to do at the time, they will cringe inwardly, grow confused, and plot revenge.

That is why your victory is actually a failure.

Chapter 43: Gentle Interventions

Gentle interventions, if they are clear, overcome rigid resistances.

If gentleness fails, try yielding or stepping back altogether. When the leader yields, resistances relax.

Generally speaking, the leader's consciousness sheds more light on what is happening than any number of interventions or explanations. But few leaders realize how much so little will do.

Chapter 46: Nothing to Win

The well-run group is not a battlefield of egos. Of course there will be conflict, but these energies become creative forces.

If the leader loses sight of how things happen, quarrels and fear devastate the group field.

This is a matter of attitude. There is nothing to win or lose in group work. Making a point does not shed light on what is happening. The need to be right blinds people.

The wise leader knows that it is far more important to be content with what is actually happening than to get upset over what might be happening but isn't.

Chapter 56: The Leader's Integrity

The wise leader knows that the true nature of events cannot be captured in words. So why pretend?

Confusing jargon is one sign of a leader who does not know how things happen.

But what cannot be said can be demonstrated: be silent, be conscious. Consciousness works. It sheds light on what is happening. It clarifies conflicts and harmonizes the agitated individual or group field.

The leader also knows that all existence is a single whole. Therefore the leader is a neutral observer who takes no sides.

The leader cannot be seduced by offers or threats. Money, love, or fame—whether gained or lost—do not sway the leader from center.

The leader's integrity is not idealistic. It rests on a pragmatic knowledge of how things work.

Chapter 60: Don't Stir Things Up

Run the group delicately, as if you were cooking small fish.

As much as possible, allow the group process to emerge naturally. Resist any temptation to instigate issues or elicit emotions which have not appeared on their own.

If you stir things up, you will release forces before their time and under unwarranted pressure. These forces may be emotions which belong to other people or places. They may be unspecific or chaotic energies which, in response to your pressure, strike out and hit any available target.

These forces are real. They do exist in the group. But do not push. Allow them to come out when they are ready.

When hidden issues and emotions emerge naturally, they resolve themselves naturally. They are not harmful. In fact, they are no different from any other thoughts or feelings.

All energies naturally arise, take form, grow strong, come to a new resolution, and finally pass away.

Chapter 62: Whether You Know It or Not

A person does not have to join a group or be a wise leader to work things out. Life's process unfolds naturally. Conflicts resolve themselves sooner or later, whether or not a person knows how things happen.

It is true that being aware of how things happen makes one's words more potent and one's behavior more effective.

But even without the light of consciousness, people grow and improve. Being unconscious is not a crime, it is merely the lack of a very helpful ability.

Knowing how things work gives the leader more real power and ability than all the degrees or job titles the world can offer.

That is why people in every era and in every culture have honored those who know how things happen.

Chapter 72: Spiritual Awareness

Group work must include spiritual awareness, if it is to touch the existential anxiety of our times. Without awe, the awful remains unspoken; a diffuse malaise remains.

Be willing to speak of traditional religion, no matter how offended some group members may be. Overcome the bias against the word "God." The great force of our spiritual roots lies in tradition, like it or not.

The wise leader models spiritual behavior and lives in harmony with spiritual values. There is a way of knowing, higher than reason; there is a self, greater than egocentricity.

The leader demonstrates the power of selflessness and the unity of all creation.

Chapter 81: The Reward

It is more important to tell the simple, blunt truth than it is to say things that sound good. The group is not a contest of eloquence.

It is more important to act in behalf of everyone than it is to win arguments. The group is not a debating society.

It is more important to react wisely to what is happening than it is to be able to explain everything in terms of certain theories. The group is not a final examination for a college course.

The wise leader is not collecting a string of successes. The leader is helping others to find their own success. There is plenty to go around. Sharing success with others is very successful.

The single principle behind all creation teaches us that true benefit blesses everyone and diminishes no one.

The wise leader knows that the reward for doing the work arises naturally out of the work.

References

Bynner, W. *The way of life according to Lao-tzu*. New York: Capricorn Books, 1962.

Witter Bynner lived in China for a time; he loved the Chinese. His scholarship is less important than his spirit. I must have bought ten copies of this version. He wrote it in 1944, a dark time for China.

Feng, G., & English, J. *Tao te ching*. New York: Knopf, 1972.

Both of these authors lead awareness groups. Their language is contemporary and clear. Jane English's photography and Gia-fu Feng's calligraphy evoke the spirit of Tao better than any commentary.

Medhurst, C. S. *The tao-teh-king*. Wheaton, IL: Theosophical Publishing House, 1972.

The language of this cranky old 1905 translation seems more remote than Lao Tzu himself. I like this commentary. He can relate *Tao Te Ching* to Western religious and cultural traditions. Medhurst is spiritual.

Schmidt, K. O. *Tao te ching*. Lakemont, GA: CSA Press, 1975.

Schmidt is a German metaphysical writer. He knows and loves the mysteries. His rendition makes sense. In both teaching and understanding Lao Tzu, I have relied on Schmidt most, [but he] is often inaccurate.

Suzuki, D. T., & Carus, P. *The canon of reason and virtue*. La Salle, IL: Open Court Publishing, 1974.

This translation is clear. Scholarship and commentary are very helpful. In addition, the entire text is presented in printed Chinese characters. Only Arthur Waley seems as reliable to me.

Waley, A. *The way and its power.* New York: Grove Press, 1958.

Witter Bynner said, "Arthur Waley's [Lao Tzu] is painstakingly accurate and scholarly but difficult for any but scholars to follow." Difficult, but worth it. I use Waley when I want to get close to the original. I trust him most.

14

Classic Tales of Captains, Castles, . . . and Corporations

BEVERLY KEMPTON

In this town, where the number of successful women is only a handful, it's great to walk around and, like Lear, have people say: There is the King.
—Kay Shaver, president
K. Shaver Advertising, Inc.

I'm Captain Archibald in Joseph Conrad's The Secret Sharer. *I've been doing the same job for five and a half years and I've plateaued; I'm not going to go any further up the corporate ladder. But I don't want to be Archibald; I want to find ways to sweep the cobwebs out of my mind.*
—Stan Dickson, vice president
South Central Bell Telephone Company

When was the last time you spent the day thinking?
—One participant to another
during the morning coffee break

Somehow the cast did not befit the set, a large lecture room on a properly ivied and tranquil college campus—the University of Louisville to be exact. But this was hardly the customary mélange of jocks, grinds, and rebels; no, the men and women arrayed around the square of conference tables fairly reeked authority and command. Not a professor among them—shoes were shined, neckties in place, hair coiffed, and attaché cases at hand. Gathered here, along with assorted faculty, were 18 of Kentucky's most stellar business and corporate executives. And what should emerge from their attaché cases but Shakespeare's *King Lear*, Joseph Conrad's *The Secret Sharer*, the George Orwell short stories "The Hanging" and "Shooting the Elephant," and, for the less secure

---

This chapter is an expanded version of "Classic Tales of Captains, Castles, . . . and Corporations," published by *Working Woman*, October 1987.

among them, that handy student guide to literature, *Cliff Notes*—proof that the generation gap is not always an abyss.

The name of their one-day seminar was the essence of sobriety— *Great Stories and Corporate Life: Literary Texts, Humanistic Values and the Organization*—and their assignment no less so: to ponder the complex social and moral issues confronted in their business and professional worlds. The exercise of power, acts and consequences, risk and reward, loyalty, the dimensions of responsibility, decision making, ethical conflict, and human choice were but a few of the themes. Sanford M. Lottor is cofounder and director of this traveling think tank conceived at Brandeis University in 1980. He states, "We have learned that discussing novels, plays, and short stories is a great nonthreatening way for people in responsible positions to consider what is important and not important and to ask fundamental questions about themselves and the ways in which they operate."

The introduction of the humanities into the business corridor is not simply a caprice of fashion, argues Lottor. Rather it is a reflection of the daunting complexities of our world and the fact that decisions made throughout a business hierarchy can affect the lives of thousands, in fact entire communities. If the measure of an organization is the performance of its employees, then it makes sound business sense to treat them well. Hence the importance of the study of humanistic values through which those with power, be they CEOs or supervisors of only two, can comprehend its ethical use. This is not esoterica, but a basic idea that can be adapted to all levels of management in a multitude of businesses and professions. To this end, Lottor and Dr. Michael Kaufman, the program's academic director, have conducted 100 day-long seminars on the Brandeis campus in Massachusetts and a dozen other states, accumulating thus far some 50 texts that meet their criteria: complete works of fiction of no more than 100 pages—timeless, well-told tales with themes appropriate for the particular business or professional group being addressed. Close to 2,000 people—administrators, teachers, clerk magistrates, managers, mental health workers, physicians, entrepreneurs, and so on—have elected to take part, representing such diverse corporations as John Hancock Life Insurance, Advertising to Women, Mobil Corporation, Manufacturers Hanover Trust Co., Wrangler Men's Wear, Charles of the Ritz, and Data Language Corporation. Indeed this management "training" tool is proving as valuable as it is unique, even in a society such as ours that has discovered how neatly the arts lend themselves to mass marketing techniques.

Essentially, Lottor explains, the program has two texts: the literary work and the personal work drawn from each participant's experiences in organizational life. A productive seminar is the result of an open intermingling of both. "This program allowed me to see why some of my business associates act as they do and how I differ from them," says Joseph Corradino, president of his own engineering firm and an acknowledged workaholic. "And that, in turn, will improve my performance as a business person, a father, a husband, and a member of the community."

But what possible relevance does a play, set in a remote time and place, have to the universe of today's businessman or woman? Is there practical wisdom to be gleaned from the tale of the tragic King Lear, who, willfully and despite the admonitions of his faithful and loving advisor, the Earl of Kent, elected to divide his realm among his three daughters, the largest portion to be bestowed on the one who swore the greatest love? We may not ask the people we supervise if they like us; nevertheless we are mindful of their signals. Do we reward those who flatter us, who "love" us, and punish those who do not? A parallel theme in *King Lear*, chronicling the vicissitudes of Gloucester's sons, Edgar—naive, perpetually deceived but of good heart, and Edmund— pragmatic, crafty, talented, and a planner, generates questions about which personality is most apt to be hired and promoted in business.

In short, this 300-year-old play is grist for toilers in the commercial mill. We find the characters serving in roles with attributes that help define the dimensions of leadership. These ancient characters remind us of people on the stage of leadership today, as illustrated in the following quotes taken from the seminar.

DETERMINED REALIST: Lee Iacocca could have been Kent, and in my opinion would have been the greatest executive vice president any open-minded and secure chief executive could ever have. If you examine companies that are in trouble, you'll find executives who are surrounded by people who court them and don't give them the facts, and sometimes the facts are pretty tough to take from your employees when they tell you you've screwed up. But you need a guy like that. Lear is a great failure as an employer not to have had the wisdom to understand that. I don't think Lear's objective to divide his kingdom was crazy in the sense of orderly transition, but his rationale was horrible: In effect, who sings the best song is the one who's going to get the next promotion.

ORGANIZATIONAL LOYALIST: I don't think Lear intended to walk away but rather to give away the tangible assets while retaining the power.

CONFIDENT RISK-TAKER: I don't see much difference between what Lear did and the sort of thing we do. When we get ready to step down, many of us make darn sure that certain perks will follow. After all, I ran this company; I deserve the things that go with it—including the corporate jet.

STEADY TRADITIONALIST: The Earl of Kent, on the other hand, was loyal to his boss and believed in the system, and he did not want to see the system ruined.

ELDER STATESMAN: There was a total failure on Lear's part to do what all managers know they must do and that's not only find a successor but train that person. It's in the training that you discover whether someone can do the job; with a little market research, Lear could have found out what his girls were going to do.

SEMINAR LEADER: Shakespeare's point is that there are so many emotions, circumstances we can't control, chance events that come between us and our goals, that the great charts and plans we draw up don't always work for us.

REALIST: Maybe we have to build them in a different way—make those three-year strategic plans, or whatever, but leave a lot of white space in them for contingencies and develop alternatives.

LOYALIST: If you're in control, the way to prevent disaster is to slow things down and call time-out. If you could do that in a corporate setting when you think, "Oh, God, I've got myself in a box," you could show that when you make a decision, it's something you believe in and that if it has a flaw, you can bend.

THOUGHTFUL MORALIST: As leaders we are so rewarded for action that we begin to think the action is what defines the job. But if you have no underlying concept of what you and the organization are about, you're just problem solving in the situational sense. You keep stumbling and falling into traps. That's where introspection, which Lear lacked in the beginning, becomes so crucial.

LEADER: What about Edmund? He'd be perfect in our society. This guy is all three-year plans, a Horatio Alger type who may not run a business but sorta puts contracts out on people . . .

REALIST: The Shakespearean political consultant . . .

LEADER: Are the people who are cunning—the infighters and hatchet men—the ones who move up the corporate ladder? Would you pick an Edmund over an Edgar?

REALIST: If you're interested in earnings per share, you might. However, I don't believe any company consciously hires someone immoral. But a lack of morality doesn't necessarily stifle progress up certain corporate ladders. It might even facilitate it. The answer reflects the personal morality of the top management. In all honesty, you'll probably find equal numbers of Edmunds and Edgars in key positions in corporate life.

RISK-TAKER: Actually I can imagine certain kinds of jobs for which you *would* hire an Edmund, even knowing his questionable character.

MORALIST: I think a trap many of us fall into is wanting to hire the Edmunds because of the extraordinary gifts, believing we can work around the flaws or clean up after them. That's a real danger.

For Kay Shaver, president of her own advertising agency, this discussion produced a moment of "smashing insight." As she remarked recently, she had gone to the seminar burdened by a particularly thorny personnel problem. An aggressive, ambitious employee, the most talented member of her staff, was so encumbered with insecurities that she not only disrupted the harmony of the firm but also made commitments on its behalf that were difficult to meet. "When one of the participants said he had learned through long experience that no matter how talented the employee, if he is severely insecure, he is impossible to work with and must be gotten rid of, a light went on and I thought, he's right. Several weeks later, after Christmas, I brought the matter to a head, and by mid-January the employee was gone. I feel good that I was able to make the move, and I'm not sure I would have done it quite so clearly had it not been for the seminar." It seems the classics do bear messages for us from time past.

This was not a day for conclusions; it was one, however, that summoned up several of the participants' most worrisome concerns. *Risk* was paramount. When is it reasonable? Unreasonable? Does our society look kindly on risk-takers? Do organizations tolerate them? It was one of the day's most potent themes, exemplified in Conrad's *The Secret Sharer* and Orwell's "Shooting the Elephant."

Although in essence "Shooting the Elephant" is a political and anti-colonial tale, Lottor and Kaufman focus on the problem of risk that it raises. Its hero, if such he be, is a functionary in a complex system— a police officer serving the British Raj in Burma. He detests his work and the Empire with equal passion. Nevertheless, in the line of duty, he shoots an elephant that has killed a coolie, because: "The people expected it of me. . . . A sahib has got to appear resolute, to know his own mind and do definite things." "The story raises such questions as: Why didn't the narrator take the risk of *not* shooting the elephant, and if he didn't like the system, why didn't he leave it?" says Lottor. "Do employees have the freedom to take risks, to fail? Say you're a middle manager and find something unethical is being done. Do you blow the whistle, or do you do what most of us would, a bit of 'hedonistic calculus.' If I go to my supervisor with this, people will call me a fool because I'll probably lose my job, and with a family and mortgage I can't afford that. Middle managers are not called middle for nothing; they really are caught in a whiplash."

Discussion turned to our sometimes mistaken tendency to do and say what we *think* is expected of us. As one participant suggested, the manager at any level is often torn between the safety of approved conduct and the action for which there is no organizational sanction but that nonetheless is the ethical course. And chances are, added another executive, employees will opt for safety because they know the organization will "shoot" them for taking the risk and perhaps making a mistake. This led, as it must in a decent Platonic dialogue, to the question of how the sense of being unfree and shut out from ownership in the process lowers our self-esteem as workers and affects both our loyalty to our employers and the moral responsibility we take for our actions on their behalf. ("Loyalty is almost a naive word today and has all but left corporate life," one CEO observed.)

During another discussion, there was sharp disagreement in the group as to how authoritative and controlling an organization is by nature. To several people, it seemed arbitrary, ready to trample on those who dared to speak out; if its workers undervalue themselves, blame a milieu that is uneasy with independence and creativity. Not so, countered a more zealous executive, suggesting that employees who have integrity and the courage to criticize his work will advance further, and faster, than their silent and deferential colleagues. *Risk* again, a tangled concept for so tiny a word.

The protagonist of *The Secret Sharer* is the "nameless captain," the youngest man on board a ship under his command. It is his first command, and he begins this initial test of leadership by relieving the night crew and standing watch alone, allowing aboard a stranger—who confesses that to save the ship he has just fled, he murdered a sailor—hiding him in his cabin, and risking the safety of his crew and ship by sailing in the dead of night to within inches of the land to set the fugitive free. The stranger, Leggatt, thus achieves his freedom and the "nameless captain" his self-confidence.

Once again the story translates to our world of business. The initiation of the captain is akin to the challenge faced by a new manager. Before she can win the support of her staff, she must prove to herself that she has the courage to lead.

> RISK-TAKER: I think this situation is more common than not. A young person thrust into a very senior position with a crew—i.e., a staff—she's unfamiliar with but who are very familiar with each other, and the first tendency, being young, is to try and win their favor as the captain does by relieving the night watch. It's a mistake, but as a result the captain meets Leggatt. Because the captain's so insecure, he embraces Leggatt to the point of hiding him and seeking counsel with him. But his maturation and growth in the process show in the end when he does the right thing. He effectively disposes of the problem. He commands the ship and gets the crew knowing that, dammit, he's in charge.
>
> REALIST: Maybe he's in charge in one sense, but in another he's not at all; he exercises authority but totally lacks responsibility.

LEARNING FROM THE MASTERS

Leading isn't easy. Everyday problems often defy answers. But you don't always have to turn to modern-day management gurus for advice. Try turning the pages of classic literature instead. From Homer to Hemingway, great writers can offer insight into age-old problems.

PROBLEM	REFERENCE
You are president of a biomedical company. Some proprietary information about your company landed on the front page of today's *Wall Street Journal.* The head of research insists that the leak must have come from the head of manufacturing. You consider confronting the manager with the accusation, but after working with her for four years you cannot believe she would betray the company. Besides, the two managers have had problems in the past, and you start to question the researcher's motives. What should you do?	Shakespeare's *Othello* is the story of a high-powered military officer betrayed by one of his subordinates, Iago, who is passed over for a promotion. To get back at Othello, Iago tries to convince him that his wife has been unfaithful. Othello's intuition tells him that his wife has been true and that he should not doubt her. But the vengeful Iago puts on a convincing show—so convincing that Othello, never questioning Iago's motives, kills his wife and then kills himself. If only Othello had listened to to his heart instead of his head.
You are a workaholic. Each day you are consumed by the tasks that call you to the office, staying late into the night until each and every piece of paper is off your desk. Nothing excites you more than the thought of hitting the top of the corporate ladder. But your family and friends are begging you to take a vacation—or at least a long lunch. Do you book a trip to St. Bart's or a conference call to London?	Tolstoy's *The Death of Ivan Ilyich* details the power-driven life of Ilyich, a Russian judge. At the height of his success Ilyich contracts a fatal disease. On his deathbed he takes a long look at his life only to realize that the last time he knew happiness was in his childhood. He received no fulfillment from his years at work. But Ilyich makes this discovery too late.
You have just been brought in to resuscitate a troubled company's sales effort. You have the authority to reorganize the operation and fire and replace personnel, but you adopt a wait-and-see attitude. Meanwhile you notice that the head of a rival division, a petty director who terrorizes his staff, appears to be doing well. Should you rethink your management style?	Hemingway's *For Whom the Bell Tolls* takes place during the Spanish Civil War. It contrasts the accomplishment of Robert Jordan, an American who fights for the Loyalists, with the failure of a Fascist captain. Jordan, who listens and learns from the guerrillas, accomplishes his goal. But the captain relies on his pistols and threats and is abandoned.

You are a young, ambitious investment banker with star quality. Others on Wall Street are making fortunes overnight, and you vow that one day you'll be rich and powerful. During one of your deals you are privy to insider information. Should you call a friend and ask her to buy you 1,000 shares of stock?

Shakespeare's *Macbeth* recounts the rise and fall of Macbeth. Caught between his loyalty to the king and his swelling ambition, Macbeth murders the king and takes his throne. Consumed by guilt, Macbeth suffers horrible dreams. Eventually he is beheaded by an avenging general.

You and your partner own a large gourmet-foods business. She's the baker, you're the banker. She's also terrific with clients, while you are a cold fish on sales calls. Lately you haven't been getting along. Her expense account will drive you into the poorhouse, you charge. She accuses you of not understanding the food business. What should you do?

Homer's *Iliad* tells the story of Agamemnon, Greek king, and Achilles, his best warrior, who nearly lose the Trojan War because they cannot get along. Agamemnon cares more about proving how powerful he is than motivating Achilles to capture Troy. After the king takes Achilles' war prize, the warrior moves his army out. It takes years to finally win the war.

You're having problems with one of your best researchers. Recently she's been coming in late and staring at the walls instead of spending time at her computer. Other employees are voicing objections about "paying her for sitting around." Yet just last week, she came up with an idea that has million-dollar potential. Is it worth dealing with the gripes of many to keep this creative genius on staff?

Shaw's *St. Joan* recounts the tale of Joan of Arc, a medieval maverick who claims to hear orders from heaven. Joan defies traditionalists in the French court, dresses as a man, and leads the French army to victory. This independence leads to her condemnation. Captured by the English, she won't deny that she hears voices and is burned at the stake as a heretic. Almost 500 years later Joan is canonized by the Catholic Church.

Your ad agency is competing to represent a hot, new, preppie-sportswear company. It's up to you to select a team to create the campaign. Two art directors have expressed an interest. The first, clad in khaki, looks the part, although lately her work has been a bit flat. The second would sooner die than don a polo shirt, yet her last three campaigns have been big winners. Who should get the assignment?

Chaucer's *Canterbury Tales* looks at a handful of pilgrims about to embark on a religious journey. The seemingly simple bunch includes a friar, a cook, a monk, and a wife. But a careful read proves otherwise. The friar is money-hungry, the cook diseased, and the monk jolly. And the fat, middle-aged wife of Bath is lusty as a new bride. Together they prove that you shouldn't judge a book by its cover.

—*Michelle Morris*

Source: Reprinted with permission from *Working Woman* magazine. Copyright ©1987 by Working Woman, Inc.

TRADITIONALIST: I'd challenge the point that he matures. On the last page he brings the ship under the very shadows of the trees on an island and is about to run it aground, endangering his cargo and the lives of his crew.

MORALIST: I find it troubling that he lucked out. Was it strong of him to keep the course right up to the edge of the island or was it fixated behavior? To me, it's strong if you weigh all the evidence and pick a target that's clearly worth the risk and then take great risk to achieve it. But he didn't think through the perils and the gain; all those risks, and what was the reward—that he could deliver his passenger a few feet closer to shore? That's not strong. It's stupid.

RISK-TAKER: I'm surprised there's such a polarized difference of opinion here about whether or not he succeeded. I think he did. After a lot of early missteps, he made a decision, right or wrong, and carried it through. It was risky but when he accomplished it he felt better about himself. And whether it was lucking out or not, there isn't one of us who's ever been successful without a large degree of luck.

TRADITIONALIST: But can a leader simply act out his own needs, or does he have the responsibility for the stewardship with which he's been entrusted—in this case the ship, its cargo, and crew? He puts it all at terrible risk; for what purpose? To make himself feel better. I think he ought to be hanged.

RISK-TAKER: Every one of us, at one time or another, risks a lot because in that situation we think it's the right thing to do.

STATESMAN: I think there's an organizational lesson in this text. When you put a person in a position of responsibility, you ought to watch his early behavior with extreme care. In my experience, those who have good leadership traits show them early and those with bad judgment show it just as early, and just as clearly, if we pay attention.

LOYALIST: If someone's first action is a radical change of plan, it signals a potential problem with that individual.

REALIST: But what happens if someone comes to you and says, "Instead of banking in the old-fashioned way, let's do it this way: no interest rates whatsoever"? Isn't there room in business for radical departure?

RISK-TAKER: If you want to look at the big picture, societies progress when the risk-takers get in positions of authority and can do things. We teach children to blend in. We don't cherish our eccentrics; in organizations we all dress alike and look alike. When you think about it, though, the people who change society usually deviate from custom. In a business situation, they're the ones who see ways to do things that others might consider senseless.

REALIST: True, but the nameless captain risked many lives to protect one life, and I submit it was a bad trade. You encourage risk, but reasonable risk.

LOYALIST: I'd like to say a word in favor of Archibald, the captain of Leggatt's ship, which almost sank. For 25 years he subscribed to all

the rules and never risked anything, including personal growth. I think
to keep society and our organizations on an even keel, we need those
people who are steady and can be relied on to follow a defined set of
rules.

REALIST: But in this situation, it's Archibald who almost loses his ship.
The man has fallen into complacency and ineptness. He's a failure.

LOYALIST: Yes, but he's a good example of what I was once taught:
When we promote a person to a position he can't handle, it's our fault,
not his. It's the old Peter Principle; we think the only way to reward
someone who's a damn good bean counter is to make him something
else instead of making sure he has a better life as a bean counter.

"*The Secret Sharer* really grabbed me," says Corradino. "I related to
the captain's aggressiveness and risk-taking, and I was stunned that
some of the participants were so critical of his actions. It made me feel
very different, but I realized that their viewpoint is shaped by their
coming from large corporations that give them established patterns to
follow, whereas a small business person, I made my own niche from
scratch without the aid of set procedures. My role is to do the risky
thing. However, now I'm more sensitive to the positions of people in
the establishment, and it has affected the way I do business with them.
I'm far more laid back. It doesn't help me to have a reputation as a
maverick and wild risk-taker. There's a lot of room for guys like me to
get ahead, but I will pick and choose my shots more carefully and use
them only when I know I'll win."

There is something poignant about these doyens of industry, the need
to give voice to their humanness, to forswear the image of business
people as blackhearted creatures of profit and loss. They are caught in
the system's metaphor—the warrior charging the hill, sword in hand,
crisp, cool, quick, and, above all, decisive. Little wonder they are drawn
to this grove of academe; there is no forum in business where they can
indulge in philosophical inquiry with their peers. The prospect of a day
devoted to material so alien to their business bibliographies appealed
to each of them. Although they did not come expecting a spiritual
rebirth, it is telling that these men and women—practiced in the
appearance of invulnerability—were ready to lay that mask aside and,
perhaps even more striking, to grope, to stammer, and, ultimately, to
risk looking foolish.

In the end, what does this new training technique add up to for
today's business community? Surprise was the shared reaction for the
executives. They were surprised that the yield of a writer's imagination
could bear directly on their own lives, that man's interior quarrel between
the honorable and venal in his nature is so timeless a theme that it was

played out on stage 300 years ago much as it is in the modern workplace. No one left with a changed set of values, yet no one left unchanged. The juices had been stirred, and a collection of dispassionate observers became active participants, reawakened to the reverberations of human history.

15

Leadership in an
Organized Anarchy

MICHAEL D. COHEN
JAMES G. MARCH

The college president faces four fundamental ambiguities. The first is the ambiguity of *purpose*. In what terms can action be justified? What are the goals of the organization? The second is the ambiguity of *power*. How powerful is the president? What can he accomplish? The third is the ambiguity of *experience*. What is to be learned from the events of the presidency? How does the president make inferences about his experience? The fourth is the ambiguity of *success*. When is a president successful? How does he assess his pleasures?

These ambiguities are fundamental to college presidents because they strike at the heart of the usual interpretations of leadership. When purpose is ambiguous, ordinary theories of decision making and intelligence become problematic. When power is ambiguous, ordinary theories of social order and control become problematic. When experience is ambiguous, ordinary theories of learning and adaptation become problematic. When success is ambiguous, ordinary theories of motivation and personal pleasure become problematic.

———— □ ————

Almost any educated person can deliver a lecture entitled "The Goals of the University." Almost no one will listen to the lecture voluntarily.

Abridged from Michael D. Cohen and James G. March, *Leadership and Ambiguity*, 2nd ed. Boston: Harvard Business School Press, 1986. Copyright © 1974 by the Carnegie Foundation for the Advancement of Teaching, © 1986 by the President and Fellows of Harvard College; all rights reserved. Reprinted by permission.

For the most part, such lectures and their companion essays are well-intentioned exercises in social rhetoric, with little operational content.

Efforts to generate normative statements of the goals of a university tend to produce goals that are either meaningless or dubious. They fail one or more of the following reasonable tests. First, is the goal clear? Can one define some specific procedure for measuring the degree of goal achievement? Second, is it problematic? Is there some possibility that the organization will accomplish the goal? Is there some chance that it will fail? Third, is it accepted? Do most significant groups in the university agree on the goal statement? For the most part, the level of generality that facilitates acceptance destroys the problematic nature or clarity of the goal. The level of specificity that permits measurement destroys acceptance.

Efforts to infer the "real" objectives of a university by observing university behavior tend to be unsuccessful. They fail one or more of the following reasonable tests. First, is the goal uniquely consistent with behavior? Does the imputed goal produce the observed behavior and is it the only goal that does? Second, is it stable? Does the goal imputed from past behavior reliably predict future behavior? Although it is often possible to devise a statement of the goals of a university by some form of revealed preference test of past actions, such goal statements have poor predictive power.

The difficulties in imputing goals from behavior are not unique to universities. Experience with the complications is shared by revealed preference theorists in economics and psychology, radical critics of society, and functionalist students of social institutions. The search for a consistent explanation of human social behavior through a model of rational intent and an imputation of intent from action has had some successes. But there is no sign that the university is one of the successes, or very likely to become one.

Efforts to specify a set of consciously shared, consistent objectives within a university or to infer such a set of objectives from the activities or actions of the university have regularly revealed signs of inconsistency. To expose inconsistencies is not to resolve them, however. There are only modest signs that universities or other organized anarchies respond to a revelation of ambiguity of purpose by reducing the ambiguity. These are organizational systems without clear objectives; and the processes by which their objectives are established and legitimized are not extraordinarily sensitive to inconsistency. In fact, for many purposes the ambiguity of purpose is produced by our insistence on treating purpose as a necessary property of a good university. The strains arise from trying to impose a model of action as flowing from intent on organizations that act in another way.

College presidents live within a normative context that presumes purpose and within an organizational context that denies it. They serve on commissions to define and redefine the objectives of higher education. They organize convocations to examine the goals of the college. They accept the presumption that intelligent leadership presupposes the rational pursuit of goals. Simultaneously, they are aware that the process of choice in the college depends little on statements of shared direction. They recognize the flow of actions as an ecology of games (Long, 1958), each with its own rules. They accept the observation that the world is not like the model.

———— □ ————

Power is a simple idea, pervasive in its appeal to observers of social events. Like *intelligence* or *motivation* or *utility*, however, it tends to be misleadingly simple and prone to tautology. A person has power if he gets things done; if he has power, he can get things done.

As students of social power have long observed, such a view of power has limited usefulness. Two of the things the simple view produces are an endless and largely fruitless search for the person who has "the real power" in the university, and an equally futile pursuit of the organizational locale "where the decision is *really* made." So profound is the acceptance of the power model that students of organizations who suggest the model is wrong are sometimes viewed as part of the plot to conceal "the real power" and "the true locus of decision." In that particular logic the reality of the simple power model is demonstrated by its inadequacy.

As a shorthand casual expression for variations in the potential of different positions in the organization, *power* has some utility. The college president has more potential for moving the college than most people, probably more potential than any one other person. Nevertheless, presidents discover that they have less power than is believed, that their power to accomplish things depends heavily on what they want to accomplish, that the use of formal authority is limited by other formal authority, that the acceptance of authority is not automatic, that the necessary details of organizational life confuse power (which is somewhat different from diffusing it), and that their colleagues seem to delight in complaining simultaneously about presidential weakness and presidential willfulness.

The ambiguity of power, like the ambiguity of purpose, is focused on the president. Presidents share in and contribute to the confusion.

They enjoy the perquisites and prestige of the office. They enjoy its excitement, at least when things go well. They announce important events. They appear at important symbolic functions. They report to the people. They accept and thrive on their own importance. It would be remarkable if they did not. Presidents even occasionally recite that "the buck stops here" with a finality that suggests the cliché is an observation about power and authority rather than a proclamation of administrative style and ideology.

At the same time, presidents solicit an understanding of the limits to their control. They regret the tendency of students, legislators, and community leaders to assume that a president has the power to do whatever he chooses simply because he is president. They plead the countervailing power of other groups in the college or the notable complexities of causality in large organizations.

The combination is likely to lead to popular impressions of strong presidents during good times and weak presidents during bad times. Persons who are primarily exposed to the symbolic presidency (e.g., outsiders) will tend to exaggerate the power of the president. Those people who have tried to accomplish something in the institution with presidential support (e.g., educational reformers) will tend to underestimate presidential power or presidential will.

The confusion disturbs the president, but it also serves him. Ambiguity of power leads to a parallel ambiguity of responsibility. The allocation of credit and blame for the events of organizational life becomes—as it often does in political and social systems—a matter for argument. The "facts" of responsibility are badly confounded by the confusions of anarchy; and the conventional myth of hierarchical executive responsibility is undermined by the countermyth of the nonhierarchical nature of colleges and universities. Presidents negotiate with their audiences on the interpretations of their power. As a result, during the recent years of campus troubles, many college presidents sought to emphasize the limitations of presidential control. During the more glorious days of conspicuous success, they solicited a recognition of their responsibility for events.

The process does not involve presidents alone, of course. The social validation of responsibility involves all the participants: faculty, trustees, students, parents, community leaders, government. Presidents seek to write their histories in the use of power as part of a chorus of history writers, each with his own reasons for preferring a somewhat different interpretation of "Who has the Power?"

--- □ ---

College presidents attempt to learn from their experience. They observe the consequences of actions and infer the structure of the world from those observations. They use the resulting inferences in attempts to improve their future actions.

Consider the following very simple learning paradigm:

1. At a certain point in time a president is presented with a set of well-defined, discrete action alternatives.
2. At any point in time he has a certain probability of choosing any particular alternative (and a certainty of choosing one of them).
3. The president observes the outcome that apparently follows his choice and assesses the outcome in terms of his goals.
4. If the outcome is consistent with his goals, the president increases his probability of choosing that alternative in the future; if not, he decreases the probability.

Although actual presidential learning certainly involves more complicated inferences, such a paradigm captures much of the ordinary adaptation of an intelligent man to the information gained from experience.

The process produces considerable learning. The subjective experience is one of adapting from experience and improving behavior on the basis of feedback. If the world with which the president is dealing is relatively simple and relatively stable, and if his experience is relatively frequent, he can expect to improve over time (assuming he has some appropriate criterion for testing the consistency of outcomes with goals). As we have suggested earlier, however, the world in which the president lives has two conspicuous properties that make experience ambiguous even where goals are clear. First, the world is relatively complex. Outcomes depend heavily on factors other than the president's action. These factors are uncontrolled and, in large part, unobserved. Second, relative to the rate at which the president gathers experimental data, the world changes rapidly. These properties produce considerable potential for false learning.

We can illustrate the phenomenon by taking a familiar instance of learning in the realm of personnel policies. Suppose that a manager reviews his subordinates annually and considers what to do with those who are doing poorly. He has two choices: he can replace an employee whose performance is low, or he can keep him in the job and try to work with him to obtain improvement. He chooses which employees to replace and which to keep in the job on the basis of his judgment about their capacities to respond to different treatments. Now suppose that, in fact, there are no differences among the employees. Observed variations in performance are due entirely to random fluctuations. What would the manager "learn" in such a situation?

He would learn how smart he was. He would discover that his judgments about whom to keep and whom to replace were quite good. Replacements will generally perform better than the men they replaced; those men who are kept in the job will generally improve in their performance. If for some reason he starts out being relatively "humane" and refuses to replace anyone, he will discover that the best managerial strategy is to work to improve existing employees. If he starts out with a heavy hand and replaces everyone, he will learn that being tough is a good idea. If he replaces some and works with others, he will learn that the essence of personnel management is judgment about the worker.

Although we know that in the hypothetical situation it makes no difference what a manager does, he will experience some subjective learning that is direct and compelling. He will come to believe that he understands the situation and has mastered it. If we were to suggest to the manager that he might be a victim of superstitious learning, he would find it difficult to believe. Everything in his environment tells him that he understands the world, even though his understanding is spurious.

It is not necessary to assume that the world is strictly random to produce substantially the same effect. Whenever the rate of experience is modest relative to the complexity of the phenomena and the rate of change in the phenomena, the interpretation made of experience will tend to be more persuasive subjectively than it should be. In such a world, experience is not a good teacher. Although the outcomes stemming from the various learned strategies in the personnel management example will be no worse because of a belief in the reality of the learning, the degree of confidence a manager comes to have in his theory of the world is erroneously high.

College presidents probably have greater confidence in their interpretations of college life, college administration, and their general environment than is warranted. The inferences they have made from experience are likely to be wrong. Their confidence in their learning is likely to have been reinforced by the social support they receive from the people around them and by social expectations about the presidential role. As a result, they tend to be unaware of the extent to which the ambiguities they feel with respect to purpose and power are matched by similar ambiguities with respect to the meaning of the ordinary events of presidential life.

———— □ ————

Administrative success is generally recognized in one of two ways. First, by promotion: An administrator knows that he has been successful by virtue of a promotion to a better job. He assesses his success on the current job by the opportunities he has or expects to have to leave it. Second, by widely accepted, operational measures of organizational output: A business executive values his own performance in terms of a profit-and-loss statement of his operations.

Problems with these indicators of success are generic to high-level administrative positions. Offers of promotion become less likely as the job improves and the administrator's age advances. The criteria by which success is judged become less precise in measurement, less stable over time, and less widely shared. The administrator discovers that a wide assortment of factors outside his control are capable of overwhelming the impact of any actions he may take.

In the case of the college president all three problems are accentuated. As we have seen earlier, few college presidents are promoted out of the presidency. There are job offers, and most presidents ultimately accept one; but the best opportunity the typical president can expect is an invitation to accept a decent version of administrative semiretirement. The criteria of success in academic administration are sometimes moderately clear (e.g., growth, quiet on campus, improvement in the quality of students and faculty), but the relatively precise measures of college health tend neither to be stable over time nor to be critically sensitive to presidential action.

An argument can be made, of course, that the college president should be accustomed to the ambiguity of success. His new position is not, in this respect, so strikingly different from the positions he has held previously. His probable perspective is different, however. Success has not previously been subjectively ambiguous to him. He has been a success. He has been promoted relatively rapidly. He and his associates are inclined to attribute his past successes to a combination of administrative savoir-faire, interpersonal style, and political sagacity. He has experienced those successes as the lawful consequence of his actions. Honest modesty on the part of a president does not conceal a certain awareness of his own ability. A president comes to his office having learned that he is successful and that he enjoys success.

The momentum of promotion will not sustain him in the presidency. Although, as we have seen, a fair number of presidents anticipate moving from their present job to another, better presidency, the prospects are not nearly as good as the hopes. The ambiguities of purpose, power, and experience conspire to render success and failure equally obscure. The validation of success is unreliable. Not only can a president not assure himself that he will be able to lead the college in the directions in which others might believe, he also has no assurance that the same criteria will be applied tomorrow. What happens today will tend to be rationalized tomorrow as what was desired. What happens today will have some relation to what was desired yesterday. Outcomes do flow in part from goals. But goals flow from outcomes as well, and both goals and outcomes also move independently.

The result is that the president is a bit like the driver of a skidding automobile. The marginal judgments he makes, his skill, and his luck may possibly make some difference to the survival prospects for his riders. As a result, his responsibilities are heavy. But whether he is convicted of manslaughter or receives a medal for heroism is largely outside his control.

One basic response to the ambiguities of success is to find pleasure in the process of presidential life. A reasonable man will seek reminders of his relevance and success. Where those reminders are hard to find in terms of socially validated outcomes unambiguously due to one's actions, they may be sought in the interactions of organizational life. George Reedy (1970) made a similar observation about a different presidency: "Those who seek to lighten the burdens of the presidency by easing the workload do no occupant of that office a favor. The 'workload'—especially the ceremonial work load—are the only events of a president's day which make life endurable."

———— □ ————

The ambiguities that college presidents face describe the life of any formal leader of any organized anarchy. The metaphors of leadership and our traditions of personalizing history (even the minor histories of collegiate institutions) confuse the issues of leadership by ignoring the basic ambiguity of leadership life. We require a plausible basic perspective for the leader of a loosely coupled, ambiguous organization.

If we knew more about the normative theory of acting before thinking, we could say more intelligent things about the functions of management and leadership when organizations or societies do not know what they are doing. Consider, for example, the following general implications.

First, we need to reexamine the functions of management decision making. One of the primary ways in which the goals of an organization are developed is by interpreting the decisions it makes, and one feature of good managerial decisions is that they lead to the development of more interesting value premises for the organization. As a result, decisions should not be seen as flowing directly or strictly from a preexistent set of objectives. College presidents who make decisions might well view that function somewhat less as a process of deduction or a process of political negotiation, and somewhat more as a process of gently upsetting preconceptions of what the organization is doing.

Second, we need a modified view of planning. Planning can often be more effective as an interpretation of past decisions than as a program for future ones. It can be used as a part of the efforts of the organization to develop a new consistent theory of itself that incorporates the mix of recent actions into a moderately comprehensive structure of goals. Procedures for interpreting the meaning of most past events are familiar to the memoirs of retired generals, prime ministers, business leaders, and movie stars. They suffer from the company they keep. In an organization that wants to continue to develop new objectives, a manager needs to be tolerant of the idea that he will discover the meaning of yesterday's action in the experiences and interpretations of today.

Third, we need to reconsider evaluation. As nearly as we can determine, there is nothing in a formal theory of evaluation that requires that criteria be specified in advance. In particular, the evaluation of social experiments need not be in terms of the degree to which they have fulfilled our prior expectations. Rather we can examine what they did in terms of what we now believe to be important. The prior specification of criteria and the prior specification of evaluational procedures that depend on such criteria are common presumptions in contemporary social policy making. They are presumptions that inhibit the serendipitous discovery of new criteria. Experience should be used explicitly as an occasion for evaluating our values as well as our actions.

Fourth, we need a reconsideration of social accountability. Individual preferences and social action need to be consistent in some way. But the process of pursuing consistency is one in which both the preferences and the actions change over time. Imagination in social policy formation involves systematically adapting to and influencing preference. It would be unfortunate if our theories of social action encouraged leaders to ignore their responsibilities for anticipating public preferences through action and for providing social experiences that modify individual expectations.

Fifth, we need to accept playfulness in social organizations. The design of organizations should attend to the problems of maintaining both playfulness and reason as aspects of intelligent choice. Since much of the literature on social design is concerned with strengthening the rationality of decision making, managers are likely to overlook the importance of play. This is partly a matter of making the individuals within an organization more playful by encouraging the attitudes and skills of inconsistency. It is also a matter of making organizational structure and organizational procedures more playful. Organizations can be playful even when the participants in them are not. The managerial devices for maintaining consistency can be varied. We encourage organizational play by insisting on some temporary relief from control, coordination, and communication.

———— □ ————

Contemporary theories of decision making and the technology of reason have considerably strengthened our capabilities for effective social action. The conversion of the simple ideas of choice into an extensive technology is a major achievement. It is, however, an achievement that has reinforced some biases in the underlying models of choice in individuals and groups. In particular, it has reinforced the uncritical acceptance of a static interpretation of human goals.

There is little magic in the world, and foolishness in people and organizations is one of the many things that fail to produce miracles. Under certain conditions, it is one of several ways in which some of the problems of our current theories of intelligence can be overcome. It may be a good way, for it preserves the virtues of consistency while stimulating change. If we had a good technology of foolishness, it might (in combination with the technology of reason) help in a small way to develop the unusual combinations of attitudes and behaviors that describe the interesting societies of the world. The contribution of a college president may often be measured by his capability for sustaining that creative interaction of foolishness and rationality.

References

Adams, Jesse E., and Herman Lee Donovan: "The Administration and Organization in American Universities," *Peabody Journal of Education*, vol. 22, May 1945.

Allison, Graham T.: *Essence of Decision: Explaining the Cuban Missile Crisis*, Little, Brown and Company, Boston, 1971.

Baldridge, J. Victor: *Power and Conflict in the University*, John Wiley & Sons, Inc., New York, 1971.

Baldridge, J. Victor (ed.): *Academic Governance: Research on Institutional Politics and Decision Making*, McCutchan Publishing Corporation, Berkeley, 1971.

Beard, John L.: "A Study of the Duties Performed by College Administrators," Ph.D. dissertation in education, University of Texas at Austin, June 1948.

Bolman, Frederick de W.: *How College Presidents Are Chosen*, American Council on Education, Washington, D.C., 1965.

Bryan, William Lowe: "The Share of Faculty in Administration and Government," in Guy P. Benton (ed.), *Transactions and Proceedings of the National Association of State Universities in the United States*, Free Press Printing Company, Burlington, Vt., 1914.

Carnegie, Dale: *How to Win Friends and Influence People*, Simon and Schuster, New York, 1936.

Cohen, Michael D., James G. March, and Johan P. Olsen: "A Garbage Can Model of Organizational Choice," *Administrative Science Quarterly*, vol. 17, no. 1, pp. 1–25, March 1972.

Cyert, Richard M., and James G. March: *A Behavioral Theory of the Firm*, Prentice-Hall, Inc., Englewood Cliffs, N.J., 1963.

Demerath, Nicholas J., Richard W. Stephens, and R. Robb Taylor: *Power, Presidents, and Professors*, Basic Books, Inc., Publishers, New York, 1967.

Donovan, Herman Lee: "The State University Presidency: 1955," in C. P. McCurdy, Jr. (ed.), *Transactions and Proceedings of the National Association of State Universities in the United States*, National Association of State Universities, Washington, D.C., 1955.

Faculty Efforts and Output Study, University of California, Berkeley, 1970.

Ferrari, Michael R.: *Profiles of American College Presidents*, Michigan State University Business School, East Lansing, 1970.

Foote, Caleb, and Henry Meyer: *The Culture of the University—Governance and Education*, Jossey-Bass, Inc., San Francisco, 1968.

Frey, Frederick W.: "Comment: On Issues and Nonissues in the Study of Power," *American Political Science Review*, vol. 65, pp. 1081–1101, 1971.

Green, Paul E., and Frank J. Carmone: *Multidimensional Scaling and Related Techniques in Marketing Analysis*, Allyn and Unwin, Boston, 1970.

Hayes, Denis A., and James G. March: "The Normative Problems of University Governance," Assembly on University Goals and Governance, Stanford University, 1970. (Mimeographed.)

Hemphill, John K., and Herbert J. Walberg: *An Empirical Study of the College and University Presidents in the State of New York*, Regents Advisory Committee on Educational Leadership, Albany, 1966.

Hodgkinson, Harold L.: *Institutions in Transition: A Profile of Change in Higher Education*, McGraw-Hill Book Company, New York, 1971.

Hodgkinson, Harold L., and Richard L. Meeth (eds.): *Power and Authority* (Transformation of Campus Governance . . . Conference Papers) Jossey-Bass, Inc., San Francisco, 1971.

Iklé, Fred C.: *How Nations Negotiate*, Harper & Row, Publishers, Incorporated, New York, 1964.

Ingraham, Mark H.: *The Mirror of Brass: The Compensation and Working Conditions of College and University Administrators*, University of Wisconsin Press, Madison, 1968.

"The Invitational Seminar on Restructuring College and University Organization and Governance," *The Journal of Higher Education*, vol. 42, no. 6, pp. 421–542, June 1971.

Kerr, Clark: "Governance and Functions," *Daedalus*, vol. 99, no. 1, pp. 108–121, Winter 1970.

Kerr, Clark: "Presidential Discontent," in David C. Nichols (ed.), *Perspectives on Campus Tensions*, papers prepared for the Special Committee on Campus Tensions, American Council on Education, Washington, D.C., September 1970.

Kerr, Clark: *The Uses of the University*, Harvard University Press, Cambridge, Mass., 1963.

Klahr, David: "A Monte Carlo Investigation of the Statistical Significance of Kruskal's Nonmetric Scaling Procedure," *Psychometrika*, vol. 34, pp. 319–330, 1969.

Knode, Jay C.: "Presidents of State Universities," *Scientific Monthly*, vol. 58, March 1944.

Kruse, S. A., and E. C. Beck: "Study of the Presidents of State Teachers Colleges and of State Universities," *Peabody Journal of Education*, pp. 358–361, May 1928.

Kruskal, J. B.: "Nonmetric Scaling: A Numerical Method," *Psychometrika*, vol. 29, pp. 115–129, June 1964.

Kruskal, J. B.: "Multidimensional Scaling by Optimizing Goodness of Fit to a Nonmetric Hypothesis," *Psychometrika*, vol. 29, pp. 1–28, March 1964.

Long, Norton A.: "The Local Community as an Ecology of Games," *American Journal of Sociology*, vol. 44, pp. 251–261, 1958.

McNeil, Kenneth, and James D. Thompson: "The Regeneration of Social Organizations," *American Sociological Review*, vol. 36, pp. 624–637, 1971.

McVey, Frank, and Raymond A. Hughes: *Problems of College and University Administration*, Iowa State College Press, Ames, 1952.

March, James G.: "The Power of Power," in David Easton (ed.), *Varieties of Political Theory*, Prentice-Hall, Inc., Englewood Cliffs, N.J., 1966.

March, James G., and Herbert A. Simon: *Organizations*, John Wiley & Sons, Inc., New York, 1958.

March, James G. (ed.): *Handbook of Organizations*, Rand McNally & Company, Chicago, 1965.

Mayhew, Lewis B.: *Arrogance on Campus*, Jossey-Bass, Inc., San Francisco, 1971.

Monson, C. H., Jr.: "Metaphors for the University," *Educational Record*, vol. 48, pp. 22–29, Winter 1967.

Perkins, James A.: *College and University Presidents: Recommendations and Report of a Survey*, New York State Regents Advisory Committee on Educational Leadership, Albany, 1967.

Peter, Laurence J.: *The Peter Principle*, William Morrow & Company, Inc., New York, 1969.

Rauh, Morton A.: *The Trusteeship of Colleges and Universities*, McGraw-Hill Book Company, New York, 1969.

Reedy, George E.: *The Twilight of the Presidency*, The World Publishing Company, New York, 1970.

Riesman, David: "Vicissitudes in the Career of the College President," Speech given at the dedication of the O. Meredith Wilson Memorial Library at the University of Minnesota, Minneapolis, May 13, 1969.

Selden, William K.: "How Long Is a College President?" *Liberal Education*, vol. 46, no. 1, pp. 5–15, March 1960.

Simon, Herbert A.: "The Job of a College President," *Educational Record*, vol. 48, no. 1, pp. 68–78, Winter 1967.

Singletary, Otis A. (ed.): *American Universities and Colleges*, American Council on Education, Washington, D.C., 1968.

Stephens, Richard W.: "The Academic Administration: The Role of the University President," Ph.D. dissertation, University of North Carolina, Chapel Hill, 1956.

Walton, Richard E., and Robert B. McKersie (eds.): *Behavioral Theory of Labor Negotiations*, McGraw-Hill Book Company, New York, 1965.

Warren, Luther E.: "A Study of the Presidents of Four-Year Colleges in the U.S.," *Education*, vol. 58, pp. 427–438, March 1938.

Weiner, Stephen S.: "Educational Decisions in an Organized Anarchy," Ph.D. dissertation, Stanford University, Stanford, Calif., 1972.

White, Harrison C.: *Chains of Opportunity: System Models of Mobility in Organizations*, Harvard University Press, Cambridge, Mass., 1970.

Wolfinger, Raymond: "Nondecisions and the Study of Local Politics," *American Political Science Review*, vol. 65, pp. 1063–1080, 1971.

Wolfinger, Raymond: "Rejoinder to Frey's 'Comments,'" *American Political Science Review*, vol. 65, pp. 1102–1104, 1971.

16

Transactional and Transformational Leadership: A Constructive/Developmental Analysis

KARL W. KUHNERT
PHILIP LEWIS

James MacGregor Burns, in his book *Leadership* (1978), identified two types of political leadership: Transactional and transformational. Transactional leadership occurs when one person takes the initiative in making contact with others for the purpose of an exchange of something valued; that is, "leaders approach followers with an eye toward exchanging" (p. 4). Transformational leadership is based on more than the compliance of followers; it involves shifts in the beliefs, the needs, and the values of followers. According to Burns, "the result of transforming leadership is a relationship of mutual stimulation and elevation that converts followers into leaders and may convert leaders into moral agents" (p. 4).

Bass (1985) applied Burns' (1978) ideas to organizational management. He argued that transactional leaders "mostly consider how to marginally improve and maintain the quantity and quality of performance, how to substitute one goal for another, how to reduce resistance to particular actions, and how to implement decisions" (p. 27). In contrast, transformational leaders

> attempt and succeed in raising colleagues, subordinates, followers, clients, or constituencies to a greater awareness about the issues of consequence. This heightening of awareness requires a leader with vision, self-confidence, and inner strength to argue successfully for what he [sic] sees is right or

Reprinted by permission from *The Academy of Management Review*, 12:4 (1987), pp. 648–657.

good, not for what is popular or is acceptable according to established wisdom of the time. (Bass, 1985, p. 17)

Both Burns (1978) and Bass (1985) identified leaders by their actions and the impact those actions have on others. Missing from their works, however, is an explanation of the internal processes which generate the actions of transactional or transformational leaders. That is, neither author provided a framework for understanding the motivational states or personality differences that give rise to these two types of leadership.

In this paper, an attempt to alleviate this shortcoming is made. The authors propose a framework for examining the processes through which transactional and transformational leaders develop. It is based on the idea that transactional and transformational leaders are qualitatively different kinds of individuals who construct reality in markedly different ways, thereby viewing themselves and the people they lead in contrasting ways. The framework used here to explain the differences between transactional and transformational leaders is constructive/developmental personality theory (Kegan, 1982; Selman, 1980).

Transactional and Transformational Leadership

Transactional leadership represents those exchanges in which both the superior and the subordinate influence one another reciprocally so that each derives something of value (Yukl, 1981). Simply stated, transactional leaders give followers something they want in exchange for something the leaders want. Transactional leaders engage their followers in a relationship of mutual dependence in which the contributions of both sides are acknowledged and rewarded (Kellerman, 1984). In these situations, leaders are influential because doing what the leaders want is in the best interest of the followers. Effective transactional leaders must regularly fulfill the expectations of their followers. Thus, effective transactional leadership is contingent on the leaders' abilities to meet and respond to the reactions and changing expectations of their followers (Kellerman, 1984).

Although transactional leadership can be described as the exchange of valued outcomes, closer examination of the literature suggests that all exchanges are not equivalent (e.g., Dienesch & Liden, 1986). Indeed it appears that two "levels" of transactions can be distinguished. Graen, Liden, and Hoel (1982), for example, studied the impact that both high-quality and low-quality exchange relationships had on the turnover of employees. They found that employees who engaged in relationships that involved support and the exchange of emotional resources (high-quality) were less likely to leave an organization than employees who engaged in relationships that involved contractually agreed upon elements such as eight hours of work for eight hours of pay (low-quality). The work reported by Graen et al. suggests low-quality transactions are based on the exchange of goods or rights, whereas high-quality transactions are augmented by an interpersonal bond between leaders and followers (Landy, 1985).

Burns (1978) and Bass (1985) similarly distinguished between levels of transactional leadership. Burns suggested that the kinds of transactions leaders and followers engage in range from the obvious (jobs for votes, subsidies for campaign contributions) to the less obvious (exchanges of trust, commitment, and respect). Similarly, Bass noted that transactional leaders have various transactions available to them. Transactions based on leaders' knowledge of the actions subordinates must take to achieve desired personal outcomes (e.g., working overtime for a paid vacation) are most common. In these exchanges, transactional leaders clarify the roles followers must play and the task requirements followers must complete in order to reach their personal goals while fulfilling the mission of the organization.

A less common form of transactional leadership involves promises or commitments that are rooted in "exchangeable" values such as respect and trust. Burns (1978) referred to these values as modal values; modal values bond leaders to followers in an attempt to actualize the needs of both parties. Thus lower-order transactions depend upon the leaders' control of resources (e.g., pay increases, special benefits) that are desired by the followers (Yukl, 1981). If such rewards are not under the leaders' direct control, their bargaining power is diminished. Higher order transactional leadership, on the other hand, relies on the exchange of nonconcrete rewards to maintain followers' performance. In this relationship, the leaders directly control such exchanges since they rely upon nontangible rewards and values.

Transformational leadership also originates in the personal values and beliefs of leaders, not in an exchange of commodities between leaders and followers. Both Bass (1985) and Burns (1978) indicated that transformational leaders operate out of deeply held personal value systems that include such values as justice and integrity. Burns refers to these values as *end values*—those that cannot be negotiated or exchanged between individuals. By expressing their personal standards, transformational leaders are able both to unite followers and to change followers' goals and beliefs. This form of leadership results in achievement of higher levels of performance among individuals than previously thought possible (Bass, 1985).

Perhaps the concept of *charisma* (House, 1977; Weber, 1947) comes closest in meaning to Burns' (1978) and Bass' ideas of transformational leadership. House described charismatic leaders as those 'who by force of their personal abilities are capable of having a profound and extraordinary effect on followers" (p. 189). He further contended that the term "is usually reserved for leaders who by their influence are able to cause followers to accomplish outstanding feats" (p. 189).

Both transformational leaders and charismatic leaders gain influence by demonstrating important personal characteristics. Many of these characteristics were described by Bass (1985; Avolio & Bass, 1986); some of them are self-confidence, dominance, and a strong conviction in the moral righteousness of one's beliefs. Thus, key behaviors of successful transformational leaders may include articulating goals, building an image, demonstrating confidence, and arousing motivation. These behaviors can convince and motivate followers without bartering for goods and rights, which characterizes transactional leadership.

A Model of Transactional and Transformational Leadership

Bass (1985) identified a number of personality variables believed to distinguish transformational from transactional leaders. Except for a brief foray into psychoanalytic theory, however, he failed to explain how particular traits cohere to produce different types of leaders. It appears that constructive/developmental personality theory can provide a framework for understanding the processes through which different types of leaders emerge.

Constructive personality theories hold that people vary in the ways in which they construct or organize experiences about themselves and their social and interpersonal environments. According to this view, events and situations do not exist, psychologically, until they are experienced and composed privately (Kegan, 1982). Thus, understanding the processes through which people construct meaning out of their experiences may advance our knowledge of how leaders understand, experience, and approach the enterprise of leading.

It appears, from this perspective, that the organizational and perceptual structures of transactional leaders are quite distinct from those of transformational leaders. Also, it can be argued that the constructive/developmental framework can be used to distinguish between lower order and higher order transactional leadership by focusing on the personality mechanisms that induce leaders to engage in one level of exchange versus the other. Thus, while the behaviors of leaders may change under different circumstances, the underlying personality structures that produce the behaviors are quite stable.

Constructive/Developmental Personality Theory

Constructive/developmental theory, as outlined by Robert Kegan (1982), describes a critical personality variable that gives rise to the range of an individual's experience (the growth of interpersonal and intrapersonal understanding). The constructive part of the theory assumes that humans construct a subjective understanding of the world that shapes their experiences as opposed to their directly experiencing an objective "real" world.

Constructive/developmental theory extends the constructivist view by highlighting sequential regularities or patterns in ways that people construct meaning during the course of their lives, and by showing how individuals progress from simple to more complex (encompassing) modes of understanding. Kegan (1982) argued that these regularities are the *deep structure* of personality which generate people's thoughts, feelings, and actions in the same way that linguistic *deep structures* generate grammatical language (Chomsky, 1968). Throughout this developmental process (which extends into adulthood for most individuals), there is an expansion of people's abilities to reflect on and understand their personal and interpersonal worlds. This expansion is made possible by increasing differentiation of oneself from others and by simultaneously integrating the formerly undifferentiated view into a more complex and encompassing view.

To understand the nature of these personality stages and how they relate to transactional and transformational leadership, it is necessary to distinguish between two personality structures which Kegan (1982) termed *subject* and *object*. The structure by which people compose experience is termed subject; it is so basic to human functioning that typically people are not aware of it. It is, in other words, the lens through which people view the world and their inner experiences, and they are unable to examine that lens.

Piaget (1954) demonstrated this phenomenon by showing that the typical four-year-old child is subject to his/her perceptions. In his now famous experiment, the typical four-year-old reported that there was more liquid in a taller, thinner beaker than there was in the shorter, wider beaker, even when the same amount of water was poured from one container to the other. For this preoperational child, the perceptual process is subject: Perceptions are the organizing process, and these perceptions cannot be made object.

Only when the child has moved to Piaget's concrete operational stage is he/she able to take a perspective on his/her perceptions, recognizing that even though the level of liquid is different in the two beakers, they actually contain the same amount. With this new organizing process,

TABLE 1
**Stages of Adult Development Showing the Organizing Process ("Subject")
and the Content of that Organizing Process ("Object")**

Stage[a]	Subject (Organizing Process)	Object (Content of Experience)
2 Imperial (Lower-order Transactional)	Personal goals and agendas	Perceptions, immediate needs, feelings
3 Interpersonal (Higher-order Transactional)	Interpersonal connections, mutual obligations	Personal goals and agendas
4 Institutional (Transformational)	Personal standards and value system	Interpersonal connections, mutual obligations

Note: When individuals progress from one stage to the next, what was formerly subject becomes the object of a new organizing process.

[a]Stage numbers and names are taken directly from Kegan (1982).

the child can make his/her perceptions the object of that organizing process; this opens up a new way of viewing the world.

Constructive/developmental theory supports a similar view of the personality structure of adults. What is subject for some is object for those at higher stages of development, freeing adults to examine new ways of interpreting themselves and their interpersonal relationships. Indeed, the process of development of the personality from this theoretical perspective is one of qualitative restructuring of the relationship between the subject and the object of experience.

It is important for adult development (and consequently for leadership) to determine what is subject and what is object at various developmental stages and then to understand what implications this distinction has for leaders' behavior. Kegan (1982) described six developmental stages, three of which are characteristic of the level of interpersonal understanding of most adults (see Table 1). Since it will not be possible to discuss Kegan's highest stage (5), and lowest stages (0 and 1) here, interested readers may consult Kegan's book (1982) for a description.

In stage 2, individuals' frames of reference (subject) are personal goals or agendas. This frame of reference becomes the lens through which stage 2 adults view their interpersonal world; everything they "witness" is experienced and evaluated in those terms. For example, a stage 2 leader whose goal is becoming the youngest manager to be promoted in the unit can be expected to view his or her followers largely in terms of whether they are advancing or thwarting this aspiration.

Enmeshed in personal goals as an organizing process, the stage 2 leader also assumes, often incorrectly, that others operate because of similar motives. It follows that leaders who have failed to progress beyond Kegan's second developmental stage are apt to use lower level transactional leadership, an approach that motivates followers through trade-offs of the leaders' and followers' personal goals. Constructive/ developmental theory suggests that stage 2 individuals are able to use only lower level transactional leadership techniques.

Stage 2 leaders may *say* that they aspire to higher order transactions (e.g., team spirit, mutual respect), but from the perspective of cognitive/ developmental theory they have not developed the organizing processes (subject) necessary for understanding or participating in mutual experiences and shared perceptions. Although wanting to be the youngest manager to be promoted in the unit may be an acceptable goal, such single-minded vision may have negative consequences for co-workers, the unit, or the organization. Even though one cannot be certain how this leader's behavior will affect the unit's effectiveness, it is certain that his/her commitment to the organization is one of reciprocity.

Stage 2 leaders, from a constructive/developmental perspective, lack an ability to reflect on their goals; they do not *have* agendas—they are *defined* by them. When individuals reach Kegan's (1982) stage 3, they are able to reflect on their own interests and to consider these interests simultaneously with the interests of others. At this developmental stage, personal needs are no longer a part of the subjective organizing process; they become the object of a new organizing process. This is a critical point in the growth of interpersonal understanding because for the first time individuals can experience trust, commitment, respect, and mutuality—values that are central to higher level transactional leadership.

The new subjective frame of reference for stage 3 leaders (connectedness to their subordinates) is the result of their new ability to override personal needs and to coordinate their needs with the needs of others. Whereas the stage 2 leaders negotiate with their employers to satisfy personal agendas, stage 3 leaders sacrifice their personal goals in order to maintain connections with their employers. Thus, the key transactions for the stage 3 leaders are *mutual* support, promises, expectations, obligations, and rewards.

Stage 3 leaders progress to a level of understanding where personal goals are transcended by a focus on interpersonal relations. They become free to understand that for some followers the concrete payoffs they provide are not as important as the maintenance of a certain level of mutual regard. This alleviates the pressure of constantly monitoring and rewarding followers' performance and permits higher level transactional leadership. Communicating attitudes (e.g., trust or respect) becomes the critical dynamism behind this type of leadership. It is the followers' sense of these feelings that maintains their attitudes and work performance.

Higher level transactional leadership also can have serious shortcomings. Stage 3 leaders, for whom commitment and loyalty are basic, cannot take a perspective on those commitments and loyalties; in effect, they are controlled by higher order exchanges. Stage 3 leaders may feel "torn" in situations of conflicting loyalties (e.g., loyalty to the organization versus loyalty to their subordinates). Unable to take a perspective on competing loyalties because the loyalties comprise the organizing process, they find that the only satisfactory course of action is one that somehow preserves competing loyalties by being fair to all parties.

In one sense, stage 3 transactional leaders are transformational because they use relational ties to motivate followers to believe work is more than the performance of certain duties for certain concrete payoffs. Followers may perform at exemplary levels with little immediate payoff in order to maintain the respect of their leader. Still, higher level transactional leadership is not transformational in one important respect. Although followers who are persuaded by higher level transactional leaders may expend extraordinary effort to maintain a certain level of mutual regard with their leader, their beliefs and goals typically have not changed (Bass, 1985). Mutual regard also includes the liabilities of situational leadership; it requires continuous give and take between leaders and followers. The more "bargains" (concrete or interpersonal) that are struck between leaders and their followers, the more likely it is that the leader will be unable to make good on all promised transactions. More critical, stage 3 leaders are dependent on a shared sense of mutual respect, as are their followers.

In contrast, leaders who have progressed to stage 4 in the development of interpersonal understanding do not experience competing loyalties as a critical dilemma that stems from attempting to maintain the respect of everyone. This is because stage 4 leaders have developed a subjective frame of reference (organizing process) that defines their selves, not in terms of their connections to others (the hallmark of stage 3), but in terms of their internal values or standards; this is what Burns (1978) called end values. At this stage, leaders are able to take an objective view of their goals and commitments; they can operate from a personal value system that transcends their agendas and loyalties. In other words, they can operate as transformational leaders. In order to reach the transformational stage, leaders must know the limitations, the defects, and the strengths of all perspectives (Mitroff, 1978).

The hallmark of stage 4 leaders is their capacity to take a perspective on interpersonal relationships and to achieve a self-determined sense of identity. Whereas stage 3 leaders define themselves through interpersonal relationships (feel torn when conflict arises), stage 4 leaders resolve conflict based on their internal standards. Leaders at this stage of constructive/developmental maturity possess the critical requirement of acting according to end values (e.g., integrity, self-respect, equality). Because stage 4 leaders hold independent self-authored values and can carry these out despite competing loyalties while evaluating their own performance, they often can convert followers to their way of thinking and can integrate their values into the work group.

Because individuals can operate through these end values does not necessarily mean that they will always do so. Sometimes transformational leaders use transactional methods to lead, but stage 4 leaders have the ability to understand the available leadership options and to act in the manner that is most appropriate to the situation. Unless leaders have progressed to stage 4 personality structures, they will be unable to transcend the personal needs and commitments of others and they will be unable to pursue their own end values.

Transformational leaders motivate followers to accept and accomplish difficult goals that followers normally would not have pursued. Transforming leadership is made possible when leaders' end values (internal standards) are adopted by followers, thereby producing changes in the attitudes, beliefs, and goals of followers. It is end values such as integrity, honor, and justice that potentially can transform followers. Further, the commitment of followers to their leaders' values causes leadership influence to cascade through the organization (Bass, Waldman, & Avolio, 1986).

The literature on contingency theories of leadership (see Hunt, 1984, for an overview) suggests that leader personality is not nearly as important to leader effectiveness as selecting the right behavior or style for a given situation. However, Lord, DeVader, and Alliger (1986) argued that the relationship between personality and leadership is stronger and more consistent than many contemporary writers believe. A reconciliation of these competing views could come from a better understanding of differences in how individuals process information about situations. The constructive/developmental personality theory presented here, which explains both individual differences in perceptual processing and differential responsiveness to situations, may provide that understanding.

Implications

Methodological Issues

Constructive/developmental theory has been used here as a heuristic for distinguishing between transactional and transformational leadership. The success this theory has in furthering researchers' understanding of the leadership process is contingent upon accurately measuring leaders' developmental stages. Kegan (1982) described a methodology for determining adults' levels of perceptual processing in which a structured interview is used to determine how adults organize their values and how they use language to describe their level of interpersonal understanding. Although research which measures developmental stages has increased (Kegan, 1982; Lewis, Kuhnert, & Maginnis [1987]), more empirical research is needed.

Vital to transformational leadership are the articulation by the leader of end values and the acceptance of those values by followers. Since the communication of values depends upon language (e.g., Pondy, 1978), it is crucial that researchers analyze (a) how transformational leaders convey values to followers, and (b) the processes by which followers internalize their leaders' value systems. Behavioral modeling (Manz & Sims, 1986) may provide a tool for investigating the possible link between transformational leaders' conduct and their followers' actions; it also may be useful for determining the behaviors of transformational leaders.

Clearly, longitudinal research is needed. If leaders develop as the constructive/developmental perspective suggests, then a longitudinal approach is necessary to help discover/decipher the variables that influence how this leadership emerges and how it is expressed. Thus, studies are needed that span leaders' careers; at the same time, these studies should identify the ways in which experiences are reflected in changes in the leaders' cognitive organizing processes.

It is important to expand the criterion variables studied in leadership research. In past research, effective leadership has been defined too narrowly. That is, too many researchers have limited effective leadership to its impact on task performance. Although task performance is important, neglecting other variables such as group or organizational effectiveness misses the potential transforming contribution of higher stage leaders. In fact, increased focus on transactional and transformational leaders may help to identify the outcome variables that are necessary to effectively evaluate the different leadership styles.

Substantive Research Issues

Applying constructive/developmental theory to transactional and transformational leadership liberates researchers from a static view of leadership; it emphasizes leaders' development over the course of their lives. Rather than categorizing behaviors and inferring the presence of transactional or transformational leadership based on those behaviors, constructive/developmental theory focuses on changes and growth in leaders' perspective-taking abilities as the means for understanding changes in their behaviors.

According to Kegan and Lahey (1984), leaders who are at different developmental levels use different systems for construing reality (implying differences in their approach to leadership issues and problems). If it can be demonstrated that perceptual processes of leaders change over time, concomitant behavioral changes also should be explored. An important question for empirical study is "are there observable changes in leaders' behaviors as a function of their own personality development, or do changes in leaders' behaviors merely reflect changes in the leadership context?" As stated earlier, this question cannot be answered unless longitudinal investigations of leaders' cognitive processes are undertaken along with studies of the situations in which leaders' decisions are made.

If a pattern of how leaders develop can be determined reliably, the constructive/developmental framework may have implications for selecting and developing leaders. It may be possible to select individuals for particular leadership positions on the basis of their stage in the development process and the needs of the organization. That is, stage 2 leaders may work well when contingency management is needed, particularly in an organization in which goals are clearly defined and rewards are controlled by the leader (Sims, 1977). In contrast, stage 4 leaders may be necessary at upper levels of such an organization because they possess perspective-taking abilities that have not yet been attained by individuals at lower constructive/developmental levels (Jacobs & Jaques [1986]). That is, we might expect stage 4 leaders to be skilled at resolving organizational conflict because they can transcend interpersonal allegiances. Therefore, research on the degree to which organizations can manage the fit of leaders to positions is called for.

A second question of interest is "are the hypothesized stages of development invariant?" That is, do all leaders advance through the developmental stages in the same manner, or do the patterns differ for different leaders?

If leaders progress through the four stages in order, related questions would be "is it possible for all leaders to advance to the highest level of structural maturity, or are some leaders limited to lower levels? If so, by what means?" Researchers need to identify the processes by which leaders develop from one stage to another and to understand the mechanisms necessary for transition of subject (the organizing process of experience) to object (the content of experience). Such research also may help to identify the extent to which cognitive processing can be learned and, consequently, the potential effectiveness of leadership training programs.

Another focus for research is the question "what happens when leaders and followers operate at different developmental levels?" Because constructive/developmental theory is a general theory of human development (not a theory of leaders' personalities), both leaders and followers can be examined from the same theoretical perspective; it may be that developmental fit between leaders and followers explains the successes and failures of leaders. For example, it may be that leaders who function at developmental levels *beyond* the levels of their followers are better able to motivate their followers. Alternately, similarity in perceptual processing may lead to leader effectiveness. Even more intriguing is the question "can transactional leaders be effective in motivating subordinates whose organizing processes are more developed and encompassing than their own?"

This focus on the relationship between leaders and followers gives rise to still other areas for research. In particular, the distinction between transactional and transformational leaders as defined by their constructive/developmental stage may help to define a crucial determinant of the work environment. It may be that interactions between leaders and followers, as described above, influence characteristics of the work environment such as the organizational culture. Perhaps the culture of an organization is determined by the quality of co-worker interactions in organizations characterized by transactional leadership, but it may be influenced significantly by the values and standards of leaders when the dominant mode of leadership is transformational. Again, the constructive/developmental framework provides us with unique challenges for the study of leadership.

References

Avolio, B. J., & Bass, B. M. (1986) *Transformational leadership, charisma, and beyond* (Tech. Rep. No. 85-90). Binghamton: State University of New York, School of Management.

Bass, B. M. (1985) *Leadership and performance beyond expectations.* New York: Free Press.

Bass, B. M., Waldman, D. A., & Avolio, B. J. (1986) *Transformational leadership and the falling dominoes effect* (Tech. Rep. No. 86–99). Binghamton: State University of New York, School of Management.

Burns, J. M. (1978) *Leadership.* New York: Harper & Row.

Chomsky, N. (1968) *Language and mind.* New York: Harcourt, Brace & World.

Dienesch, R. M., & Liden, R. C. (1986) Leader-member exchange model of leadership: A critique and further development. *Academy of Management Review,* 11, 618–634.

Graen, G. B., Liden, R. C., & Hoel, W. (1982) The role of leadership in the employee withdrawal process. *Journal of Applied Psychology,* 67, 868–872.

House, R. J. (1977) A 1976 theory of charismatic leadership. In J. G. Hunt & L. L. Larson (Eds.), *Leadership: The cutting edge.* Carbondale: Southern Illinois University Press.

Hunt, J. G. (1984) Organizational leadership: The contingency paradigm and its challenges. In B. Kellerman (Ed.), *Leadership: Multidisciplinary perspectives* (pp. 113–138). Englewood Cliffs, NJ: Prentice-Hall.

Jacobs, T.O., & Jaques, E. [1986] Leadership in complex systems. In J. A. Zeidner (Ed.), *Human productivity enhancement, Volume II: Organizations, personnel, and decision making.* New York: Praeger.

Kegan, R. (1982) *The evolving self: Problem and process in human development.* Cambridge, MA: Harvard University Press.

Kegan, R., & Lahey, L. L. (1984) Adult leadership and adult development: A constructivist view. In B. Kellerman (Ed.), *Leadership: Multidisciplinary perspectives* (pp. 200–230). Englewood Cliffs, NJ: Prentice-Hall.

Kellerman, B. (1984) *Leadership: Multidisciplinary perspectives.* Englewood Cliffs, NJ: Prentice-Hall.

Landy, F. L. (1985) *Psychology of work behavior.* Homewood, IL: Dorsey Press.

Lewis, P., Kuhnert, K. W., & Maginnis, R. [1987] Defining military character: A new perspective. *Parameters: Journal of the U.S. Army War College.*

Lord, R. G., DeVader, C. L., & Alliger, G. M. (1986) A meta-analysis of the relation between personality traits and leadership: An application of validity generalization procedures. *Journal of Applied Psychology,* 71, 402–410.

Manz, C. C., & Sims, H. P., Jr. (1986) Beyond imitation: Complex behavioral and affective linkages resulting from exposure to leadership training models. *Journal of Applied Psychology,* 71, 571–578.

Mitroff, I. (1978) Systemic problem solving. In M. W. McCall & M. M. Lombardo (Eds.), *Where else can we go?* (pp. 129–143). Durham, NC: Duke University Press.

Piaget, J. (1954) *The construction of reality in the child.* New York: Basic Books (first published in 1939).

Pondy, L. R. (1978) Leadership is a language game. In M. W. McCall & M. M. Lombardo (Eds.), *Where else can we go?* (pp. 87–99). Durham, NC: Duke University Press.

Selman, R. (1980) *The growth of interpersonal understanding: Developmental and clinical analyses.* New York: Academic Press.

Sims, H. P. (1977) The leader as manager of reinforcement contingencies: an empirical example and a model. In J. G. Hunt & L. L. Larson (Eds.), *Leadership: The cutting edge* (pp. 121–137). Carbondale: Southern Illinois University Press.

Weber, M. (1947) *Theory of social and economic organization* (T. Parsons & A. M. Henderson, Trans.). New York: Oxford University Press.

Yukl, G. A. (1981) *Leadership in organizations.* Englewood Cliffs, NJ: Prentice-Hall.

PART FOUR

VISION: A FOCUS ON THE FUTURE

Contemporary writers regard vision, power, self-confidence, tenacity, intuition, and even humor as necessary for strong leadership. Our need to understand the leadership process becomes more urgent as the world changes at a frenetic pace and rational systems of logic no longer prevail. People are overloaded with data yet starved for timely and meaningful information. The challenge for leaders is to "know." Somehow they must seek out from all of the data those pieces that make the most sense in terms of their vision. The increasing complexity of our world calls for the leaders of tomorrow to have a clear sense of purpose and direction.

Vision is the ability to create a mental image of the possible and to identify a desirable future state of affairs. It is intuitive and often appears to be irrational. Furthermore, it is not a serendipitous phenomenon but a cumulative force that sets leaders apart from others. However, vision alone is not sufficient; leaders must have a strong sense of purpose. In addition, leaders must build cohesiveness and commitment by sharing their ideals and visions. It takes courage and inspiration to create a shared vision, but even more to persevere when the vision is not transformed into reality as quickly as others would like.

Visionary leadership is a term that has crept into our vocabulary in recent years. We know it under the more traditional rubric of "organizational culture," meaning what people feel about themselves and their group or organization. The leader's task is to create the vision in such a way that all believe it to be their own. This concept is important because successful leadership in today's environment comes from the strength of those who seek a common goal.

Power, which will always be an element of leadership, will be shared in the future. Because of the difficulties that face us, it is less likely that a single individual will be able to bring to bear all of the resources necessary for effective leadership. Although there will always be a central figure, the necessary power will be dispersed, and the ownership of ideas will be widely shared. No longer will others in the group or organization be followers. Everyone will participate in the leadership process through networks and consensus. Leadership will be more collective than ever before. And in this sense, our notion of "co-creating" the vision is more realistic.

Nonetheless, we will always find the stimulus for change in an individual or a small group within the larger one. Adapting to the environment means that groups and organizations are constantly altering their paths and perspectives as they seek to achieve a desired state of affairs. Coping with this change means constant readjustment, and individuals who can anticipate the necessary changes, propose outcomes, and help us to actively pursue our dreams will be those ultimately held accountable as leaders.

Leadership Perspectives

In Part 4, we conclude this study of leadership with some provocative perspectives about the visioning process. Our intent is to give examples of successful leaders who started out with dreams and turned them into realities. In each case, an individual energized a group to perform specific actions that resulted in significant change. The cause went beyond the leader, but it is the initial process that is best remembered—this phenomenon we call leadership.

In Chapter 17, "Absentee Charismatic Leadership: Khomeini, Gandhi, and Mandela," William Rosenbach and Sharon Hayman explore how these men changed the societies in which they lived in very different and profound ways. In each case, the leader envisioned a desired state of affairs and communicated that vision to those affected. Effective communication was key to the success of these leaders—the physical being was absent, but the magic of language convincingly conveyed the ideas.

Marshall Sashkin, in "Visionary Leadership: A Perspective from Education" (Chapter 18), explores leadership as it relates to the field of education. In a pragmatic fashion, Sashkin shows how the vision influences organizational culture. Once again, the focus is on change; however, his contribution provides some practical approaches for those who want to better understand the leadership process.

Communication is the theme of Chapter 19, "The Language of Leadership." Charles Handy offers a perspective of how we view leadership today. At the same time, he provides insights into the future of collective leadership. He presents some interesting concepts about dealing with groups and organizations that may provide aspiring leaders with important insights into how they can effect significant change.

The final chapter concludes our study with one of the most compelling visions of our time, Martin Luther King, Jr.'s, "I Have a Dream." There is no finer modern example of vision and how it can be communicated. The message, although associated with Dr. King, is one that has captured individuals and societies regardless of race, color, or creed. It is clear that these simple, yet eloquent, words triggered many changes in society, organizations, and individuals.

With this, we conclude our view of the contemporary issues in leadership and our discussion of personality, style, and values. As long as there are people who dream, leaders will capture those dreams and empower others to transform them into reality so that we continue to achieve our potential.

Absentee Charismatic Leadership: Khomeini, Gandhi, and Mandela

WILLIAM E. ROSENBACH

SHARON HAYMAN

Charisma is both powerful and mysterious. In fact, the dictionary defines it as an extraordinary gift from God or a personal magic of leadership—a form of personal power. Max Weber defined charisma in both psychological and sociological terms as a quality of an individual's personality by virtue of which he or she is set apart from ordinary people and treated as endowed with supernatural, superhuman, or at least specifically exceptional, powers or qualities. Weber viewed charisma as a form of authority or influence dependent upon the recognition of a group and its validity of revelation, hero worship, and absolute trust in the charismatic leader (Weber 1922). House (1977) described charismatic leaders as having high self-confidence, a strong conviction in their own beliefs and ideals, and a strong need to influence people (need for power).

Charismatic leaders effectively articulate ideological goals for their followers. They relate the mission of the group to deeply rooted values, ideals, and aspirations shared by the followers. In addition, charismatic leaders use role modeling; they set an example by their own behavior. Furthermore, they are likely to communicate high expectations and simultaneously express confidence in their followers. Charisma, then, results from behaviors that leaders engage in to communicate their visions.

Although there is an increasing amount of interest in and study of charismatic leadership, relatively little is known about a somewhat unusual form of charismatic leadership—absentee leadership. There is no formal definition of absentee leadership, but in general terms it is the process through which a person has unusual influence with a population or mass of people despite that person's absence from their everyday lives. Even if the leader is imprisoned or exiled, the leader's presence can be felt.

This chapter examines the lives of three charismatic leaders in an attempt to learn more about absentee leadership. Mahatma Gandhi, Ayatollah Ruhollah Khomeini, and Nelson Mandela are leaders whose missions involved revolutionary change in their countries. All three of these leaders have described their leadership role as one that requires

- the leader to be the most important articulator of his own ideology,
- conviction that these ideals must be shared by his followers,
- that these ideals be promoted by a mass movement that aims at the breakdown of the old order, and
- an effective and rational organization to bring about the final collapse of the obsolete order.

All three men met these objectives, although their motives and situations were very different. We will examine each man's achievements in the context of their leadership styles.

The Ayatollah Khomeini

Ayatollah Khomeini is a controversial figure in the United States because of the powerful revolt he led against the former Shah of Iran and his role in allowing the seizure of hostages from the American Embassy. Khomeini, however, exemplifies absentee leadership. His first conflict with the Iranian government occurred in 1962 over the local council law. Khomeini and other religious leaders opposed the law because it allowed women to vote; it did not require adherence to Islam as a necessary qualification for either voters or candidates; and it specified that elected councillors would not take their oath of office on the Koran but on "the holy book." After that law passed in 1963, another law on land reform was passed causing Khomeini to begin to question the government. He started by organizing protests within seminaries; the government retaliated by attacking students at the Faiziyyeh seminary. Khomeini then accused the shah of crushing the nation and personally attempting to take over the economy, commerce, and agriculture. Within days after his speech, Khomeini was placed in jail for ten months. When the country first heard of his imprisonment, violent demonstrations resulted. Many people tried to release him from jail, giving an early indication of Khomeini's growing following.

In April 1964, Khomeini was released. Soon after, he gave three speeches describing the shah as a lackey of foreign powers and proclaimed his determination to continue to resist the shah and his government. Finally, after distributing a leaflet demanding that the people bring down the shah's government, Khomeini was arrested and exiled.

Khomeini began his exile in Turkey and after a year moved to Najaf, Iraq, where his absentee leadership began. Within weeks of his banishment, tapes of his declarations were smuggled from Turkey into Iran, which kept Khomeini and his ideals before the people. Many of the tapes urged his followers to deny the existing government and its institutional legitimacy by refusing recognition and by directing their loyalty to other Islamic institutions. He not only recorded tapes, he also wrote appeals such as, "We have no choice but to shun wicked governments, governments that give rise to wickedness, and to overthrow governors who are traitorous, wicked, cruel and tyrannical" (Heikal 1981, p. 39). While working to gain and keep the support of his followers inside Iran, Khomeini also took advantage of his exile to try to win attention from those people who opposed the shah outside of Iran.

He accomplished these ends through an extensive network. Khomeini's network consisted of three basic groups. One group maintained a moderate position; the second encouraged people to protest (some were sentenced to jail, and others to internal exile); the members of the third group plotted assassinations (many were executed). Because he was a religious figure, this network included the 80,000–90,000 mosques within Iran and their 180,000–200,000 clerics. The clerics not only provided communications with his people but also helped organize many demonstrations to control the masses. For instance, when the shah set a curfew on a religious holiday, Khomeini urged his followers to defy the curfew— almost immediately, thousands filled the streets. Unfortunately, police opened fire on the crowds, and many people died. Khomeini responded,

> Do not attack the army in its breast, but in its heart. You must appeal to the soldiers' hearts even if they fire on you and kill you. Let them kill five thousand, ten thousand, twenty thousand—they are our brothers and we will welcome them. We will prove that blood is more powerful than the sword. (Heikal 1981, p. 167)

This quote, like his other speeches and writing, illustrates the power Khomeini had over people who had not seen him for years and his incredible ability to communicate his vision to his followers.

Khomeini's abilities to network, communicate, and achieve his goals while absent from his country are examples of his effective absentee and charismatic revolutionary leadership.

Mahatma Gandhi

Mahatma Gandhi was one of the most powerful leaders the world has known. W. W. Pearson described him: "small dark eyes, a small frail man, with a thin face and rather large protuding eyes, his head covered with a little white cap, his body clothed in a coarse white cloth, barefooted" (Rolland 1924, p. 3). This description does not seem as if it could apply to the man who freed India from Britain's grasp.

Gandhi grew up in India, and at 19 he went to London to study law. He returned to India, but later received an assignment in South Africa where he started a law practice. His compassionate nature contributed to his success as a lawyer and led him to become involved in politics. During his time in South Africa, Gandhi's life was transformed both in terms of his style of living as well as his acquisition of new values. These new values were developed in the process of leading the Indian people of South Africa to a less oppressed life. The government passed a law that required all Indians to register and have their fingerprints recorded. Gandhi instructed the people to picket the registration offices, be nonviolent, and cheerfully submit to arrest.

For this, Gandhi and some of his followers spent two months in jail. Once released, still determined not to submit, Gandhi started a huge bonfire in which everyone burned their registration cards. As a result of this act, Gandhi was again jailed, this time to serve hard labor. While in jail, he boosted the morale of the prisoners, and "his personality developed and took on that steely strength which was to become a powerful force in years to come" (Nanda 1965, p. 53). Finally, Gandhi's long-time friend and mentor, Gokhale, came to tour South Africa. Gokhale had great influence in Africa, and when he left he believed that the government was going to improve the conditions of the Indians. Nothing changed, however, but his visit added force to the momentum for change.

Gandhi's final effort began when groups of Indian miners attempted to cross into other areas without their registration cards. The first group was arrested, but the second group was successful, thus convincing the Indian miners to go on strike. As the miners and Gandhi's people walked back to Gandhi's farm, which he had founded to support the satyagraha (firmness in truth) nonviolence movement, the miners were arrested. As part of their sentence they were forced to go back to work. When word reached the other Indians, they went on strike and forced the government to meet their demands. Gandhi had accomplished his goals with little or no violence and was ready to return home to India.

When Gandhi returned to India he was well known for his activities in South Africa. Gokhale had written that Gandhi "is without doubt made of the stuff of which heroes and martyrs are made. Nay, more, he has in him the marvellous spiritual power to turn ordinary men around him into heroes and martyrs" (Nanda 1965, p. 83). Despite this, Gokhale believed that before Gandhi assumed a leadership role in India's politics he should be silent for one year until he was fully aware of the situation. Gokhale did offer Gandhi the opportunity to join the Servants of India Society of which he was president, but before Gandhi could become a member Gokhale died.

After a year's wait Gandhi could not resist becoming involved in politics because "his capability for leadership, for identification with the masses and for personal sacrifice was extraordinary" (Buultjens 1983, p. 277). His first opportunity came in 1918 when the government tried to pass the Rowlatt Bills that were

> aimed to establish definitely the provisions of the Defense Act imposed on India during the War, and made secret police services, censorship, and all the tyrannical annoyances of a real state of seige into permanent reality. There was one burst of indignation all over India. The revolt began. Gandhi led it. (Rolland 1924, p. 28)

In February 1919, Gandhi began his movement based upon the important principles of love and nonviolence because "their appeal transcends cultural and national differences" (Buultjens 1983, p. 275). April 6 was set aside as a day of prayer and fasting to begin the peaceful protests, which, tragically, were anything but peaceful. The police opened fire on the mass of people, killing five to six hundred of them. At this point, Gandhi courageously attempted to keep his followers from turning to violence. During this episode he demonstrated his power as a leader through his own sacrifices and his ability to control crowds. Early in 1922 he began to feel that the country was not ready for his nonviolent tactics, so he terminated civil disobedience. However, the government still viewed him as a threat and arrested him on March 22, 1922. Gandhi told his outraged followers,

> I desire that the people should maintain perfect self-control and consider the day of my arrest a day of rejoicing. The government believes that I am the soul of all this agitation and that if I am removed it will be left in peace. (Rolland 1924, p. 28)

Thus he provided direction to his followers before physically leaving them. He pleaded guilty to the charge of openly assembling to overthrow the government and was sentenced to six years' imprisonment.

While Gandhi was in jail, violence erupted. The government wanted him to speak to the people, but he refused because he had not been given a hearing. This situation prompted his famous 21-day fast. His followers became concerned about him and continued to protest. As a result, the government permitted the crowds to pass through the jail to see the Mahatma for themselves. Finally he was released. Although violence was still rampant throughout the country, he took time to rest and stayed out of politics for a while. In an attempt to still the violence, Gandhi decided to walk through the troubled areas and, wherever he went, the violence stopped and peace was restored. One area was an exception, so he vowed to fast until everyone stopped fighting; the rioters stopped to pray for Gandhi's life. These two instances demonstrate the power of his charisma and presence. However, the violence soon rekindled, and Gandhi felt he had lost his influence. He was assassinated soon after; yet, through his death, his power was restored, bonding everyone together in peace.

Gandhi was an extraordinary leader who not only possessed the typical charismatic characteristics but was also willing to make personal sacrifices and model high standards for his followers. Gandhi's success as a leader was a result of his capacity to act bravely, to inspire people, and to instill in them a new sense of their own capacities. He also had great organizational ability and paid attention to detail. His dominant charismatic characteristic was his ability to speak and move a crowd to incredible action. Gandhi said, "My speeches are intended to create 'disaffection' as such, that people might consider it a shame to assist or cooperate with a government that had forfeited all title to respect or support" (Sharp 1979, p. 53). Gokhale, Gandhi's mentor, patiently taught and developed these attributes in Gandhi and helped Gandhi win respect for his principles within his own country, where such behavior was not valued.

Nelson Mandela

Nelson Mandela, considered the most potent symbol of South Africa's long black liberation struggle, has been imprisoned since July 11, 1962. It seems incredible that he could still have such influence and power after 26 years in prison, especially considering that for the past two decades it has been a crime in South Africa to print anything that the African National Congress leader has said or written. Mandela's charismatic absentee leadership, however, has been powerful enough to survive.

Mandela has been interested in politics and law since his youth. After his father died, Mandela became a ward of David Dalindyebo, who provided him with a proper education because, even then, he demonstrated unusual leadership potential. In 1936, at the time Mandela was attending college, pass laws and segregation bills were enacted that severely restricted black movement. When the authority of the student government was reduced, he protested along with others and was suspended from college. When his guardian told Mandela to return and obey college rules, he declined. Adding to his unrest was the discovery that a marriage had been arranged for him. He fled to Johannesburg to escape.

He arrived in Johannesburg at age 22 and met Walter Sisulu, who arranged for Mandela to attend law school. Johannesburg is where, with the help of Sisulu, Nelson Mandela became the leader of the oppressed nonwhites of South Africa. It was there that Mandela, who had never experienced oppression, was able to learn firsthand how the blacks were treated by the white government. Mandela joined the African National Congress and was soon elected the general secretary. The Afrikaner Nationalist government came to power in 1948, bringing apartheid laws, which caused protests to break out. During 1952, the Defiance Campaign began with Nelson Mandela as volunteer-in-chief. This campaign resulted in

> a great surge of protest against many of the unjust laws. In disciplined groups men and women all over the country went through "EUROPEAN ONLY" entrances to railway stations and post offices; Africans broke curfew laws, which applied only to them; a number of whites joined Indians illegally entering African townships. In all, 8,500 went to jail until government legislation halted the campaign. (Mandela 1978, p. 2)

The fact that Mandela was able to create such massive demonstrations testifies to the effect his leadership had on people early in the fight for freedom. Mandela did not ask any more of his followers than he expected from himself. He was arrested with many of his followers, but Mandela was given a suspended sentence.

The African National Congress elected Nelson Mandela as its president, demonstrating the trust and loyalty the members had for him as their leader. His role, however, was severely restricted when the government issued a banning order that confined him to a small section of the country. During this time, Mandela said, "I found myself restricted and isolated from my fellow men, trailed by officers of the Special Branch wherever I went. . . . I was made, by the law, a criminal, not because of what I had done, but because of what I stood for" (Mandela 1986, p. 3). The restrictions, however, did not stop his messages from getting to the people. At various conventions and meetings, his followers delivered speeches that he wrote. On March 21, 1960, a crowd protesting the pass laws was fired upon by police and 69 protestors died. Mass riots erupted, and more protestors were killed. The government used this incident as justification to arrest and imprison anyone; naturally, Mandela was one of the 20,000 arrested. Later Mandela was released, and his banning orders were not renewed, allowing him to go where he wanted for the first time in years. The government, however, had outlawed the African National Congress. At the All-in-African Conference, Mandela unexpectedly appeared and delivered the keynote address, which had and electric effect on the delegates. Inspired by his strength and courage, the people elected him to lead their protest and their demand for a truly representative National Convention to establish, not a white republic, but a new union of all South Africans.

The government responded by arresting masses of people. Mandela went underground. He had to assume disguises, travel about the country secretly, and find places to live that were not likely to be under surveillance. Many problems resulted when Mandela went underground—the largest was communication with his followers. Mandela, however, learned when and how to surface to lead and advise his people and then to disappear again; he was extremely careful not to put others at risk when he appeared. Sisulu, once again, helped him as he had many times previously. From the underground, Mandela was able to arrange press conferences and demonstrations; he distributed leaflets stressing that the protest must go on despite recent governmental arrests. "I shall fight the government side by side with you until victory is won," he promised his people (Benson 1986, p. 99). While Mandela was underground he had to make one of his most difficult decisions—because nonviolence was not affecting the government's policies he decided that the movement would turn to violence. During October 1961, Mandela rejoined his family and worked out the details of a new campaign with his advisers and followers. They decided that sabotage was the best policy because it did not cause the loss of life. Mandela was smuggled out of the country to attend conferences, gain support for the movement from the outside, and study military action. Mandela returned to South Africa and after reporting on his travels was suddenly arrested and brought to trial.

During his trial Mandela spoke about unfair and violent treatment by the government and stressed that one day the oppressed people would be freed and the government would then go on trial. He was sentenced to five years' hard labor and was ushered to prison amidst chants of "Amandla Ngawethu!" (Power to the people!). Within the next year the government passed a 90-day law that allowed detention without trial, solitary confinement, and people to be held incommunicado for periods of up to 90 days. Some of the people arrested broke under interrogation, incriminating some of the underground's leaders, including Mandela. The Rivonia trial, as it was called, resulted in Mandela being released from the prison term he was serving to stand trial for sabotage. Mandela's appearance at the trial shocked everyone; he had lost 40 pounds, and his face was a sickly color. Although, during the trial, many false statements were made solid evidence was also produced. Mandela took the stand for one last speech. He spoke of the reasons for choosing sabotage, how violent the government had become, even with the nonviolent protest, and finally stated:

> During my lifetime I have dedicated myself to this struggle of the African people. I have fought against white domination, and I have fought against black domination. I have cherished the ideal of a democratic and free society in which all persons live together in harmony and with equal opportunities. It is an ideal which I hope to live for and to achieve. But if need be it is an ideal for which I am prepared to die. (Benson 1986, p. 159)

This was the last time most people saw Mandela, for he was then sentenced to life imprisonment. The people, however, still heard from their beloved absentee leader. Various speeches and messages were smuggled out of jail to continue support for his vision of black freedom. Others have now taken over to continue the struggle, but there is no doubt that if Mandela were released, he would become the visible leader once again. Most of his continued influence comes from the power of his charisma and the loyal followers and strong policies he developed before he was imprisoned. Mandela, symbol of his nation's freedom, effectively led and organized people even through the difficult period. His journey outside the country demonstrated his vision of the future of his people; he realized that outside influences would be needed to secure that future. All the qualities of a charismatic leader are demonstrated in Nelson Mandela, notwithstanding his absence from his followers.

Dimensions of Absentee Leadership

The similarities and differences of these three leaders can be examined in Table 1. First, 4 of the 11 characteristics of charismatic revolutionary leadership can be attributed to all three leaders. Khomeini, Gandhi, and Mandela all had the ability to communicate their ideology and visions effectively. This was demonstrated frequently by each of the leaders.

Next, because of the leaders' superb ability to articulate their vision, followers were committed to and shared their convictions and ideas. The ability to break down an old form of government especially applies to Khomeini, who succeeded in overthrowing the shah. Ghandi led his people to freedom from oppression, and Mandela has the potential for accomplishing the same. Khomeini had an organized group ready to take control over the government, and it appears Mandela will also, if

TABLE 1
Comparison of Leadership Characteristics

Characteristic	Khomeini	Gandhi	Mandela
Charismatic Leadership			
Did not possess or claim any unusual characteristics	No	Yes	Yes
Communicated ideas and values	Yes	Yes	Yes
Convictions shared by followers	Yes	Yes	Yes
Promoted mass movement with breakdown of old government or order	Yes	Yes	Yes
Organized group to effectively control new order	Yes	Yes	Yes
Helped by a mentor	No	Yes	Yes
Developed an effective network	Yes	Yes	Yes
Able to choose successor	Yes	Yes	N/A
Ability to communicate while in exile/prison	Yes	Yes	Yes
Able to influence country without being present	Yes	Yes	Yes
Joined followers and did not expect anything of them he would not do himself	Yes	Yes	Yes
Political Leadership			
Practiced nonviolence	No	Yes	Yes
Involved strongly in religion	Yes	Yes	No
Fought against racial oppression	No	Yes	Yes
Fought against religious oppression	Yes	No	No

he succeeds in his attempts at governmental reform. Gandhi had problems in organizing a group to control the new order but eventually was successful.

The only difference between the three leaders is the characteristic of claims to be godlike. Khomeini fits that description because "he regards himself as the supreme figure of the Islamic revolution, to whom obedience and devotion naturally flow because of his religious qualities" (Stempel 1981, p. 47). However, Gandhi and Mandela both stressed to their followers that there was nothing godlike about them.

All three leaders were similar in terms of two absentee characteristics. However, the ability to communicate while in prison or in exile was demonstrated by each of them in different ways. Khomeini used his network to smuggle tapes and written documents into Iran. He also used the press in Paris to his advantage to get his messages into Iran. Gandhi communicated through letters and his famous fast that focused worldwide attention on him during his prison term. Mandela has had more difficulty in his attempts to smuggle instructions and speeches out of jail because there has been a ban on talking, printing, or even referring to him in public. All three leaders remained influential even during their exile or imprisonment because of their inspiring communication skills, the commitment of their followers, and a belief in a common vision. Neither Khomeini, Gandhi, nor Mandela ever asked their followers to do anything they would not do themselves. They were jailed or exiled, primarily, because they were doing what they had instructed their followers to do. When Gandhi asked his people to fast, he often did it for a longer period than he asked of them. He also employed role modeling by being cheerful when he was led off to prison.

Other qualities that allow a person to be a more effective leader are the presence of a mentor, development of a network, and the ability to chose a successor. Gandhi was the only one of the three that had a formal mentor relationship. Gokhale helped Gandhi direct his career—first in South Africa, then back in India. Gokhale also informed people about Gandhi's unusual leadership ability and advised Gandhi to wait a year before becoming involved in India's politics after his return so that he could learn the political climate. Mandela had an informal mentor relationship with Sisulu who helped him get into law school and the African National Congress and also aided him a great deal when he was underground. All three leaders developed extensive networks. Khomeini started out with a natural network of mosques and clerics that he gradually improved upon. Mandela's network, which included the underground, was amazingly effective in its accomplishments, especially while he was underground. Both Khomeini and Gandhi were able to designate successors, whereas Mandela is still capable of accomplishing the leadership role himself. Khomeini is said to be preparing his son to assume his leadership role. And Gandhi chose Nehru, his protégé, as his successor.

The most striking differences between the three leaders are their political beliefs, particularly concerning nonviolence. Gandhi was totally committed to nonviolence throughout his lifetime; Mandela embraced the concept of nonviolence until it became ineffective. However, even when Mandela abandoned his nonviolent strategy, his followers turned to sabotage as an alternative because of their belief that it would not result in death. Khomeini, on the other hand, was committed to overthrow the shah at all costs, no matter how many lives were lost. When returned to power in Iran, Khomeini is said to have executed many of those who opposed him. Deep religious convictions motivated both Gandhi and Khomeini's visions. Khomeini fought for religious reasons. Gandhi and Mandela protested racial oppression.

These three—Khomeini, Gandhi, and Mandela—are examples of successful absentee leaders. Throughout their lives, they have been able to influence people through the power of their charisma and vision, to create dreams, and lead people in achieving those dreams. The overwhelming power of their charismatic leadership has allowed them to overcome tremendous obstacles and to empower their followers to translate their visions into realities even in their absence.

References

Bakkash, Shaul. *The Reign of the Ayatollahs.* Basic Books. New York, 1984.

Benson, Mary. *Nelson Mandela.* W. W. Norton and Co. New York, 1986.

Brotz, Howard. "Bring ANC Out of the Closet." *Wall Street Journal,* August 26, 1986.

Brown, Judith M. *Gandhi's Rise to Power.* Cambridge Press. New York, 1972.

Buultjens, Ralph. "Another Side of Gandhi. *America,* April 9, 1983, pp. 274–278.

Cobb, David. "A Champion Behind Bars." *Macleans,* May 14, 1984, p. 5.

Doob, Leonard W. *Personality, Power and Authority.* Greenwood Press. Connecticut, 1983.

Heikal, Mohamed. *The Return of the Ayatollah.* Andre Deutsch. London, 1981.

House, R. J. "1976 Theory of Charismatic Leadership." In J. G. Hunt and L. L. Largon (eds.). *Leadership: The Cutting Edge.* Southern Illinois University Press. Carbondale, 1977.

Mandela, Nelson. *The Struggle Is My Life.* International Defence and Aid Fund for Southern Africa. London, 1978.

Nanda, B. R. *Mahatma Gandhi.* George Allen and Unwin Ltd. London, 1965.

"Pinning Blame in South Africa." *New York Times,* July 7, 1985, p. 2E.

Rolland, Roman. *Mahatma Gandhi.* The Century Company. New York, 1924.

Sampson, Anthony. "The Invisible Leader." *Newsweek,* September 9, 1985, p. 32.

Schweitzer, Arthur. *The Age of Charisma.* Nelson-Hall. Chicago, 1984.

Sharp, Gene. *Gandhi as a Political Strategist.* Porter Sargent Publishers, Inc. Boston, 1979.

Sheean, Vincent. *Mahatma Gandhi.* Alfred A. Knopf. New York, 1970.

Stempel, John D. *Inside the Iranian Revolution.* Indiana University Press. Bloomington, 1981.

Weber, Max. *On Charisma and Institution Building.* S. N. Eisenstadt (ed.). Chicago University Press. Chicago, 1922.

18

Visionary Leadership: A Perspective from Education

MARSHALL SASHKIN

To some, history is the story of great leaders. Throughout the first half of this century, most managers and scholars probably accepted the basic premises of the "great person" theory of leadership. But, by the late 1940s, studies at Harvard, in human relations and group dynamics, had shown that only a small proportion of leaders actually fit this theory. Subsequent theories of leadership centered on behavior; perhaps if one were to act like a great leader, the act would become real. As we began to understand how leaders behaved, perhaps it was reasonable to train people to act that way.

But the next 30 years of research failed to yield substantial evidence that leaders who behaved in a task-directed manner, while simultaneously behaving in a relationship-directed manner, were especially successful or "great." Thus, researchers turned to situational factors in the hope of finding that different behavioral approaches would be effective for different situations. Although these situational or "continuing" approaches were somewhat more successful in helping to guide managers, they did little to improve our understanding of top-level, creative leadership. Researchers were still at a loss to explain outstanding leadership at the top—leadership characterized by vision.

My theory of effective executive leadership, or visionary leadership, considers not only the leader's personal characteristics, not only the leader's behavior, and not only the situation; it considers all three. Only by looking at each of these factors as they relate to one another can we truly understand visionary leadership. Visionary leaders share certain

The views expressed are those of the author and do not necessarily represent the position or policies of the Office of Educational Research and Improvement or the United States Department of Education.

222

characteristics that are different from the personality traits on which early leadership research was focused. In addition, they have a deep, basic awareness of key situational factors that dictate what leadership approach and actions are required. Furthermore, these leaders not only know what behaviors are required, they can also carry out those behaviors.

Visionary Leadership in Action

There are three major aspects to visionary leadership. The first consists of constructing a vision, creating an ideal image of the organization and its culture. The second involves defining an organizational philosophy that succinctly states the vision and developing programs and policies that put the philosophy into practice within the organization's unique context and culture. The third aspect centers on the leaders' own practices, the specific actions in which leaders engage on a one-to-one basis in order to create and support their visions.

Visioning: Creating a Cultural Ideal. The process of conceiving a vision calls for certain cognitive skills. Central to the ability to conceive a vision is the ability to think in terms of a period of time, that is, not just in terms of daily or weekly goals but in terms of actions carried out over a period of years. Elliott Jaques (1979) has shown that there are reliable differences among individuals in terms of the span of time over which they think and work. Effective executive leaders must, according to Jaques, be able to think clearly, to "vision," over periods of at least 5 years and, more often, 10 years or longer. In more recent work, Jaques (1986) has constructed a theory of cognitive development, based on Piagetian concepts, specifying in detail the series of hierarchical cognitive tasks required to construct visions over increasingly long spans of time. But whether one is involved in creating a 10-year or 10-week vision, the ability to do so involves four distinct actions, each requiring certain thinking skills.

The first such cognitive skill is in *expressing* the vision—behaving in a way that advances the goal of the vision. Consider the case of a manufacturer's chief executive who wishes to create a plant-level operation to involve all employees in managing the firm. To make this vision real, the CEO must be able to perform these steps:

- write a proposed set of policy actions that would create a plant-level worker involvement program;
- meet with relevant parties—plant-level managers as well as workers—to develop a document detailing the new policy and program;

- meet with, and arrange meetings of, all plant-level managers and all employees to review and revise the program and to plan for its implementation;
- work with relevant managers to identify ways to track the program's effects and effectiveness; and
- oversee the monitoring of the program and work with relevant parties on any further modifications needed.

Leaders must understand and express by their behavior the sequence of actions to be taken to make a vision real.

The second important thinking skill is *explaining* the vision to others—making the nature of the vision clear in terms of its required action steps and its aims. Let us return to the example of the CEO who envisions worker involvement at the plant level. The CEO who can express this vision still may not succeed in implementing it unless he or she can clearly explain to others the steps involved in carrying it out. Unless the CEO can clearly explain the vision to the program manager, uncertainty will arise as to the steps and handling of problems and issues. And unless the CEO can explain the program to plant managers, their support for the vision will fade as the CEO loses touch with the day-to-day program details (as is inevitable for any chief executive). Explaining involves more than mere restatement of the vision's nature or aim. The visionary leader must be able to describe how the actions required for the vision link together until, step by step, the goal is reached.

The third required thinking skill is *extending* the vision—applying the sequence of activities to a variety of situations so that the vision can be implemented in several ways and places. To continue with the above example, the CEO will probably, at some point, wish to extend the vision to other parts of the organization. This might mean working with the program manager to revise the worker involvement plan and apply it to the headquarters staff departments as well as to the plant. Doing so will call for changes in how the program is implemented and may even require alterations in the worker involvement program itself. The expressed vision is an important frame of reference, but the visionary leader must be able to adapt it to varied circumstances, as required. Again, he or she must be able to explain these changes to others and to demonstrate the steps necessary to carry them out.

The fourth thinking skill involves *expanding* the vision—applying it not just in one limited way, and not even in a variety of similar ways, but in many different ways and in a broad range of circumstances. The CEO who has a vision of worker involvement at the operating level, and who goes about implementing this vision in the manner outlined above, still may not be a visionary leader. The true visionary leader will also have the conceptual skill needed to look at the overall plan and effects of worker involvement in the organization. This means more than extending the program to another unit. The visionary leader will think through the effects of the worker involvement vision throughout the organization, consider different ways the program might be spread (for example, unit by unit, or by divisions), and speculate about how to "revise" the entire organization in consistence with the new employee involvement system.

Just about anyone can carry out the four skills of visioning—expressing, explaining, extending, and expanding—with respect to short-range visions—those implemented in a day, a week, or a month. Many individuals can do this over time spans as long as a year. Few people, however, can do so over periods of 1 to 3 years, and fewer still can vision over periods of 5 to 10 years. The person who can think through a vision over a time span of 10 to 20 years is the rare, visionary leader.

In addition to these thinking skills, visionary leaders must also possess the personal conviction that what they do can make a difference. Without this belief these actions would be no more than "going through the motions." Nor will their efforts suffice or their visions endure unless those visionary leaders desire and can use power and influence in positive ways, so that followers are "empowered" to carry out the leaders' visions (Burke 1986; McClelland and Burnham 1976).

 Implementing the Vision Organizationally. Elsewhere I have detailed the process by which visionary leaders turn their cultural ideals into organizational realities (Sashkin 1985, 1988). The most important part of this process is creating an explicit organizational philosophy and then enacting that philosophy by means of specific policies and programs. The specific statement of the philosophy is best developed by the leader and his or her key subordinates. In this manner, the visionary leader begins the process of implementing the vision with a strong base of support from the key actors in the system. The statement of philosophy must then be put into practice by means of actual, operational policies and programs. That is, the philosophy must be articulated through action, not just words. Deal (1987) offered some insight as to how this process of articulating the vision takes place. He spoke of identifying heroes, of creating rituals and ceremonies, and of telling stories that support and strengthen the philosophy—and the values behind it—and that make more visible the policies and programs derived from the philosophy. Deal also noted that this process is best accomplished if the visionary leader can identify an "informal network of cultural players"—informal advisers (or even just gossips) and secretaries, for example—who, in effect, preside over the organization's culture, serve as key links to the community, and are keepers of the organization's history. These are the keys to organizational implementation of the leader's vision.

Implementing the Vision Through Personal Practices. Finally, effective visionary leaders put their visions into practice by means of their own specific interpersonal behaviors on a one-to-one basis. Warren Bennis (1984; Bennis and Nanus 1985) studied 90 exceptionally effective CEOs and identified several sets of characteristics common to many of these visionary leaders. Based on this work I defined five specific behavior categories (Sashkin 1984, 1988; Sashkin and Fulmer 1985, 1987). These behaviors have since proven to be strongly associated with organizational performance (Major 1988).

The first category of behavior consists of focusing others' attention on key issues—helping people grasp, understand, and become committed to the leader's vision. A second group of behaviors is centered on effective communication: listening for understanding, rephrasing to clarify, giving constructive feedback (e.g., being descriptive and not evaluative, being specific and not general), and summarizing when appropriate. These behaviors are easy to describe, but they take tremendous skill to perform.

The third behavior category concerns consistency and trustworthiness. Bennis found that outstanding CEOs exhibited consistent behavior. They did not ever flip-flop on their positions; it was always clear where they stood on issues. People might not agree with the leader, but they could trust that what the leader said was, in fact, what was really meant. Visionary leaders do not shift their positions with every shift in the political winds.

Displaying respect for self and others is the fourth type of visionary leadership behavior and is similar in essence to what Carl Rogers called "unconditional positive regard." Leaders must start with self-respect because they cannot really care about others without caring first about themselves. Visionary executive leaders are self-assured, certain of their abilities. This trait is not manifested in an arrogant or superior attitude, but in a simple display of self-confidence. This sense of self-respect, of confidence in themselves and their abilities, comes across not only in leaders' attitudes but also in how they treat others. One of the characteristics of visionary leaders is that we feel good around them because they boost our sense of self-worth by paying attention to us, by trusting us, by sharing ideas with us, by making it clear how important we are as persons. They tell us we are important—"I really value your ability to do that, John; we need you"—and they demonstrate what they say through their behavior.

The final category of behavior involves taking calculated risks and making a commitment to risks once they are decided on. Visionary leaders have no energy to spare for recouping their losses; all their efforts go toward achieving their goals. Moreover, these leaders build into their risks opportunities for others to buy in, to take the risks with the leaders and share in the effort and the rewards. These leaders motivate by "pulling" us along with them, as Bennis put it, rather than by trying to push us in the direction they want to go. Franklin D. Roosevelt displayed this sort of behavior often; he took risks and made commitments and inspired others to join him.

Behaviors of a kind other than these five types surely contribute to the sense of inspiration and commitment we feel when responding to visionary leadership. Most important, however, is what visionary leaders are trying to accomplish through their behavior. They attempt to create cultures that will guide their organizations into the future.

Visionary Leadership in Schools

The importance of school leadership can be better appreciated by noting that more than 50 percent of all current school principals will have retired by the end of the next decade. The Office of Educational Research and Improvement's *Principal Selection Guide* (1987) is one step in the direction of improving the increasingly important selection process (which many agree is generally poor, e.g., see Southern Regional Education Board 1986). But regardless of how they are selected, the next "generation" of principals will be faced with unprecedented opportunities and with exceptional new challenges. Using these opportunities and meeting these challenges will call for a deeper understanding of the role of the principal and the skills needed to carry out that role effectively. Principals will need to be "organizational leaders," but, even more important, they will have to be *visionary* leaders. We have already discussed the sort of cognitive and personal characteristics needed by visionary leaders. We now turn to the sort of specific values that must underlie a vision of school excellence, the sort of values that define and support an effective school "culture." In other words, we shall focus on the specific energizing value content of principals' visions.

The Principal as a Visionary Leader

What is this vision? What are its elements, of what does it consist, and to what does it refer? The vision of which I speak is a cultural ideal. It defines the shared values that support certain critical functions of the school organization, functions that must be carried out effectively in any organization if that organization is to survive. These functions have been identified by sociologists and consist of *adapting* to the environment, *achieving* goals, and *coordinating* or integrating the various activities that take place in the organization (Parsons 1960). There is even some hard evidence that schools in which these functions are accomplished well are, by objective assessment, actually more effective (Hoy and Ferguson 1985).

But what exactly are these shared values? Can they be specified? I think the answer is yes, to a degree. I base this opinion on the recent work on leadership and organizational culture by Edgar Schein (1985), a professor of organizational psychology at the Massachusetts Institute of Technology. Schein discussed the specific content of values in each of the three domains identified above, along with some additional values that are even more basic and general. Recognizing that (1) we are now in the realm of theory rather than fact; (2) even values that appear to be very different may support effectiveness in the same organizational function; and (3) it is difficult at best to pin down and specify a value, we can, nonetheless, use Schein's discussion as the basis for exploring the values that might support the three organizational functions in schools and that might, therefore, be related to school effectiveness. We can then suggest that these are some of the values that should be built into principals' visions for their schools.

Adapting. Schein noted that members of organizations differ in viewing their environments as controllable, as situations that can be "lived with" in peaceful coexistence, if not outright harmony, or as circumstances to which the members of the organization must concede control. I suggest that the values most likely to support effective adaptation are those emphasizing the organization's control or, perhaps, values centered on the importance of harmonious coexistence. Schein observed that with respect to the question of what value position is best, the answer must depend on which is most accurately oriented to reality. There is obvious truth to this point: only if the organization believes it can control its destiny is it likely to try to do so. Recall that we earlier observed that unless leaders believe they can make a real difference by their reactions, even the most advanced visionary skills are worthless. We must begin with the premise that we *can* exert some degree of influence over our environment, before it becomes possible to "control" the environment as a result of our efforts. Thus, although it is foolish, and perhaps even destructive, to hold to values that are in obvious conflict with reality, there is much to be said for taking "optimistic" positions, even when we realize that there may be some question about whether the value is, in fact, consistent with objective reality.

I suggest that to support the adaptation function and to achieve optimal organizational effectiveness, visionary leaders build into their visions the value of control over the organization's destiny and over critical factors in its environment. What are these factors? In most organizations and schools, they consist of technology and technological change, of political factors in the government bureaucracy as well as at the local organizational level, of the community culture (the school's equivalent of the private-sector organization's marketplace), and of economic conditions. Can school leaders really control all these things? Certainly not, at least not all the time nor completely. Yet they probably can exercise some control in each area. New teaching methods can be sought out and implemented. Effective relations can be built at the district level. Finances can be enhanced in a variety of ways. And, one of the critical culture-building tasks of the principal, positive community relations can be developed.

Achieving Goals. Schein suggested that organizational values may emphasize doing and achieving, being, or being-in-becoming, a sort of compromise position. For the school, it would seem that the central values supporting achievement of goals should be doing and achieving, supplemented by being-in-becoming (which is related to the issue of growth and development, one of the key reasons for the existence of schools). Unlike the case of adapting, there would appear to be little likelihood of a conflict with reality, regardless of which value position is taken.

Internal Coordination. It is clear that we think of and treat school organizations as though the many different activities were relatively independent of one another, as though the organization could be coordinated by rather simple methods, such as rules, procedures, and perhaps a few plans. In fact, the work of sociologist James Thompson (1967) implied that schools represent extremely complex systems, in which what one teacher or administrator does with regard to a particular student will affect the impact of every other teacher's or administrator's actions with regard to that same student. Under these conditions effective coordination can only be achieved by what Thompson referred to as a process of "mutual adjustment," involving all relevant parties in understanding what each is doing and in working together, explicitly, to make mutual adjustments in their activities in order to achieve their common goals—in this case learning and development.

Schein (1985) noted that the cultural values relevant to internal coordination center on issues of influence and power. Specifically, the organization may operate under the assumption that all power and decisions are centrally located and that the system is and should be autocratic. Alternatively, the values involved may be those of democracy and participation or may reflect "in-between" positions such as paternalism, consultative management, a delegative style, or even a sort of laissez-faire abdication, with everyone pretty much "doing their own thing."

Barth (1987), for example, has characterized collegiality among school faculty as typically analogous to the activity of 3-year-olds that is called "parallel play." However, the sort of coordination needed in schools—coordination by mutual adjustment—calls for a rather high degree of involvement in the process of management and decision making by those who depend on one another, even requiring consensus at times, with everyone explicitly "buying into" a particular decision or plan of action. It seems, then, that strictly from the pragmatic viewpoint of achieving effective coordination (and thereby contributing to goal achievement), and ignoring the broader sociocultural value of participation in our society, it makes sense to build into school organizations the value of involvement and participation of the faculty and staff in operational decision making.

Schein also observed that organizations take internal coordinative stances emphasizing competition, collaboration, or collateral action on the part of managers and organization members generally. This observation is relevant to this discussion for several reasons. First, the nature of the school organization and its coordinative needs would seem more in line with a collaborative stance. Second, it has become increasingly evident that though schools emphasize competitive values, the real world—for which children are being prepared—is far more oriented toward collaboration; most people today work *with* others to accomplish tasks and attain goals rather than on their own in competition with peers. Richard Walton (1985) of the Harvard Business School has recently said that the shift to group-based, instead of individual-based, work activity in American organizations represents a revolution in the workplace. If children are to be prepared to live and work effectively in the organizations of the next century it would seem sensible to build values that support collaborative and collateral activities, along with competition.

I have concentrated on the values underlying effective internal coordination because they are so evidently lacking in American schools. Visionary school leaders must pay special attention to making these values part of their visions.

Maintaining the Culture

Earlier I referred to certain broader cultural beliefs that provide general support for the three critical functions—adapting, achieving goals, and coordinating. At least three such beliefs can be derived from Schein's (1985) presentation. One centers on the assumption that people are "perfectible"—or if we cannot be perfect, at least we can move in that direction. For example, the belief that all children can achieve is consistently found in effective schools. A second concept has to do with how we define and determine what is real. Schein described three ways of defining and determining what is real. The first way is based on physical evidence and the scientific method. The second is based on what others—especially those we trust, respect, and identify with—say is real. This is called "social reality." And the third test of reality is based on our own personal viewpoints and beliefs, on what we believe to be real for ourselves, regardless of what others may say and even regardless of physical evidence or science. Of course, the latter two tests of reality are much easier to apply when there is a lack of scientific evidence, when there is no empirical proof of whether something is true or not.

There is little support in schools, organizations, or society for the third belief, the assumption that what is real is what one personally believes to be real (although there is a disturbing trend in the thinking of many identified with "New Age" philosophies toward just such an assumption, e.g., MacLaine 1983). There is much reinforcement, however, for the second assumption, that what "everyone" agrees is real is what is real. This is especially the case when the issue is complex and when there is little or no scientific evidence in the matter. Now, it should be clear that there is a conflict of sorts here. Most educators and the public might agree that the importance of science as a test of truth, of what is real, should be emphasized in schools. To some degree, however, this emphasis might undercut the values that support the critical organizational functions of adapting, achieving goals, and internally coordinating activities.

This conflict is resolved to a degree by a third general issue raised by Schein, centering on the distinction between moralism and pragmatism. Former Secretary of Education William Bennett has argued that schools are responsible for the development of character in children, for their basic moral education with regard to societally accepted values such as honesty or responsibility. One aspect of the development of moral character is understanding the difference between what is right and what works. Such an understanding can reduce, if not eliminate, the sort of conflict referred to above. For example, recognize that, as Schein noted, the environment exerts more control over members of the school and its activities than members of the school do over their own "destiny." At the same time, we must insist that it is right, if not totally accurate, that school participants exercise some control over their own actions and achievements. With this understanding, the visionary principal can act to move the school toward that desired state.

In summary, effective school leaders create visions that construct and support cultures of excellence (Peters and Waterman 1982). They do so by building into their visions values that support the critical organizational functions of adapting, achieving, and coordinating.

Conclusion

I have tried to make the case that effective schools must have effective leaders who can create and implement a vision of the school's culture that contains within it the values on which excellence is built. As organizational leaders, principals cannot simply be administrators (although effective administration is critical); they must be culture-builders as well. The principal's task as culture-builder is easier if he or she understands both the key functions of a school's culture—helping the organization adapt to change, achieve goals, and coordinate the tasks of its members—and the specific values that support these functions. But more than understanding is needed. Effective school leaders must be able to conceive of a vision, a cultural ideal, for the school. They must be able to generate schoolwide support for this vision by involving others in articulating a philosophy that summarizes the vision and by creating policies and programs that turn the philosophy (and the vision) into action. Finally, effective school leaders carry out their visions through their own behavior. None of this is easy, conceptually or behaviorally. Yet it is only through the actions of visionary principals that we can work toward the ideal of effective schools.

In the general introduction of this review I sketched the outline of a new theory of organizational leadership. Over the past decade a variety of leadership research and practice work has come together, forming the basis for a new vision of leadership. I have used the work of David McClelland and Elliott Jaques on leaders' personality traits, of Talcott Parsons and Edgar Schein on organizational culture, and of Warren Bennis and myself on leaders' behaviors as the three primary elements of my theory.

Visionary leadership provides the basis for organizations that are extremely effective in terms of performance or profit, that contribute a vision to society that benefits clients as well as the larger public, and that provide an extremely high "quality of organizational life" for all of the organization's workers. It's hard to imagine what more one might ask of organizations . . . or leaders.

References

Andrews, R. I., and R. Soder. 1987. Principal leadership and student achievement. *Educational Leadership*, 44 (6), 9–11.

Barth, R. 1987. "Personal vision and school improvement." Address before the annual convocation of the Academy for the Advancement of Teaching and Management, Princeton, NJ.

Bennis, W. 1984. The four competencies of leadership. *Training and Development Journal*, 38 (8), 15–19.

Bennis, W., and B. Nanus. 1985. *Leaders*. New York: Harper & Row.

Burke, W. W. 1986. Leadership as empowering others. In S. Srivastra et al. (eds.), *Executive power*. San Francisco: Jossey-Bass.

Deal, T. E. 1987. The culture of schools. In L. T. Sheive and M. B. Schoenbeit (eds.), *Leadership: Examining the elusive: 1987*. Yearbook of the Association for Supervision and Curriculum Development (pp. 3–15). Alexandria, VA: ASCD.

Firestone, W. A., and B. L. Wilson. 1985. Using bureaucratic and cultural linkages to improve instruction. *Educational Administration Quarterly*, 21 (2), 7–30.

Hoy, W. L., and J. Ferguson. 1985. A theoretical framework and exploration of organizational effectiveness of schools. *Educational Administration Quarterly*, 21 (2), 117–134.

Jaques, E. 1979. Taking time seriously in evaluating jobs. *Harvard Business Review*, 57 (5), 124–132.

_____. 1986. The development of intellectual capability: A discussion of stratified systems theory. *Journal of Applied Behavioral Science*, 22, 361–383.

MacLaine, S. 1983. *Out on a limb*. New York: Bantam.

Major, K. D. 1988. Dogmatism, visionary leadership, and effectiveness of secondary principals. Unpublished doctoral dissertation, University of LaVerne, LaVerne, CA.

McClelland, D. C., and D. H. Burnham. 1976. Power is the great motivator. *Harvard Business Review*, 54 (2), 100–110.

Office of Educational Research & Improvement. 1987. *Principal selection guide*. Washington, DC: Government Printing Office.

Parsons, T. 1960. *Structure and process in modern societies*. New York: Free Press.

Peters, T. J., and R. H. Waterman. 1982. *In search of excellence: Lessons from America's best run companies*. New York: Harper & Row.

Sashkin, M. 1984. *The leadership behavior questionnaire*. Bryn Mawr, PA: Organization Design and Development.

_____. 1985, August. "Creating organizational excellence: Developing a top management mind set and implementing a strategy." Paper presented at the annual meeting of the Academy of Management, Organization Development Division, San Diego.

_____. 1986. True vision in leadership. *Training and Development Journal*, 40 (5), 58–61.

_____. 1988. The visionary leader: A new theory of organizational leadership. In J. A. Conger and R. N. Kanungo (eds.), *Charismatic leadership in management*. San Francisco: Jossey-Bass.

Sashkin, M., and R. M. Fulmer. 1985. "A new framework for leadership: vision, charisma, and culture creation." Paper presented at the Biennial Leadership Symposium, Texas Tech University, Lubbock, TX.

———. 1987. Toward an organizational leadership theory. In J. G. Hunt et al. (eds.), *Emerging leadership vistas*. Boston: Lexington Press.

Sashkin, M., and G. Huddle. 1987. A synthesis of job analysis research on the job of the school principal. Unpublished report, Office of Educational Research and Improvement, U.S. Department of Education, Washington, DC.

———. 1988. Recruit top principals: Tips for spotting and coaching key players. *School Administrator,* 45 (2), 8–13, 15.

Schein, E. H. 1985. *Organizational culture and leadership.* San Francisco: Jossey-Bass.

Southern Regional Education Board. 1986. *Effective school principals.* Atlanta, GA.

Thompson, J. D. 1967. *Organizations in action.* New York: McGraw-Hill.

Walton, R. E. 1985. From control to commitment in the workplace. *Harvard Business Review,* 63(2), 77–84.

19

The Language of Leadership

CHARLES HANDY

Leadership is back in fashion. No longer does the word carry overtones of militarism and macho heroics. Gone are the days when it conjured up images of an officer class, of glory linked to privilege. Today leadership is the stuff of best-selling tracts on business and the theme of ambitious researchers and of expensive training conferences! How has this situtation come about? Is it a passing fashion, or should we take it seriously? What does it take to be a leader? Can one learn, develop, or only recognize leadership when it is there?

The rise of a leadership industry is, I suggest, an indication of a deeper and more far-reaching change in our thinking about organizations. We have exchanged the language of engineering for the language of political theory, and the study of organizations will never be quite the same again. Organizations used to be thought of as pieces of engineering—flawed pieces maybe but capable in theory of perfectability, of precision, of full efficiency. Organizations were things to be designed, planned, and managed—full of human resources, feedback loops, and control systems. The very word *management*, with its origins in the running of the household or, some say, of the army mule trains, implies control backed by authority (which is perhaps why it is a word much disliked in all those professional and voluntary bodies that value autonomy).

The new language of organizations is different. The talk today is of networks and alliances, of adhocracy and federalism, of shared values, cultures, and consensus. The key words are options not plans, possible rather than perfect, involvement instead of compliance. These are the words of political systems, not engineering; they are the language of leadership, not management.

Let us look at two of these words and their implications. The first is *federalism*. Federalism is a way of describing what we increasingly see as the necessary paradox of organizations—how to make things big while keeping them small. Paradox is something that *managers* abhor but that *leaders,* being more politically attuned, know is part of the grist of life. All of us hate the things we love, want to be both free and yet belong, to have our cake and eat it.

Federalism manages the paradox of big and small by gathering into the center only the things that really matter and by letting go of the rest, by being "tightloose" in the new language. And it results in *reverse-thrust* organizations in which the energy and initiative come from the bits, not from the center. The center does not direct or command; it coordinates, facilitates, and enables; and it is a center, not a head. These organizations at their best are living examples of *subsidiarity,* that moral principle enshrined in papal encyclicals that holds that a higher-order body should not do anything that can be done by a lower-order body. Subsidiarity is delegation turned into moral imperative; it is trust in action because you have to let other people make decisions that may be mistakes, and you have to forgive them, as long as they are genuine mistakes, lest you destroy that trust. These organizations are fun to work in; they attract the best people and are alive with energy. But when did you last read the words trust and forgiveness in a management manual? This is the language of leadership.

Trust, however, cannot be unbounded. Federal organizations keep ultimate control through the principle of *limited tenure* and the practice of *inverted doughnuts.* Limited tenure is a principle of political theory, one that holds that real responsibility is only given to a person for a limited period of time, in case that responsibility is abused, the decision to give it was wrong, or the individual turns out to be incapable or becomes corrupted. Unlimited tenure is a recipe for dictatorship; therefore, democracies insist that presidents and prime ministers be reelected and that when organizations give real power to people (by, for example, combining the roles of chairman and chief executive), they do so only for a fixed period. Fixed-term contracts, in other words, are becoming more a feature of organizations as a necessary counterpart to increased responsibility and power.

The inverted doughnut is a pictorial way of describing the new jobs. Imagine a doughnut of the American kind; the kind that is a ring with an empty hole in the middle. In this picture, however, the doughnut is inverted. The hole is filled in, and the ring is empty but has a boundary. The new jobs are similar in that they have a core of essentials—if you do not do the essentials, you have failed. But not failing is not enough. These new jobs allow for discretion and require initiative ("intrapreneuring," if you like the jargon). The doughnuts need filling but only up to the boundary. You are trusted—but to a limit. The job of the leader in the center is to design the doughnuts so that the core is understood; there is room for discretion, but the responsibility has clear boundaries. The new organizations work best with large doughnuts and small cores. Old organizations liked small doughnuts and large cores—that way they kept control; they "managed."

The second word is *networks*. Networks depend on *making connections*. Organizations have always known about the so-called informal organization that lay behind the neat array of boxes on their organizational charts, but this informal organization was somehow seen as undesirable—illicit even—in well-run places. Networks are now respectable. You are expected, if you are any good, to have your own alliances and connections. Organizations like "gatekeepers"—people with connections to the world outside.

Networks, however, are unlike managed organizations. They depend on influence, not authority. They are shifting and changing, more like plants than objects. They do not exist for you until you create or join them. Indeed, they are like clubs, and like clubs they have a center and a secretary rather than a head office and a manager. Some networks have even turned their offices into clubs, recognizing that not all networkers work at the same place or at the same time. Why, after all, provide people with private spaces, almost apartments of their own, in an office block when often all they need is an "occasional" space and "occasional" use of facilities? A club provides privileged access to resources, not private spaces, and it is privileged access that is the key to a network.

The language of federations and networks is new—full of new images and metaphors. It requires us to learn new ways and habits, to live with more uncertainty but more trust, less control but more creativity. To those of us reared in another tradition, it can be a strange and a frightening language; but I think that we have to recognize that it is the *right* language. No one, after all, has ever liked being managed, even if they did not mind being the manager, and anyone who has tried to run an organization knows that it was more like running a small country than a machine. It was only the theorists who tried to apply the hard rules of numbers, logic, and mechanics to an essentially soft system. Few people paid heed to managing until people like Peters and Waterman started talking the new language in *In Search of Excellence*, a book that obviously touched some chord.

As a result, leadership is now fashionable, and the language of leadership is increasingly important, but, as Warren Bennis says in his own book on leaders, it remains the most studied and least understood topic in all the social sciences. Like beauty, or love, we know it when we see it but cannot easily define it or produce it on demand. Again, like beauty and love, the writings on it are fun, sexy even, with their pictures of heroes and stories that can be our private fantasies. To read

MacGregor Burns, Maccoby, Alistair Mant, Warren Bennis, Cary Cooper, or Peters and Waterman is to escape into a private world of might-have-beens.

These fun books may even do a disservice, with their tales of heroes and their myths of the mighty, by suggesting that leadership is only for the new and the special. The significance of the new language is, I believe, that leadership has to be endemic in organizations—the fashion, not the exception. Everyone with pretensions to be anyone must begin to think and act like a leader. Some will find it comes naturally and will blossom; some will not enjoy it at all, but unless you try and are allowed to try, one will never know, for leadership is hard if not impossible to detect in embryo—it has to be seen in action to be recognized by oneself as much as by others.

So what is this mysterious thing, and how does one acquire it? The studies agree on very little, but what they do agree on is probably at the heart of things: A leader shapes and shares a vision that gives point to the work of others. Would that it were as easy to do as to say! Think on these aspects of that short sentence.

- The vision must be different. A plan or a strategy that is a projection of the present or a replica of what everyone else is doing is not a vision. A vision has to reframe the known scene, to reconceptualize the obvious, connect the previously unconnected, dream a dream. Alistair Mant talks of the leader as a builder working with others toward a "third corner," a goal. Those who are interested only in power or achievement for its own sake he calls "raiders" or mere "binary" people. MacGregor Burns talks of the transforming leader as opposed to the more transactional one, the busy fixer.
- The vision must make sense to others. Ideally it should create the "aha effect," as when everyone says "aha—of course, now I see it." What oft was thought but ne'er so well expressed. To make sense it must stretch people's imaginations but still be within the bounds of possibility. To give point to the work of others the vision must be *related* to their work and not to some grand design in which they feel they have no point. If "vision" is too grand a word, try "goal" or even "manifesto."
- The vision must be understandable. No one can communicate a vision that takes two pages to read or is too full of numbers and jargon. It has to be a vision that sticks in the head. Metaphor and analogy can be keys because they provide us with vivid images with room for interpretation—low-definition concepts as opposed to the more precise high-definition words of engineering and management.

- The leader must live the vision. He or she must not only believe in it but must be seen to believe in it. It is tempting credulity to proclaim a crusade for the impoverished from a luxury apartment. Effective leaders, we are told, exude energy. Energy comes easily if you love your cause. Effective leaders, again, have integrity. Integrity, being true to yourself, comes naturally if you live for your vision. In other words, the vision cannot be something thought up in the drawing office; to be real it has to come from the deepest parts of you, from an inner system of belief. The total pragmatist cannot be a transforming leader.
- The leader must remember that the vision remains a dream without the work of others. A leader with no followers is a voice in the wilderness. Leaders like to choose their teams but most inherit them and must then make them their own. Trust in others is repaid by trust from them. If it is to be *their* vision too, then their ideas should be heeded.

Such arts and skills cannot, I think, be taught. But they can be learned, or, rather, you can discover them within you, foster them, and let them grow. Leaders may well be born or shaped by early experience, but how do we know if we possess the capacity to become leaders unless we try. Some say that firstborns or those who had to struggle more when young, or those who needed to prove something to parents or significant elders strive harder. Yet this idea relates more to achievement than to leadership. For leadership to flower, the following things are necessary.

- Room to move. Space for responsibility and experiment is essential. Without freedom to change things there is no call for leadership. Without the room to make mistakes there is no point in experiment. Early responsibility is essential to the discovery of leadership ability, so is the readiness to *forgive* yourself, and be forgiven, for any mistakes made in the process. No one can learn from mistakes unless they are prepared to write them off to experience.
- A belief in self. No one with an inferiority complex is going to start creating visions or dreaming dreams. You have to believe that you can influence events and people. Carried too far this belief is arrogance, but unless you believe in yourself it is unlikely that others will. Warren Bennis describes how Wallenda, the great tightrope walker, never fell until he started to think about *not* falling, and then he fell to his death. Belief in yourself is boosted by early success but is also rooted in a greater belief that gives some sense of the meaning of life and the purpose behind doing

things. Those who see no point in things will see no need to change things, no need to make a difference.

- An awareness of other worlds. Reframing is hard to do without perspectives from other worlds. People with long experience in one field have the blinkers of that experience. To see yourself and your situation as others see it, it is necessary to stand outside your world at times. To use metaphor, analogy, and words effectively you need to know those metaphors and words. John Kennedy read history and biography. Others travel, enjoy theatre or music, read novels or study literature. There must be time to live in the other worlds.

- A capacity for loneliness. Leaders are, by definition, out front. They may be respected, trusted, and believed in, but they will not always be loved. Leaders are often lonely, with only their own convictions to hold onto. Furthermore, wise leaders take time to be by themselves; they understand that retreats, stability zones, and quiet times are needed or they might lose themselves in activity and become blinkered by their busyness—oscillation, Mant calls it, withdrawing so that one may better reenter. Cooper found that his leaders were, without exception, self-defined "loners."

Not all who possess these qualities will end up leaders. They are necessary but not sufficient conditions. They are not the stuff of training courses, but they are a sort of highway code for those who would spend their lives in organizations. Pay heed to these things if you want to make a difference or if you want to encourage others to make a difference.

Leadership is not without pain. Mistakes, even when forgiven, can hurt and cost. To be alone is often to be depressed. A belief in self goes with and comes from constant reflection about oneself and about the point of things. Leaders are not invulnerable and should not be if they want the empathy of others. To train the leaders they so badly need, organizations must take more risks with more people, be more understanding, and be more forgiving. Only then will they discover what leadership talents exist.

But there is more to the overall picture than just spotting leaders. Organizations would be wise to embrace the new languages of leadership and politics and begin to think of themselves as societies of citizens. They should be run as societies, not as machines, with leaders at the head. There is managing to be done and it needs to be done effectively, but it is subordinate to the proper *leadership* of the bits that make up the whole.

References

Bennis, Warren, and Burt Nanus. *Leaders.* London: Harper & Row, 1985.

Burns, James MacGregor. *Leadership.* New York: Harper & Row, 1978.

Cooper, Cary, and Peter Kingley. *The Change Makers: Their Influence on British Business & Industry.* London: Harper & Row, 1985.

Maccoby, Michael. *The Leaders.* New York: Simon & Schuster, 1981.

Mant, Alistair. *Leaders We Deserve.* Oxford: Martin Robertson, 1983.

Peters, Thomas, and Robert Waterman, Jr. *In Search of Excellence.* London: Harper & Row, 1982.

20

I Have a Dream

MARTIN LUTHER KING, JR.

. . . I say to you today, my friends, that in spite of the difficulties and frustrations of the moment I still have a dream. It is a dream deeply rooted in the American dream.

I have a dream that one day this nation will rise up and live out the true meaning of its creed: "We hold these truths to be self-evident, that all men are created equal."

I have a dream that one day on the red hills of Georgia the sons of former slaves and the sons of former slaveowners will be able to sit down together at the table of brotherhood.

I have a dream that one day even the state of Mississippi, a desert state sweltering with the heat of injustice and oppression, will be transformed into an oasis of freedom and justice.

I have a dream that my four little children will one day live in a nation where they will not be judged by the color of their skin but by the content of their character.

I have a dream today.

I have a dream that one day the state of Alabama, whose governor's lips are presently dripping with the words of interposition and nullification, will be transformed into a situation where little black boys and black girls will be able to join hands with little white boys and white girls and walk together as sisters and brothers.

I have a dream today.

I have a dream that one day every valley shall be exalted, every hill and mountain shall be made low, the rough places will be made plains, and the crooked places will be made straight, and the glory of the Lord shall be revealed, and all flesh shall see it together.

Reprinted by permission from *The Words of Martin Luther King, Jr.*, Coretta Scott King, ed., pp. 95–98. Copyright © 1963 by Martin Luther King, Jr.

This is our hope. This is the faith with which I return to the South. With this faith we will be able to transform the jangling discords of our nation into a beautiful symphony of brotherhood. With this faith we will be able to work together, to pray together, to struggle together, to go to jail together, to stand up for freedom together, knowing that we will be free one day.

This will be the day when all of God's children will be able to sing with new meaning "My country 'tis of thee, sweet land of liberty, of thee I sing. Land where my fathers died, land of the pilgrim's pride, from every mountainside, let freedom ring."

And if America is to be a great nation this must become true. So let freedom ring from the prodigious hilltops of New Hampshire. Let freedom ring from the mighty mountains of New York. Let freedom ring from the heightening Alleghenies of Pennsylvania!

Let freedom ring from the snowcapped Rockies of Colorado!

Let freedom ring from the curvaceous peaks of California!

But not only that; let freedom ring from Stone Mountain of Georgia!

Let freedom ring from every hill and molehill of Mississippi. From every mountainside, let freedom ring.

When we let freedom ring, when we let it ring from every village and every hamlet, from every state and every city, we will be able to speed up that day when all of God's children, black men and white men, Jews and Gentiles, Protestants and Catholics, will be able to join hands and sing in the words of that old Negro spiritual, "Free at last! Free at last! Thank God almighty, we are free at last!

About the Editors
and Contributors

Editors

William E. Rosenbach is professor and chairperson in the Department of Management at Gettysburg College. Formerly, he was professor and head of the Department of Behavioral Sciences and Leadership at the U.S. Air Force Academy. He is the author or coauthor of numerous articles and books and is a member of the Editorial Board of *The Leadership Quarterly*. His special interest is in leadership development of youth.

Robert L. Taylor is dean of the School of Business at the University of Louisville. He has also taught at the U.S. Air Force Academy and the University of Wisconsin. He is a consultant, researcher, and prolific writer on managerial leadership.

Contributors

Warren G. Bennis is the Joseph DeBell Professor of Management at the University of Southern California. Formerly he held professorships at MIT's Sloan School of Management and Harvard and was president of the University of Cincinnati. His books include *The Unconscious Conspiracy: Why Leaders Can't Lead, Leaders*, and *Why Leaders Can't Lead: The Unconscious Conspiracy Continues*.

Michael D. Cohen is a professor at the Institute of Public Policy Studies at the University of Michigan, Ann Arbor.

Thomas E. Cronin is McHugh Professor of American Institutions and Leadership at The Colorado College and is the author, editor, or coauthor of numerous publications, including *The State of the Presidency, The Government by the People*, and *Direct Democracy: The Politics of Initiative, Referendum and Recall*. He is working on a book about leadership theories and leadership strategies.

John W. Gardner has held many esteemed positions, including president of the Carnegie Corporation and of the Carnegie Foundation for the Advancement of Teaching and secretary of the U.S. Department of Health, Education, and Welfare (1965–1968). He was a founder of Common Cause. In 1964 he was awarded the Presidential Medal of Freedom, the highest civil honor in the United States. Mr. Gardner is the author of *Excellence, Self-Renewal,* and *Leadership: The Release of Human Possibilities* (forthcoming).

Charles Handy is a visiting professor at the London Business School, a writer, teacher, broadcaster, and consultant. He is the author of *Understanding Organizations* and *Gods of Management.*

Sharon Hayman, a 1987 graduate of Gettysburg College, was a member of a senior seminar on leadership when she collaborated with Professor Rosenbach to write "Absentee Charismatic Leadership: Khomeini, Gandhi, and Mandela."

John Heider is a group leader and a teacher of group leaders. Formerly, he studied and helped to direct long-term training programs, taught at the Menninger Foundation School of Psychiatry, served as a staff psychologist at the Veterans Administration Hospital in Topeka, Kansas, and was director of the Human Potential School of Mendocino, California.

Robert E. Kelley teaches at the Graduate School of Industrial Administration, Carnegie Mellon University. He is the author of *Gold-Collar Worker: Harnessing the Brainpower of the New Work Force, Consulting: The Complete Guide to a Profitable Career,* and *Followership-Leadership-Partnership* (forthcoming).

Beverly Kempton is a free-lance writer based in New York City. A former newspaper feature writer, she has reported on a wide range of subjects for a number of magazines, among them *Working Woman, Self, McCalls,* and the *Washington Monthly.*

Martin Luther King, Jr., is perhaps the most significant leader of this century. His ability to articulate his vision and empower others changed all of our lives.

James M. Kouzes is president of TPG/Learning Systems, a company in the Tom Peters Group, and former director of the Executive Development Center at Santa Clara University. He is coauthor of *The Leadership Challenge.*

Karl W. Kuhnert is an assistant professor in the Applied Psychology Program at the University of Georgia in Athens. Formerly, he taught at Auburn and Ohio State universities. His research interests and publications are in the areas of organizational leadership, job security, and personnel selection.

Philip Lewis is professor in the Department of Psychology at Auburn University and has served on the faculties of the University of Georgia and the University of Pittsburgh. In 1989–1990, he will serve as a National Research Council senior research associate at the U.S. Army Research Institute for the Behavioral and Social Sciences, where he will be pursuing his interests in the development of perspective-taking in senior military officers.

Morgan W. McCall, Jr., is a senior research scientist at the Center for Effective Organizations and a visiting professor in the Department of Management and Organization in the School of Business Administration, University of Southern California. Formerly, he held a variety of research and management positions at the Center for Creative Leadership in Greensboro, North Carolina, including three years as director of research. He is the author of several books and numerous articles about leadership and executive development ranging from leadership of professionals to managerial decision making to executive derailment and success.

James G. March is a Fred Merrill Professor of Management and director of the Public Management Program at Stanford University. He is a senior fellow at the Hoover Institution.

David A. Nadler is president of Delta Consulting Group and former professor at the Graduate School of Business, Columbia University.

Marshall Sashkin is a senior associate in the Office of Educational Research and Improvement, U.S. Department of Education. He has taught and conducted research at several universities, including the University of Michigan, Wayne State University, the State University of New York at Binghamton, and the University of Maryland. He is the author or coauthor of numerous books, monographs, and articles. His most recent books are *Experiencing Management* and *A Manager's Guide to Performance Management*. He recently completed a seven-year term as editor of the journal *Group & Organization Studies*.

Virginia E. Schein is professor of management at Gettysburg College. She is a former associate professor at the Wharton School and has held professorial positions at Yale University, the City University of New York, and Case Western Reserve University. She has held managerial positions at Metropolitan Life Insurance Company and the American Management Association. She is the coauthor of *Power and Organization Development*.

Michael L. Tushman is professor of management at Columbia University. His research interests focus on managing strategic innovation, R&D laboratories, and strategic change. He has lectured throughout Europe, Japan, and Brazil and has published several books and articles.

David D. Van Fleet is professor of management at Texas A&M University and a fellow of the Academy of Management. Formerly, he taught at the University of Akron and the University of Tennessee. He is the author or coauthor of numerous publications dealing with leadership and is the editor of the *Journal of Management*.

Gary A. Yukl is professor of management at the State University of New York in Albany and a fellow of the Society for Industrial-Organizational Psychology and the American Psychological Association. He has written many articles on leadership, is the author of *Leadership in Organizations,* and is the coauthor of *Military Leadership.* He serves on the editorial boards of several journals.

Abraham Zaleznik is the Konosuke Matsushita Professor of Leadership at the Harvard Business School. He is the author of numerous articles and books, including *The Managerial Mystique: Restoring Leadership in Business.*